COMMON COURAGE

COMMON COURAGE

Bill Wassmuth, Human Rights, and Small-Town Activism

ANDREA VOGT

Foreword by **MORRIS DEES**

University of Idaho Press | Moscow, Idaho

Visit our website at www.uidaho.edu/uipress

First published 2003 by the University of Idaho Press
Published with the support of the Schreck Family Foundation
Printed in Canada by Houghton Boston, Saskatoon using vegetable-based inks on 100% post-consumer recycled, chlorine- and acid-free paper stock produced by New Leaf Paper.

Library of Congress Cataloging-in-Publication Data
Vogt, Andrea, 1971–
Common Courage : Bill Wassmuth, human rights, and small-town activism / Andrea Vogt ; foreword by Morris Dees.
   p. cm.
Includes bibliographical references and index.
   ISBN 0-89301-264-5 (pbk. : alk. paper)
1. Wassmuth, Bill. 2. Human rights workers—West (U.S.)—Biography.
3. Catholic Church—West (U.S.)—Clergy—Biograpny. 4. Human rights—West (U.S.) 5. Social justice—West (U.S.) I. Title.
JC 599.U52 W388 2003
323'.092—dc21   2003010644

Paperback printing   5 4 3 2

For Bill

CONTENTS

FOREWORD *by Morris Dees*

I FIRST MET Bill Wassmuth shortly after the Aryan Nations had bombed his house and several downtown buildings in Coeur d'Alene, Idaho, during the fall of 1986. At the Southern Poverty Law Center we had been following what was developing in Idaho because our Klanwatch intelligence project had been tracking former Ku Klux Klan Grand Dragon Louis Beam and other members of the Aryan Nations with KKK connections.

I flew out to Idaho a few weeks after the bombings to meet with community activists and lawyers about possibly filing a lawsuit. I will never forget. It was frigid there in the wintertime. We eventually did draft a nuisance complaint against the Aryan Nations, but it never got off the ground. I was reluctant to get involved at the time because we did not have the connections with former Aryan Nations members we needed.

I remember one night we all met at Bill's house to discuss it. After we had finished all our talking, Wassmuth turned to us and said, "Hey, would you guys like a beer?" I was shocked. I said, "Man, you're a Catholic priest, aren't you? Well I'm going to convert from Baptist to Catholic because you all have beer-drinking priests. You're just a regular kind of guy, aren't you?" And I drank the one he offered me, even though I don't generally drink beer.

Noted civil rights lawyer and co-founder of the Southern Poverty Law Center Morris Dees has been at the forefront of dozens of successful civil legal battles against racist organizations. In 2000, he led the legal team that won a 6.3-million-dollar judgment against the Aryan Nations in Idaho, effectively bankrupting the organization.

I think his having grown up in a small, rural town in Idaho speaks volumes about how he was able to relate with regular people. We had that in common. I also was born in a tiny farming community in rural Alabama. When you grow up in a small town you know the rich and the poor, the drunks and the saints. You learn fast that a reputation lost is hard to win back. You learn not to evaluate people by their social class but rather by what they stand for, you learn to treat your neighbors with respect, and you gain a good solid sense of right and wrong. Wassmuth, through his effective consensus-building system, won over the community, and eventually people in positions of power, by gradually building, block by block, a solid wall of opposition to Butler and his ideas. I remember being particularly impressed by how he was able to build a coalition that included community residents, law enforcement officers, religious leaders, and city council members. His coalition building—especially among religious groups—was a key factor that cannot be overstated. America is a church nation. During the civil rights struggles, when Dr. King wrote his famous letter from the Birmingham jail, he wrote it to the white ministers in Birmingham, Alabama. Wassmuth, like King, was a minister, and this gave them a certain moral high ground to operate from, which was effective. "Rev." Richard Butler was no more a minister than my dog. He just mailed away for a fifty-cent piece of paper. Yet he picked three powerful words to name the religious arm of his hate group: Jesus Christ Christian. Those words made some churches timid about speaking out against him. If every church in the community had locked arms twenty years earlier and said "Putting Jews down is not Christian and is what led to the Holocaust," the Aryan Nations might not have lasted as long as it did.

But Idaho is not alone in its struggle against hate. Every part of the country has gone through traumatic experiences—anti-Irish uprisings in New York, World War II internment of Japanese in the West, race riots in Los Angeles, and the civil rights struggle in the South, to name just a few. There is a legacy of hate across America. I do not think people in Idaho have any more obligation than others in the nation to make a place for everybody at the table. We all share that duty. But those who experience acts of intolerance in their midst do owe an extra responsibility to make sure people do not forget. There are a lot of young people in the South today who do not remember that fifty years ago blacks could not go into certain restaurants or vote. These rights today are taken for granted. It is important that even when people in Idaho do not have the Aryan Nations to deal with anymore, that they not take that fact for granted.

As Americans, we take great comfort that we are not like the Klan or neo-Nazis. But the truth is, less than 5 percent of the thousands of hate crimes committed annually are perpetrated by members of these hate groups. The vast majority are committed by ordinary citizens who just do not like the interracial or homosexual couple next door. You might stamp out the hate group in the community, but it is the systemic bias against Native Americans, African Americans, Hispanics, or other minorities that is problematic. They suffer the daily indignity of being treated differently. Bill Wassmuth understood that when a community hears messages of hatred and nobody responds, the seeds of that systemic bias begin to grow.

To me, his legacy is not unlike Rosa Parks', . . . it is an inspiring story of how one person can make a major difference. The message he got across is, "We're better than these people. They don't represent us, they don't speak for us, and we've got to be united and speak with one voice." And that's what he did.

When I went back to Idaho to try the civil lawsuit against the Aryan Nations in 2000, I was told, "Look, you are going to have a hard time because the attitude up here is 'live and let live.' Whatever Richard Butler does on his side of the mountain is fine. Even if he's odd and eccentric, that's the American way. There is still a frontier mentality." We were able to show that this man had indeed come down off his mountain and was endangering the community. Members of the Aryan Nations threatened the paperboy, shot at a UPS driver, bombed a priest's home, and eventually assaulted a mother and son, whom we represented in court. Yet I honestly do not think our victory would have been possible without the pioneering work of Bill Wassmuth, Norm Gissel, Tony Stewart, and the other local folks working on behalf of human rights. Our lawsuit, and the jury's unanimous decision, was the culmination of their work. Together, we helped eradicate the Aryan Nations and turned their terrorist training camp into a peace park.

I am glad Bill Wassmuth lived to see the day, given that he had worked so hard and so long to help awaken the Northwest to the dangers of organized hate groups. In his own gentle way, he led the way to a meaningful community response and, in doing so, he performed a great service for the Northwest and the nation. I was privileged to know this giant among men and to call him my friend.

PREFACE

I BEGAN interviewing Bill Wassmuth in October of 2001, nearly a year after he had been diagnosed with amyotrophic lateral sclerosis (ALS), commonly called Lou Gehrig's disease. I did not know him personally at the time, but as a reporter, I thought his unique experiences and perspectives as a priest and human rights activist needed to be documented before his illness prevented him from speaking or writing any longer. We met about every two weeks in the living room of his remodeled Victorian house in Ellensburg, Washington, a small town with a big rodeo three hours from Seattle, on the sunny side of the Cascades. During our first interviews, Bill scooted across his hardwood floors in a souped-up wheelchair that he deftly operated with a joystick. Our discussions were animated and personal, often punctuated by jokes and spells of laughter, occasionally interrupted by unavoidable somber moments that filled his old house with silence. I brought him water to sip through a straw when he needed a break. He gave me license to deplete his wife's chocolate stash as I listened to his stories, often delivered with the kind of passionate oration he might have once reserved for a congregation.

Six months later, he struggled to get his tongue around certain syllables—he particularly hated the word "specificity" and had begun asking me to lift his hand and place it on the joystick of his wheelchair so he could navigate slowly across the room. He would tire after an hour, and his voice was increasingly weak and inaudible on the mini-cassette tapes I used to record the interviews. The last four meetings I brought finished chapters, which I laid on his lap so he could read them. I turned the page when he nodded to signal he had finished.

The degenerative disease was rapid and cruel; each day it took away another physical aspect of his life, atrophying muscles that allowed him to stretch, wipe a tear, even stop laughing, once he started. Lou Gehrig's essentially wastes away the motor neurons that connect brain to muscles, garbling the signals that once flowed between them. What causes the breakdown in communication is still a mystery. What is known about ALS is that approximately half of the 5,000 people diagnosed each year in the United States die within three years.

In Bill's case, during the summer when he was remodeling his Ellensburg home, it began as a tingling numbness in his left thumb that made it hard to hold the nail while he was hammering. A year later he was in a wheelchair. A year after that, he passed away.

For Roman Catholics throughout the region, Wassmuth's death marked the passing of a shining example of a good priest, at a time when the priestly image was suffering from the sexual abuse scandals in the church. Wassmuth was a beloved man of the cloth, who touched thousands of families in personal ways—confession, baptism, birth, and burial—as an honorable religious leader. For human rights activists, his death marked the loss of a leader who embraced human rights advocacy as a lifestyle and spiritual calling, and whose legacy spoke volumes about the power of love in the presence of hate.

Others who knew him more personally maintain that his message of common courage is best remembered in regular everyday ways and eschew putting him on the pedestal many insist he deserves.

Most who knew him well will miss his wit, intellectual curiosity, and the uncanny sense of humor he held onto through the end. I will always remember one lunch we ate together in the weeks before he had his feeding tube installed. I had a thick slice of gooey chocolate cake, and he had a big greasy hamburger, about which he joked: "What's it gonna do, kill me?"

Somehow, even with death in close pursuit, Bill Wassmuth not only laughed, but made others laugh, too. He also found the strength to pass on what he learned during a lifetime of fighting for human rights in rural America. Much of that is collected here. As a result, this book is not a thorough analysis of hate groups and their ideologies, but rather an examination of how small communities can combat them, and one man's story of how he did.

His story, and the greater grassroots fight against white supremacy in the rural West, unfolds in the five-state Rocky Mountain region of Washington, Oregon, Idaho, Montana, and Wyoming. At the heart of this battle was remote North Idaho, a narrow swath of achingly beautiful and sparsely populated land bordering Montana, Washington, and Canada. It is where Wassmuth was born and raised, where he worked as a priest, and where notorious white supremacist Richard Butler would move to from California in the early 1970s to establish a headquarters for his racist organization, the Aryan Nations, also known as the Church of Jesus Christ Christian. Over the course of three decades, that twenty-acre compound, just north of the resort town of Coeur d'Alene, Idaho, became a national hub of hate. The compound sheltered malcontents, spawned criminals, and gave birth to violent movements aimed at furthering a "Northwest Imperative," as racists called their failed plan to carve out a piece of American territory as their white homeland. They burned crosses and carried swastika flags down Main Street. Members of the terrorist group, The Order, sought refuge and stashed their murder weapons in North Idaho. The siege at Randy Weaver's cabin on nearby Ruby Ridge ignited a nationwide militia fervor. Bo Gritz chose North Idaho for his "Almost Heaven" haven for tax protesters and antigovernment radicals. All of that happened.

But North Idaho is also a place where regular small-town citizens (including Bill Wassmuth) waged a tenacious and monumental grassroots battle for two decades against some of the nations' most dangerous hate groups—and won. Though the media spotlight rarely shined as brightly on them as it did on the Aryan Nations, their persistent efforts on behalf of human rights outlasted the compound, which was razed in 2001 after local citizens teamed up with the Southern Poverty

Law Center to press a successful civil suit that bankrupted the Aryan Nations. Real proof of these citizens' commitment to combating hate lies not in this accomplishment alone, however, but in their continued dedication to human rights.

If there is one overarching lesson from Idaho's grassroots fight against the Aryan Nations, it is that apathy is too often interpreted as acceptance, not only by those who hate, but by the general public, and by those who have been the targets of hate. Bigotry is a scab on a community, and like any wound, if allowed to fester, it only gets worse. Had Bill Wassmuth kept quiet and not spoken up for human rights, he would not have become the target for a bomb detonated at his home by racist thugs attempting to silence him. But had he and others kept quiet, the Aryan Nations compound might still exist today.

Wassmuth's message as a priest and human rights activist was always that it is not enough to shun bigotry from the sidelines. It must be condemned publicly. Virtue, if not displayed and held up as a model for civic responsibility, does little for a community.

In the late 1990s, I worked as a reporter in the North Idaho bureau of the daily newspaper published in nearby Spokane, Washington, the *Spokesman-Review*. While working on a story about white supremacists' attempts to speak at a local college, a well-known bigot faxed several letters to my attention. The rant against journalists ended with a call to arms for white pride and a plea to "work with us to save our people."[1] By his calculation, the fact that I worked inside a newspaper that challenged such racist ideas in print meant I must be an "East Coast communist Jew." What he did not know: like Bill Wassmuth, I am a fourth-generation North Idahoan with Northern European roots. Bill's Idaho ancestors farmed. Mine, alongside those from many different ethnic and religious backgrounds, worked the mines, mills, and lumber camps across the mountainous expanse of North Idaho between the Clearwater River and Canada.

What he and other white supremacists did not know is that Idaho was the first state in the nation to elect a Jewish governor, and the first state in the nation to elect an American Indian as state attorney general.[2] Maybe they mistook the region's palpable antigovernment sentiment as a sign of support for racist fringe groups. No one told them about Idahoans' long tradition of being watchful, even suspicious of government while at the same time being supportive of civil rights: It was Idaho's Senator Frank Church whose committee in 1977 exposed the U.S. government and CIA abuses, including a host of civil rights infringements inflicted on regular Americans.[3] And before that, at the turn of the century, it was North Idaho miners who were calling for better wages and an end to child labor when the governor declared martial law and used federal troops to put down the demonstrations by force, rounding up thousands of union members and their supporters for detention in stockades.[4]

Perhaps they thought the independent "Don't Tread On Me" sentiment that runs deep through this rugged country would allow racist views to go unchallenged, overlooking the fact that this live-and-let-live sentiment is often accompanied by a humanitarian sense of justice and civic duty rooted in the hardship of rural living here in the most isolated, unpopulated portion of the Lower 48: When families fall on hard times, it is not uncommon for neighbors to fill their freezers with venison, elk, and other game hunted for sustenance in the region. We stop and pull each other out of the roadside ditch knowing that another car might not come along on these rural roads for some time, and that tomorrow, the favor might be returned. We help our neighbors when they are the victims of a logging accident, a crop-devastating hailstorm, or a hate crime.

Perhaps they had read too many urban media stories with headlines like "Backwoods Anxiety" or "Fascistville, Idaho,"[5] portraying such rural blue-collar lifestyles as the ignorant breeding ground for hate while ignoring the efforts of the thousands of North Idahoans who believe bigotry is wrong. Maybe they saw the daytime talk show when Geraldo Rivera claimed that Hayden Lake, Idaho, residents considered Timothy McVeigh a hero, or the episode in the popular NBC hospital drama *ER* when a character said she was from Idaho, then added, "not the white supremacist part."

It would be naive, however, to ignore the grain of truth underlying these portrayals: that prejudice exists and sometimes thrives in the agrarian rural regions of the Northwest, where the loss of old ways of life and the financial hardships and sense of disenfranchisement accompanying such change pose great challenges to community health.

Wassmuth believed Pacific Northwest residents must battle intolerance more vigilantly than ever in these fragile times of transition, lest their economic vulnerability, geographic isolation, "live and let live motto," and relative racial homogeneity give white supremacists, and the media watchdogs who cover them, the mistaken impression that they are welcome.

I hope this book can be a small contribution to that process, as part of the public record of what happened in my own backyard.

Since September 11, 2001, American citizens increasingly fear terrorism aimed at them from the "outside," yet students are graduating from my old Idaho high school who do not remember that homegrown terrorists set off bombs on public streets less than an hour's drive away. To be tolerant, we must treat "outsiders" the same as we do our neighbors and not forget that our neighbors can be dangerous as well if under the spell of fundamentalism.

As I write this preface, I am sitting at a plastic picnic table that serves as my desk on Lampedusa, a ten-mile-wide barren desert island in the Mediterranean that is as close to Libya as it is to the European mainland. The wind brings red sand from Africa. The bar across the street has a sign in Arabic hanging from its shutter. The nearest land is Tunisia, sixty miles away. There are few who speak with my strange accent, carry my country's passport. My fair complexion gives away that I am not from here, that I am an outsider. Yet the Lampedusans demonstrate a tolerance and friendship that I can only hope they would be shown as strangers in my land, my state, my small hometown. The eyes of a grizzled Italian sailor light up as he tells me the story of how he harvested a sea sponge from thirty meters under the sea. An African street vendor greets me with a smile and small talk each day, though I have not bought any of his wares. A local family welcomes me with a meal of blacktail fish the father caught himself.

These small but precious cultural exchanges remind me of something Bill Wassmuth said: He believed those who appreciated rather than resented diversity lived a richer, fuller life because they did not limit themselves to a narrow field of experiences. "If I choose only to deal with men," he said, "I am missing the female perspective of what life is about. If I only deal with Christians, I'm missing what Jews, Hindus, Muslims, or Native American cultures contribute. If I choose to only be with whites, I'm missing other unique perspectives. Prejudice is suffocating. It denies one the fullness of life experience."

Wassmuth urged everyone he spoke to—his friends, his family, congregations, students, public audiences—to embrace such a full life by embarking on what he called "a journey, both individually and communally, toward becoming a society accepting of diversity, a society that views diversity as a crucial source of enrichment rather than as a threat." That journey carried him into the twilight of his life. And even then, tapping some of his last reserves of strength, he gave the interviews that form the core of this book and extended an invitation to others, in hopes they might follow the path he found to common ground.

—ANDREA VOGT
Lampedusa, Italy

ACKNOWLEDGMENTS

THIS BOOK would not have been possible without many people who offered help in many ways, from editing assistance, to lodging while I was researching and writing this book between two continents, to encouragement that kept me going during the long drives to and from Ellensburg. Thanks to all those not mentioned here by name.

For their specific gestures of support along the way, I am grateful to: human rights task force members in Bonner, Kootenai, and Latah counties; my former colleague (and undisputed authority on hate groups in the Northwest), veteran *Spokesman-Review* reporter Bill Morlin; Liz Sullivan of Moscow; University of Idaho Journalism Professor Kenton Bird; Washington Association of Churches Methodist Minister John Boonstra; Rabbi Anson Laytner of Seattle; Marc Johnson of Boise; and my sister, Anna.

For his editorial vision, University of Idaho Press Director Ivar Nelson, and for her masterful fine tuning of the manuscript, editor Candace Akins.

For sage writing advice from years in the craft, Diane Pettit and Susan English; and for her friendship, brainstorming, and keen suggestions, Rebecca Huntington. Sandra Albertini and Franco Cicognani for offering cool refuge in the Apennines, and families Bittelli and Raptis for a place to write in Lampedusa.

For research assistance: Librarians, archivists, and collections at the University of Idaho, Washington State University, North Idaho College Library, Pullman's Neill Public Library, Ellensburg Public Library,

Johns Hopkins University's Paul Nitze School of Advanced International Studies, the *Spokesman-Review* and the *Lewiston Morning Tribune;* Coeur d'Alene human rights advocates Skip Kuck, Marshall Mend, and Tony Stewart.

For financial assistance: The Schreck Family Foundation, The Idaho Humanities Council, The University of Idaho Office of Diversity and Human Rights, The Washington Humanities Council, The Kootenai County Task Force on Human Relations, and the Latah County Human Rights Task Force. Thank you for believing in this work enough to help pay for it.

For giving her blessing to the project and graciously opening her home and heart to me, Mary Frances. Thanks also to Bill's caregivers in Ellensburg, Justin and Mary, for their dignified care of Bill before, during, and after our long interviews.

I am especially grateful to my husband, Marco, for his confidence and patience.

And finally, this book would have never come to fruition without the moral guidance and unwavering support of my parents, Sieg and Mabel, themselves rural Idahoans who believe in fairness and social justice.

Where, after all, do universal human rights begin? In small places, close to home—so close and so small that they cannot be seen on any map of the world. Yet they are the world of the individual person: the neighborhood he lives in; the school or college he attends; the factory, farm, or office where he works. Such are the places where every man, woman, and child seeks equal justice, equal opportunity, equal dignity without discrimination. Unless these rights have meaning there, they have little meaning anywhere. Without concerted citizen action to uphold them close to home, we shall look in vain for progress in the larger world.

—ELEANOR ROOSEVELT, 1958

1 | Greencreek

1941-1955

THE ROAD SIGN leading off Idaho's Highway 95 still points to Greencreek as if it were a destination. But it is really just the memory of a town. The old country store, AJ Wassmuth & Sons, sold its last sack of flour years ago and the taps have gone dry at Wimpy's, the local tavern, usually one of the last vestiges of a small town that is on its way toward vanishing completely.

This is where Bill Wassmuth was born, in a town so small the government would not even consider it a village, let alone a town. That year, 1941, the census referred to Greencreek, Idaho, as a "minor civil division," barely a voting precinct.

Greencreek, like many pioneering communities fading from the rural West, is now off the map. Most maps, anyway. There is no weathered wooden "Welcome to Greencreek" sign with a population count that includes dogs and cats. At the crest of the small hill overlooking Greencreek, a yellow sign with the silhouette of a tractor forewarns visitors of the only thing they might find moving if they actually drive downtown: "Farm Machinery, 35 mph." Down off to the right is the old Wassmuth place, where a rusted sign reading "Henry Wassmuth" still swings from the mailbox. The International tractor Henry bought new in 1948 sits in a patch of tall weeds outside the barn, as if it might work one more harvest after all.

The homestead looks across to the dying downtown, where the only businesses left are the church, an auto body shop, and a daycare housed in the old tavern.

But locals balk at the suggestion they are not a town. Greencreek residents point to the occasional crab feed and popular annual Fourth of July breakfast as proof. The tidy Catholic church still draws from the approximately fifty area farm families for Mass by a local priest each Sunday morning. In a pinch, you can still get your car fixed at Wassmuth's body shop (one of Bill's many cousins) or gas it up at two unmanned pumps if you are a member of the Grange or the grain growers cooperative.

Perhaps Greencreek stubbornly remains a town in the minds of many because its population, though miniscule, is still significant when considering there are less than two people per square mile living in the entire county. Idaho County is the least-densely populated county in one of the sparsest populated states in America. In a place with so few people it does not take much to be a town: a church, a crab feed, a collective memory, a handful of buildings withering along the high plateau.

This place, called the Camas Prairie after the native blue wildflowers that blossom in June, is a vast plain thirty miles long and twenty-five miles wide. The Snake, Salmon, and Clearwater Rivers carve steep canyons around the plateau's edges. The blue ridges of the Bitterroot Range and the snags of the Seven Devils Mountains rise in the distance. The county seat, Grangeville, is a small logging and farming town of 3,500, surrounded by five wilderness areas and four national forests that total more than five million acres.

Early settlers called the prairie "little Eden" and boasted that their livestock fed on native bunchgrass, and hogs could live for six months on the sweet, onionlike camas bulbs that grew in huge patches.

For centuries, the high, fertile plain had offered nourishment for the region's native inhabitants, the Nez Perce Indians, who dug the edible camas bulbs as a diet staple and grazed herds of ponies on the wild grasses while traveling from camps on the Clearwater River to hunting and fishing grounds on the Salmon.

Bill Wassmuth's great-grandfather homesteaded near Greencreek in the late 1800s on a piece of prairie that was part of the approximately 750,000 acres of what is now known as "takeback land."

Takeback land was taken from the Nez Perce and set aside for them as a reservation through treaty negotiations, but was then taken back by the U.S. government as pressure mounted to open up the reservation to settlers and speculators arriving after the discovery of gold. The takeback of Indian land was not unique to the Nez Perce. Theirs was among the nearly one-hundred-million acres of Indian landholdings nationwide that were acknowledged as Indian, but then taken over by the federal government between 1887 and 1934.[1]

Wassmuth's great-grandfather was among the many young men who staked his claim in the 1890s after Congress opened up large areas of Indian Country to homesteaders, leaving the members of the Nez Perce tribe with only a fraction of what its leaders had originally negotiated.

At the time Bill was born in 1941, Greencreek was, as it had been for four generations and still is, a small community of mostly white, Catholic farmers of German ancestry. The homesteaders were part of a surge of German immigration between 1860 and 1890, when more than 2.9 million Germans immigrated to the United States, 35 percent of them Catholic. Many of the families who settled on the Camas Prairie came after an area pioneer wrote to a German language newspaper in the Midwest urging Germans from Illinois to relocate from the flatlands to the sparsely settled farmlands of the Northwest. When recruits arrived, they named it after Greencreek, Illinois, their original hometown.

Greencreek functioned very much as a "Gemeinschaft," German for "community," with its face-to-face interactions among residents who generally shared similar values, beliefs, and ways of life. The families were large, and each family typically turned out at least one nun or man of the cloth (two of Bill's younger sisters would eventually choose to become Benedictine nuns at the nearby convent, Priory of St. Gertrude's). It was a calling that awarded automatic respect and honor, and families often had running bets among the adults about which kid would become the family's token priest or nun. The old joke goes: Everyone in town was cousins so they couldn't marry anyway.

At the time, Greencreek had half a dozen houses, a church, a school, a community hall, a workshop, and a general store offering everything from liquor to postage to laundry. The town lacked any formal political structure, but three influential groups formed the nexus of the town's unofficial leadership—the priests, who held moral superiority; the wealthiest farmers, who wielded economic power; and the road commissioners, who controlled transportation by deciding whose road was graded or plowed, when, and how often. The lack of any official governing body in town fostered a strong sense of civic responsibility: If no one governed, then everyone must. Families could count on one another for help in times of need, but the shared stewardship of the social fabric had drawbacks, too. Pressure to conform to accepted ethical norms could be stifling, a social constraint common to Catholic communalism.[2] If a couple waltzed too closely on the dance floor, the priest had the community's permission to step in and separate them.

During World War II, families patriotically rationed their sugar coupons and sat around their radios listening to Roosevelt's fireside chats, hanging on every word. In the 1950s, rocking chair money (unemployment insurance) kept the local economy afloat during the winter months when the local sawmills shut down for repairs, logging came to a halt, and farming activity slowed.[3]

As in most farm towns, a strong intergenerational continuity tied family and land together, with the youngest son expected to take over the farm. As such, Bill's father, Henry, had inherited the family farm after his mother died in the flu epidemic of 1919. Tucked into the protected hollow of a hillside, the Wassmuth place faced out over the prairie toward the spire of the Greencreek Catholic Church and its neatly landscaped grounds. Cattails in the hillside cleavage marked the small creek that fed a fish pond used to water the animals. They raised cattle, chicken and hogs, and farmed hay, wheat, and other dryland grains.

Bill was the second of nine children born over a period of twenty years, a span so long it divided the siblings into two camps of childhood memories, those of pre-television and post-television generations. It was not until 1967—at a gathering to celebrate Wassmuth's ordination as a priest—that the entire family was home together.

In the 1940s and 1950s, three items were critical to the family's survival: the garden, the Mason jar, and the deep freeze. Under matriarch Isabelle Wassmuth's direction, they raised their own vegetables, canned them for winter, and butchered their own meat. The children raised steers for 4-H and sold them every fall at the nearby Cottonwood Fair. Clothes were homemade, with fabric purchased on the occasional trips to Lewiston, which, though sixty miles away, was (and remains to be) the closest city.

The family lived a relatively self-sufficient lifestyle, through prudence, frugality, and fortitude. Every problem had at least three solutions and new things were purchased only when old things could not be fixed, and sometimes not even then. Bill's father, Henry Wassmuth, had a sturdy build and furrowed brow from years of hard labor and a stern upbringing. In addition to farming, he drove equipment for the highway district, distributed concrete products, and took other odd jobs to support his growing family. It was not just to put food on the table. Henry only completed school through the eighth grade and wanted his children to have the college education he did not. All nine Wassmuth children would eventually earn at least a bachelor's degree, with several going on to earn a master's degree.

While growing up, the Wassmuth children worked six days a week in the summer months, from dawn until dusk, with chores divided sharply along traditional gender roles—women's in the house, men's outdoors. The summer that Bill's older brother, Bob, began to consider his father's open offer of a college education, Wassmuth began to worry he would be left alone with the burden of daily farm chores, a prospect that weighed more heavily than the milk pails he lugged back and forth each day at sunup and sundown. Only his vivid imagination made the loathsome twice-daily routine bearable. He spent hours dreaming of becoming a pilot, though he reckoned it was foolish to even imagine such a vocation. Nobody in Greencreek flew. Everybody in Greencreek farmed. They were grounded for life.

The rare break from routine farm chores came during family get-togethers, the Wassmuths' primary social outlet. With such a large family and so many shirttail relatives, there was little shortage of activity. They had long picnics in the Grangeville city park. They picked blackberries along the Clearwater River until their fingers turned purple. They drove an hour south to swim at Zim's Plunge, a steamy swimming pool fed by natural thermal springs.

Visitors to the farm were infrequent. Yet they could count on certain company: Catholic volunteers dropped by every so often to conduct "convocation recruitment," inviting young Greencreek men to join the priesthood. And with Catholicism booming in America in the 1950s, they seldom went away disappointed. It was the height of the brick-and-mortar era, a period of expansion. The American Catholic Church believed that if they built more churches, more parishioners would come, and they did, for the first half of the twentieth century. The number of Catholics doubled between 1940 and 1960, and recruitment of young men into the priesthood was being met with so much success that by the end of the decade the number of priests in America had increased 25 percent to the all-time high of 53,746.[4]

The summer of 1955, volunteers left several brochures at the Wassmuth place. The pamphlets were full of illustrations depicting adventurous young black-robed priests flying single-engine airplanes to far-off missionary lands.

The tedium of farm life left room for Wassmuth's mind to drift to those exotic places. He imagined flying. He passed hours contemplating such a lifestyle—respected, yet adventurous. He decided that summer, barely a teenager, to enter the priesthood. It would be a chance to do some good in the world. It beat milking cows, and it was the only way a Greencreek boy could get his wings.

2 | The Small-Town Challenge

LIFE IN GREENCREEK, so long as things stayed the same and nobody stirred up trouble, was peaceful and uneventful for the Wassmuths. The community mores were clear: values based on tradition (the way things had been) and religion (the way things should be). But ironically, it was Henry Wassmuth's traditional and resolute ideas about right and wrong—beliefs grounded in his deep religious faith—that would put him at odds more than once with the small town.

Some members of the community blackballed him in the 1950s after he refused to ban black children from a temporary roller-skating rink he had set up in the tiny Greencreek community hall. Children could rent worn leather skates for a quarter and glide around for hours to canned organ music. The rink was popular until he invited a group of black youth from a nearby Job Corps center to join in the skating. They eagerly did, and soon after, Greencreek parents began pressuring Wassmuth to stop letting the black kids skate or they would stop bringing their own children. Henry was not aware of the growing din of calls for an end to segregation in the South. He just believed in a right and wrong way to treat people, and in this case, his was clearly the right way, the just way. If all persons are children of God, created by God, with a right to live as fully human a life as possible, he reasoned, then all should be treated equally and given the same freedoms and responsibilities: a basic tenet of Christianity. He informed town leaders he would shut the place down before refusing anyone entry. Tensions in Greencreek rose as the skating stalemate continued. People gossiped about his stubborn stance, but Henry Wassmuth kept his word. Unfortunately, so did the rest of the community. He eventually had to close the rink for lack of business. Though there was no longer a place to skate, Bill and his brothers and sisters were quietly proud of their father's courageous stance.

Henry's run-in with prejudice, and the racist alliances that turned the Greencreek community against him, underlines one of the primary challenges of defending human rights in a small town: Everybody knows everybody. And more than that, everyone depends on each other, sometimes in not-so-subtle ways. If you upset the road commissioner, your road might be plowed last next winter, or not at all. The close ties between small-town residents can be a strength or a weakness for a community trying to defend human rights, depending on the particular leadership and town dynamic.

In Greencreek, in this case, these ties exacerbated racist attitudes. And nearly fifty years later, small communities are still battling racists who have become entrenched, even popular, not because of their offensive beliefs but despite them, because of their constant public expressions of goodwill toward the community's other civic needs. Such is the case in the remote northwestern Montana town of Noxon, where Militia of Montana leader John Trochmann and his wife moved from Minnesota in 1988 to make their home and eventually to operate their militia headquarters. Trochmann claims he is not racist, yet allies himself with white supremacists, refers to "Human Wrongs Task Forces," and "free white Christians," and admits visiting the Aryan Nations on multiple occasions.[1] Though Bill Wassmuth and other human rights activists in Montana and elsewhere are convinced the Trochmanns are racist to the core, the community has not outright confronted the couple. They attend community events, even often volunteer. They are "nice folks," residents would say, shrugging their shoulders. Wassmuth said:

> It becomes those personal relationships that makes it harder for people to confront the bigotry that is there. The people you are calling names are people you know. How can you call somebody a racist when that person is taking the food basket to your grandmother on Thanksgiving when she's alone?

Though it is easy to blame such apathy toward bigots in a community on ignorance, the problem is not so much a lack of awareness as it is old-fashioned denial. There is often an unspoken recognition among small-town community members, a rural code, that certain negative sentiments might disturb their accepted web of facts and illusions that makes the community "a great place to live."

Small-town social mores tend to emphasize recognition of success and positive conversation, such as nonthreatening small talk about the weather or sports.[2] Compliments are liberally swapped back and forth. A community's failures, defeats and problems, though known to most, are rarely given equal public consideration by community members, except in small intimate chat circles or in the form of gossip.[3] It is partly for this reason local newspapers that do occasionally expose a community's problems may find themselves accused of overstating the negative and not printing enough "positive news."

This reluctance to face the negative is the basis for one of the most common arguments against taking immediate action against a bigot in a small community: the "ignore it and it will go away" theory. This camp often argues that by exposing and focusing on the problem a community gives the problem more attention and, inadvertently, more credibility, thereby making it worse.

The debate over whether to ignore the monster in their midst or attack it publicly and visibly was one of the major debates faced by residents in the small North Idaho timber and tourism town of Coeur d'Alene during the 1980s as it struggled over what to do about the presence of the notorious Aryan Nations compound near Hayden Lake, ten miles north. The compound began as twenty acres of forest and a two-story farmhouse. Over the years, Aryan Nations members erected a watchtower and guard post, a church, a guest bunkhouse, and several trailers for employees. They painted swastikas on the roofs of outbuildings, surrounded the place with barbed wire, and even posted a "Whites Only" sign at the entrance gate. It was home to German shepherds with names like Hans, Fritz, and Eva, a detail that is almost laughable if this racist retreat had not also sheltered some of the nation's most dangerous extremists over the years. The list of visitors to the compound in those years reads like a who's who of domestic terrorists: Buford Furrow, the Washington State man who shot up a Jewish community center full of children and then killed a Filipino mailman in California. Louis Beam, the renowned Texas Klansman. Robert Miles, the ex-United Klans of America leader and convicted school bus bomber. J.B. Stoner, head of the National State's Rights Party, indicted in 1977 in connection with a 1954 bombing of a church in Birmingham, Alabama. Robert Mathews, leader of The Order, the group that gunned down Denver talk show host Alan Berg and carried out a string of bombings and armed robberies. Chevie Kehoe, convicted of the 1996 murder of an Arkansas family and a 1997 shoot-out with Ohio police. Robert Pires, one of the thugs who set off the powerful pipe bomb that ripped through Bill Wassmuth's parish home in 1986. The list goes on. The common denominator linking them all was a tie to longtime Aryan Nations leader Richard Butler, one of the most visible white supremacist statesmen in the nation. Butler would eventually emerge as Wassmuth's archnemesis as the two sparred over whether the Northwest would become an increasingly tolerant place, supportive of human rights and open to all, which Wassmuth envisioned, or the white homeland Butler wanted.

The delinquents who passed through the Aryan Nations compound attempted to silence their critics through threats and harassment. Instilling fear for personal safety has long been used as an effective tool for stifling opposition to an increase in violence toward minority populations, as was the case in small towns throughout Germany during the Third Reich. In the face of hate, silence can be deadly. But speaking out in a small town is not always easy.

A number of human rights activists working alongside Wassmuth were targeted over the years, though the threats went largely unreported to police or media. Disturbing racist graffiti showed up at homes and offices. Coeur d'Alene residents received disconcerting phone calls: "We know where you live," followed by the sound of rapid machine-gun fire. One male caller left sinister messages threatening to tear out their hearts. Another caller threatened to decapitate one resident and to leave his head at a wooded rest area along Interstate 90 outside of town. The FBI showed up every now and then at activists' offices with photos of scowling white men and vague warnings to watch out for them.[4] These so-called activists were really no more than a group of good-hearted local folks—librarians, ministers, teachers, businessmen, law enforcement officials—concerned about violence and intolerance in their town. As the threats increased, they began carrying cell phones and driving nondescript vehicles void of bumper stickers or other identifying markings. They were often afraid. They watched each others' backs, did not let it show, and did not give up.

While those who spoke out feared for their personal safety, they also took financial risks. A Jewish real estate agent in Kootenai County was disturbed by the swastikas that kept turning up on his billboards and worried that the continued attacks might make it more difficult for him to do business. Fifty years ago, Henry Wassmuth refused to take part in the accepted local practice of trading alcohol with Nez Perce tribal members for the right to lease their farmland. As a result of his stand, several of his bids for farmland—acreage he desperately needed —went to other residents willing to make the barter. In this way, Henry Wassmuth was penalized financially for not bowing to pressure to participate in an accepted racist practice.

It is a theme that has not changed much over the years: Don't rock the boat, it will just make things worse.

In Coeur d'Alene, human rights activists were met over and over with this refrain as they repeatedly warned others of the need to respond more forcefully to the increasingly menacing hate group activities in the region.

The decision to fight the Aryan Nations head-on came only after months of heated town hall meetings and backroom exchanges. Wassmuth explained:

> There were two vocal groups we had to deal with. One of them argued that we were not being inclusive by opposing people that are just thinking differently from us. Our answer to that was very simple. You don't debate justice and you don't debate, or tolerate, oppression. Being inclusive does not mean being inclusive of someone who is hurting someone, or advocating violence against someone.

The tougher challenge was to convince those who said "By fighting these guys all you are doing is giving them credibility and calling attention to them and that is exactly what they want." That was the "ignore them and they will go away" theory. Our conviction was that if we ignored them they would interpret that as tolerance and acceptance. So even though you risked giving them credibility and some visibility, it had to be done in order to combat them. There are plenty of people who didn't agree with that, including some of the powerful business leaders, who fought us tooth and nail on that point.

Civil rights lawyer and Southern Poverty Law Center cofounder Morris Dees, who also joined the fight against the Aryan Nations and was crucial to its demise, bluntly refers to this approach as a head-in-the-sand attitude.[5] Dees recalls frequently encountering such perspectives in Idaho while studying the police response to the Aryan Nations and interviewing potential jurors for the court case that would later decide the Aryan Nations' fate.[6] Most people disagreed with the Aryan Nations' ideas, Dees said, but were more apt to keep their own opinions quiet so as not to rouse political or cultural divisions within the community. It was not so much malicious silence as it was apathy in the name of upholding a comforting, though delusional, sense of public harmony.

One of the dangers a small town faces when it adheres too stubbornly to its positive self-image, even in the face of crisis, is the likelihood of creating a divisive communication gap between what is said publicly and what is said privately. Positive remarks about the community are largely reserved for public conversations, while negative sentiments (including bigoted comments or beliefs) are saved for more intimate talks among like-minded parties who rarely speak these sentiments publicly.

This unspoken "etiquette of gossip,"[7] common in small towns, can create two different channels of communication that serve very different purposes and sometimes result in deep—yet rarely acknowledged—community divides. The problem is compounded when these prejudices are allowed to simmer underneath the surface, because they can be easily ignored by those who disagree (since it is rarely said publicly) in the name of maintaining the all-important sense of community cohesion, however contrived. This underlying tension may surge to the surface if the community is allowed to fracture along ethnic, class, and religious lines, as the divisions and emotions that accompany them are eventually exposed. Rather than turning away from unanswered bigotry in hopes of limiting its visibility, Wassmuth believed small towns must counter every act of hate with immediate acts of goodness, even if the immediate reward for such action is not in plain sight. The short-term result of the stand Henry Wassmuth took in support of allowing black children at the Greencreek skating rink was that no one was able to skate. But long-term, it inspired his son to stand up forcefully for human rights himself during even bigger battles. Virtue, if not displayed and held up as a public model for civic responsibility, does little for a community. History has shown that apathy is interpreted as acceptance, not only by those who hate, but by the general public and those who have been the targets of hate.

Unfortunately, an act of violence or the intent to harm another member of the community is often necessary to trigger action on the part of local residents. When white supremacists detonated a bomb outside Wassmuth's Coeur d'Alene parish home in 1986, it sparked the kind of powerful community outrage necessary to break the head-in-the-sand cycle that had prompted some to look the other way as Aryan Nations activity was intensifying. Once the unspoken social threshold of acceptable behavior has been broken, the problem often bursts into the public sphere with a fair amount of support for action and resolution. Live-and-let-live, after all, means one goes unbothered only as long as one leaves others in peace. Hate, intimidation, and violence clearly disrupt the social contract.

The perceived live-and-let-live attitude of the rural Intermountain West, along with the area's white majority population, isolated location, and natural beauty, was one of the factors that originally attracted many hate groups to North Idaho, Western Montana, Southern Oregon, and Eastern Washington. But Wassmuth believed they miscalculated the point at which the region's residents would feel the unspoken but well-defined community limits had been crossed. They did not count on Wassmuth, or the dozens of others like him.

When people would ask me why they chose this part of the Northwest I always said there are two ways to answer that question. If you are looking for a place to make the homeland for the white race, and you can choose any place in the country, you are not going to pick the deserts of Nevada. You are going to pick the most beautiful areas—so they picked North Idaho, Western Montana, and Southern Oregon, some of the most beautiful places in the country. The second thing is many of these folks felt that if they came to rural Idaho they would find that "live and let live" independent streak—which is a very real thing—and that it would let them by with this stuff, that it would translate into lax law enforcement and other areas. That people would just let them be. What they didn't count on was that "live and let live" also means don't tread on any of us, because if you come in and step on my neighbor, "my live and let live" attitude says you screwed up and I'm going to come after you. That "live and let live" attitude in Idaho turned into a fierce independence that ended up saying to these same folks, "You are stepping out of line here." I think it backfired on them. It turned on them.

The region's relatively recent frontier history has resulted in a tangible strain of rugged independence that typifies the West. But often overlooked is the enduring commitment to good neighborliness that also stems from the pioneering tradition of mutual self-help and protection.

In the rural West there is an intimate connection between culture and place, which often reveals itself as civic responsibility toward the community's shared identity. This moral code of community warm-heartedness is taken so seriously in small towns that it shows up ideologically in many aspects of organized life, reinforced through the town's institutions, including churches, schools, and civic organizations.

While a community's potential for civic goodness is most impressive during times of crisis, the rural community spirit often manifests itself in small ways, with everyday gestures of voluntarism at bake sales, car washes, raffles, spaghetti feeds, and other homegrown fundraisers that support local causes, groups, individuals, or even businesses who need a hand. Generosity is about time as much as it is about money. Residents in the small North Idaho college town of Moscow helped their favorite locally owned bookstore move to its new location across the street one evening by forming a human chain to pass hundreds of books from the old store to the new one.

But civic mindedness is an especially esteemed virtue during times of hardship. Witness how a small town mobilizes (often with lightning speed) to support a fellow community member in distress: Residents come together to make food for the recent widower or to fill a burned-out family's new freezer with donated meat from game and livestock. Farmers hold threshing bees and donate a portion of the harvest to a community charity. Timber towns give the proceeds from a day's logging to help a struggling family. These common civic gestures represent a sense of mutual obligation and dependence that says, "We depend on each other and we come through for one another in times of need."

This is done partly out of a sense of reciprocity, the idea that participating in such human exchanges secures similar help in times of need. But more often, this spirit of community develops simply because residents believe it is the right thing to do, because there is a moral expectation that the local community can take care of its own local citizens.[8] Many small-town residents have long believed that this kind of civic self-reliance is a more effective response to crisis than what any government bureaucracy or outside agency can provide.

However, it is sometimes these same community networks that can allow racism to fester under the surface if not addressed in a collective and public manner.

Personal relationships in a small town are not a one-on-one chain of independent connections but rather a complex, woven patchwork of interdependent relations that reinforce and affect each other. Human rights task forces like those Wassmuth helped form in small towns throughout the West are effective organizations for fighting hate because they provide a structure that gives the community an opportunity to recognize the problem in a collective forum and tackle it as a citizenry, instead of as individual community members confronting other individual community members.

Northwest small towns, particularly in the last decade, have displayed impressive civic responses to hate in their determination to stand up against acts of hatred against fellow community members.

Residents of Billings, Montana, successfully thwarted a groundswell of racist activity in 1993. Like North Idaho, Montana had become a favorite hideout for antigovernment extremists and radical hate groups during the 1980s. In the late '80s and early '90s, the approximately fifty Jewish families who lived in the Billings area had become more frequent targets of hate activity, the community's synagogues and Jewish cemeteries had been vandalized, and hate literature was cropping up on front porches throughout town. The homes of Native Americans were sprayed with epithets like "Die Indian." A black church congregation was harassed. Local and regional human rights groups began organizing in response.

In December 1993, the cochair of the Billings Coalition for Human Rights, Tammie Schnitzer, returned home from a meeting to find a chunk of cinder block thrown through her five-year-old son Isaac's bedroom window, which had been decorated with the Star of David and a menorah for Hanukkah. The police who responded to Schnitzer's home urged her to take the Jewish symbols down. She refused and talked about why in a story the *Billings Gazette* ran about the attack two days later. The newspaper coverage triggered an outpouring of support from several Christian churches, whose leaders encouraged the children of their churches to draw menorahs, which were photocopied and distributed throughout the congregations. Billings' residents mounted a concerted display of solidarity against the harassment of their neighbor by posting menorahs in their own windows. Then, a few days later, the *Billings Gazette* joined in the fight by publishing a full-page picture of a menorah that could be cut out of the newspaper for display. The newspaper's bold act of community activism, sometimes called civic journalism, helped ignite a smoldering grassroots movement against hate. The Jewish symbols were soon being Xeroxed all across town, even purchased at the local K-Mart. Skinheads at first responded with more vandalism and threatening acts of violence and intimidation, but Billings residents were undeterred. As hate activity increased, so did the number of menorahs being displayed in town, with nearly six thousand of them finding their way onto public and private buildings. One business even took out space on a local billboard for the following message: "Not in Our Town! No Hate, No Violence, Peace on Earth."[9] Faced with a united community unshakable in its willingness to stand up for human rights, the racists gave up the vandalism and threatening phone calls. Billings' campaign became known as Not in Our Town, and it drew nationwide press and praise.

In a similar campaign in 1994, hundreds of Idaho Falls residents protested the distribution of white supremacist flyers by displaying bright blue ribbons with the words, "If there are lines to be drawn, let them be around us and not between us."

In 1995, residents of Jordan, Montana, rallied their community against the Freemen, an antigovernment group of Christian Identity believers who holed up in a ranch called Justis Township during a standoff with federal agents. Many of those who led the grassroots community effort against the Freemen's violent rhetoric were neighbors, even relatives of members of the group.

More recently, in December 2002, residents of Riverton, Wyoming, turned to the successful grassroots task force model that Wassmuth helped develop in Idaho (and later helped spread throughout the West) to oppose a white supremacist group that had decided to move to their tiny ranching, logging, and mining town northwest of Cheyenne. When this Illinois-based World Church of the Creator announced plans to move its headquarters to Riverton (which sits on the edge of the Wind River Indian Reservation, home to thousands of Shoshone and Arapaho tribal members), community leaders quickly formed a human rights task force. Residents signed nonpartisan pledges of tolerance for publication in the local newspapers, displayed "No Hate" signs, and urged their neighbors to take a stand.

But it is the human rights activists and regular residents who stood up against hate in the two much-maligned North Idaho towns of Coeur d'Alene and Sandpoint who are perhaps most deserving of credit for their dogged community battle against the white supremacist movement. Their tireless grassroots fight against hate was more endur-ing, more persistent, and in the end, perhaps more successful than any small-town human rights campaign since the civil rights movement. At its core was the desire to hold on steadfastly to the neighborly as-pects of rural life that compel residents to place a high value on civic responsibility. If basic values such as honesty, neighborliness, charity, and tolerance of one another's differences continue to remain the core of small-town community standards, hate will have little chance to thrive. The success of these homespun campaigns against groups such as the Aryan Nations and its dwindling cadre of hangers-on is confir-mation that the Northwest's small towns are up to the civic challenge of human rights activism. It has proved that an engaged citizenry is one of the most effective tools for fighting hate. It is a reminder that the sense of grassroots civic responsibility that French philosopher Alexis de Tocqueville referred to as the "genius of American democ-racy," endures in the rural West.

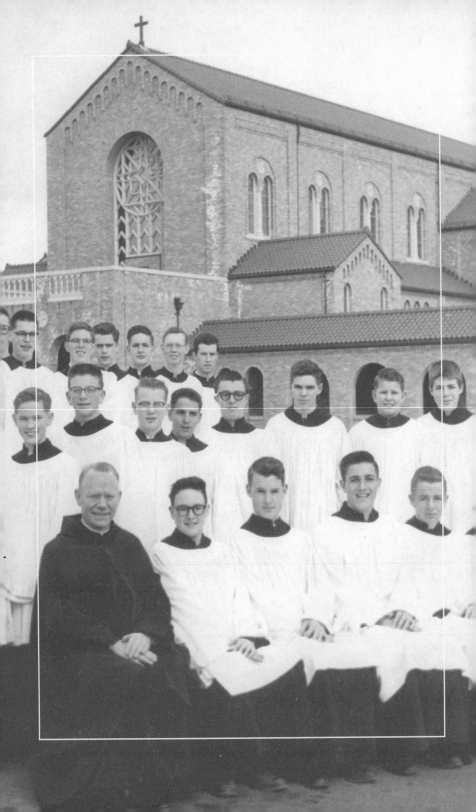

3

Mount Angel Abbey and St. Thomas Seminary

1955-1967

THE PICTURES of missionary pilots dropped off at the farm by the Catholic volunteers stayed with young Bill Wassmuth all summer. During the peak of harvest, he broke the news to his father as they were riding home on top of their load of hay, after a long, dusty day out on the prairie. He wanted to leave the farm. He wanted to be a priest. Henry, Bill recalled, nearly fell off the haywagon. But he could not say no. Greencreek residents viewed priesthood as one of the most honorable vocations. Nearly every family produced one. He would have to be proud of his son and support his decision.

That September, Henry and Isabelle loaded Bill's neatly packed suitcase into their Mercury sedan and began the day-long drive toward the Oregon coast to deliver him to the oldest seminary West of the Rocky Mountains: Mount Angel, a strict school of theology for boys located in an isolated hilltop Benedictine abbey south of Portland.

From Greencreek to Mount Angel, the roads follow rivers. They drove to Lewiston, crossed the Snake, and headed across the dry southeastern plains of Washington until they reached the wide Columbia River. They continued toward Portland, Oregon, through the steep, windswept valleys of the Columbia gorge, past The Dalles and Hood River, before turning south toward Gervais, Oregon. They wound their way through fields of wheat and hops, through apple orchards and hazelnut groves until they reached Oregon's wide Willamette Valley—Bill Wassmuth's new home.

Like its motherhouse back in Switzerland, Mount Angel Abbey was built on a wooded knoll overlooking a broad valley. A mile-long winding road led up to the red brick abbey, paralleled by a well-trodden path worn down by the abbey's monks as they walked the Stations of the Cross. As the Wassmuths turned up through the main gates, Bill noticed a series of tiny huts with depictions of scenes leading up to Christ's crucifixion: Jesus Is Condemned to Death, Jesus Falls the First Time, Jesus Meets His Mother.

Then, halfway up the hill he watched as they passed Veronica Wipes the Face of Jesus, Jesus Consoles the Women of Jerusalem, Jesus Falls a Third Time. And as they rounded the last quarter mile to the abbey: Jesus Is Nailed to the Cross, Jesus Is Taken Down From the Cross, Jesus Is Laid in the Tomb.

He recognized the depictions of the most difficult journey of Jesus' life—they were the Stations of the Cross, spiritual stops along a route that Bill would come to know well during his years at Mount Angel.

As the abbey came into view, Wassmuth peered out the sedan's side window at the imposing collection of fortress-like brick buildings flanked on either side by meticulously kept gardens and arboretums. From the abbey's high vantage point he could see five peaks, including Mount Rainier to the north and Mount Hood to the east. The colored patchwork of orchards and farm fields down below looked like an old-fashioned quilt, stitched together by fences, rivers, and trees. The monastery grounds included the hulking abbey church with the Joseph Crypt Chapel underneath it, the monk's quarters, retreat house, the two seminarian dorms Aquinas and Anselm, the Benedictine Press, the library, and the refectory, all laid out in the classic quadrangle of Benedictine monasteries. Its grandness dwarfed Bill and all his expectations. Mount Angel Abbey, one of the oldest Benedictine monasteries in the nation, was the biggest place he had ever been.

A Swiss-German Benedictine missionary monk named Father Adelhelm Odermatt founded the abbey in 1882. Odermatt was seeking out new places of refuge in America at a time when monasteries and convents in Switzerland were threatened by hostile laws being passed by the Swiss government.[1] He chose a prominent, thickly forested hill overlooking the eastern edge of the Willamette Valley, a place already considered a sacred and spiritual site for local Native Americans, who had called it *Tap-a-Lam-a-ho,* or mountain of communion.[2] The monks called it Mount Angel, a direct translation of Engelberg, the twelfth-century abbey they had fled in Switzerland. The monks developed the hilltop throughout the 1880s, establishing gardens, a college, a small press, and a seminary. The Catholic Church in America began as an immigrant church, and so the students arrived at the monastery roughly in the same order as Catholic immigrants arrived in America: Irish, Germans, Italians, Poles. As the monastery grew, the small nearby town of Fillmore that supported the monastery also grew, soon changing its name to Mount Angel.

The town's economy is still dependent on the Benedictine community of monks and nuns at Mount Angel. The monks produce everything from Gregorian chant CDs to special herbal soap. Even the local microbrewery makes an Abbey Ale. Each fall, some 350,000 tourists arrive for the community's Oktoberfest, an annual celebration of Bavarian folk culture and locally made beer, the brewing and drinking of which is still an accepted part of the monk's daily life in many German and Swiss monasteries.

Fittingly, the town's largest landmark is its Catholic church, which dominates the town center. If Mount Angel is a company town, St. Benedict is the boss.

St. Benedict founded the first twelve Benedictine monasteries in Italy fifteen centuries ago, with the first in about A.D. 529 at Monte Cassino, some eighty miles south of Rome. It is the oldest monastic order in the Catholic Church.

Its monks live a simple life of work and spiritual contemplation, with many hours of the day spent in communal prayers to foster the coordinated unity that St. Benedict believed was necessary to grow in the love of God. It was within this context that Wassmuth first developed notions about the necessity of communal action for a greater good.

Mount Angel seminary was not just an isolated religious boarding school but an integral piece of a larger Benedictine religious community devoted to prayer, work, study, charity, and self-sufficiency, in that order.

All of this seemed fine to Wassmuth as long as his parents were there, making small talk and helping him unload his few possessions to get settled. But as their car pulled out of the abbey's driveway and headed back down the hill, Wassmuth's stomach fluttered, and he wondered if he had made the right decision. In Greencreek, there had been twelve other farm kids in his class. Now he was one of several hundred men and boys living in a cloistered hilltop monastery. He felt immediately homesick.

His new digs were not exactly comforting. He had a bunk-bed cot and a locker in four-story Aquinas Hall's top floor, which housed the showers and the sleeping quarters for approximately forty young men. Two mentor priests also lived on that floor, in individual rooms, as floor supervisors.

The abbey had both a minor seminary and a major seminary. The minor seminary offered four years of high school and two years of college classes. The major seminary offered two years of philosophy and four years of postgraduate theology, which served as training for becoming a monk. After completing minor seminary at Mount Angel, Wassmuth would be sent to a major seminary in Seattle to be trained as a parish priest in the Idaho diocese, rather than as a Benedictine monk.

At Mount Angel, high-school students dormed on the fourth floor, college-age students on the third, lectures were held on the second-floor classrooms (which were actually ground level), while a daylight basement housed recreation rooms where the young seminarians played Ping-Pong, told stories, and acted out plays from which they had edited out all of the female parts. There were dingy locker rooms for athletics and a few barren music halls for practicing piano or Gregorian chants. One of the most cherished spots was the small "goody store" where seminarians, as reward for good behavior, were allowed to buy candy, gum, or basic school supplies. Meals were eaten in the basement refectory of the major seminary, connected by a long underground tunnel to the main abbey, where the kitchen was. The seminarians' strict training on the avoidance of any close relationships (including friendships) with women was reinforced by the purposeful absence of any female presence. The only women any of the residents ever saw were solemn-faced Benedictine nuns from the nearby convent who worked in the kitchen, and a very old nurse who crankily tended to the boys' minor health needs, doling out aspirin and performing regular exams. Because most of the Idaho boys could not tell a maple from an oak, poison oak became a frequent cause for trips to the elderly nurse, who referred the worst cases to a doctor in town, just down the hill.

Bill's homesickness lasted for months, assuaged only by the camaraderie of other equally lonely Idaho boys and a routine so strict it was oddly comforting. To Bill, accustomed to the rigorous daily routine of the farm, the abbey's controlled daily schedule of prayer, classes, meals, and chores seemed natural, familiar.

Each day the boys awoke before dawn and were given fifteen minutes to shower and dress in black pants, white shirts, and tie. First they went to obligatory chapel, a quiet time for meditating on the day ahead. Most slept. Then it was on to communion Mass, the first of two daily liturgies in Latin. After Mass, at about 7:30 a.m., they walked to the refectory for breakfast, the only meal of the day when talking freely was occasionally allowed. After breakfast they suited up in heavy black cassocks and white surplices and marched silently, two by two in line for several hundred yards to the main abbey church to join the older monks for High Mass. Though all the masses were in Latin, the High Mass was sung, with heavy Gregorian chants, as was Benedictine tradition. The Mount Angel choirmaster was an unusual monk named Father David, who meticulously shaved his head, spoke in a squeaky, affected voice, and held a near obsessive devotion to the art of Gregorian chanting. An expert in the high-classic chants, he worked tirelessly, though mostly unsuccessfully, to turn the nearly one hundred seminarians into world-class chanters. Most of them, especially Wassmuth, loathed this training and looked warily upon the odd manner of Father David.

After High Mass, they attended class, then shortly before noon they went back to chapel for a fifteen-minute prayer meditation called "Examination." The young men spent Examination repenting, if they had already misbehaved in the few hours they had been awake, or simply contemplating how their day was going "in relation to their faith goals." More than a few probably slept. Lunch began with a spiritual reading. If the rector felt generous, the seminarians could talk. If not, there were mandatory public readings—a dreaded lunchtime tradition. In the refectory, several tables off to the side had been designated as server tables. Those seated there served the other tables for a week. Then seats rotated. There was a similar rotation schedule for dishwashing and all the other chores necessary to keep the abbey and seminary running smoothly and self-sufficiently. The rector, the vice rector, and the dean of discipline all sat at one reserved table in the refectory, and one of them served each day in the despised role of reading critic.

A seminarian would be chosen to stand up and read, usually stories from the saints' lives or other scriptures. Halfway through, the appointed reading critic rang a small brass bell, tersely corrected pronunciation, pointed out errors, gave suggestions for improvement, and then signaled the young man to continue. The tense and often humiliating public test kept order in the dining hall, provided additional spiritual content for the day, and supposedly improved public speaking, a skill considered crucial for a successful priest.

Public discipline was also meted out at lunchtime. Those who had misbehaved were forced to "kneel out" in front of the rector's table. That meant kneeling down before the rector and his colleagues while the others ate, until given approval to stand and return to one's table. It was not uncommon for a whole crowd of boys to spend their lunch hour on their knees beneath the disciplinarian's stern gaze as he ate before them.

One level of punishment rose above kneeling out. "Swats" happened in the locker rooms. The young man who had misbehaved had to run partially clothed through a gauntlet of his peers as they swatted him with towels as censure. In the 1950s, it was considered basic character building. Today, it would be grounds for a lawsuit.

The only level of discipline above swats was being tossed out of the seminary, and the types of activities that might trigger such discipline were intentionally vague. Sexual or homosexual activity was not officially tolerated. Seminarians would sometimes do what their peers called "the disappearing act," one day vanishing from the ranks, having been shipped home because of unacceptable tendencies never acknowledged or spoken of, even outside the priests' earshot. Such developments were prudently shrouded in silence.

After lunch, the seminarians again attended classes, did the chores that kept the expansive grounds and buildings tidy, then resigned themselves to an exhaustive schedule of athletic activities designed to rid the young men of their extra adrenaline—boxing, football, basketball, track, and other sports, always played vigorously against each other. Sports served as the primary outlet for accommodating the restless young men's pent-up energy, or for releasing frustrations brought about by communal living and school pressures. Students could take walks down to the front gate or to the nearby Silverton River, but seminary officials prohibited dating, bar visiting, or going off grounds without permission.

After squeezing out all their energy in athletics, the sweaty teens returned immediately to chapel for a spiritual reading to quiet things down. They ate dinner, had a short recreational break, study hall, and then "compline" or night prayer chapel before lights out around 8:30.

Fresh off the farm, Bill Wassmuth was a model seminarian—an energetic, healthy, bright, and adaptable student. He committed to his studies, had no bad habits and rarely misbehaved. He absorbed the scripture lessons and liturgies quickly, studied hard, and aimed to please his strict monk professors.

Yet he pined for his Idaho home for much of his first year, despite the occasional weekend spent off grounds at Aunt Rosie's, his mother's sister, who worked a small chicken farm in nearby Woodburn and treated him like a son when he visited. Over the course of the year Wassmuth wrote several dreary, homesick letters to his mother and snapped pictures from atop the hill to show his dad how the Willamette Valley farmers plowed their fields in strips rather than in circles like back home. He thought about bailing out several times, but felt guilty even considering it. The guilt that followed his internal deliberations about leaving was often worse than the homesickness that prompted it. Sensing his struggle, his mother mailed him supportive letters, saying they were proud of his decision, but would love him and be proud even if he decided to leave. Sometimes pride alone kept him at Mount Angel. Other days he heard God whispering in his ear, calling him quietly, persistently into service as he walked the vast abbey grounds. The source of his motivation to stay at the abbey changed often over the course of six years. Gradually, the hilltop monastery felt more like home. He played a lead role in the seminary's drama production of "Christ in the Concrete City" and began snapping pictures of his surroundings—the abbey, the gardens, the grotto—to show folks back home.

At the end of each school year, Bill rode the Greyhound bus back to Greencreek where he worked on the farm for the summer. He hayed for his dad and then for neighbors to make extra money, taking breaks only to attend church, work on the intricate stone grotto he was building from river rock in the yard, and shoot squirrels with his buddies on Sundays. Never did he have girlfriends, nor did he even put himself within an arm's length of a woman. One Sunday afternoon his best friend brought along his girlfriend for a drive. As the three of them squeezed into the pickup cab, Wassmuth felt guilty just being in such close physical proximity to her. He was a seminarian who should avoid women at every turn. Guilt, however, proved a constant companion.

Each summer he worked hard to earn the money needed to sustain himself through the year ahead, then he returned to Mount Angel in the autumn.

In the fall of 1956, Henry and Isabelle gave him a transistor radio the size of a large encyclopedia to take back with him. He listened to it on the Greyhound the whole way to Oregon. When he arrived at the abbey, he gave it up at the main office as was required of all personal possessions. But when he went home for Christmas after a semester without popular music, he returned to the abbey with a different plan: he would stash the radio on the monastery grounds and sneak out to occasionally listen while on walks down to the river. The students were not allowed to take walks alone, so he took his two most-trusted Idaho seminarians along for the first furtive radio outing. When far enough away from the abbey, they tuned the radio to a Portland rock-and-roll station and listened for hours to the prohibited modern melodies. Inside the abbey, the only music allowed was classical or Gregorian chants. Outside the abbey, Wassmuth's clandestine radio gang snuck out every two months in hopes of hearing a single favorite tune: the Everly Brothers singing "Bye Bye Love." The monks never apprehended him. It was always one of his favorite songs.

Contraband radio aside, Seminarian Bill proved such a model student and natural leader his peers voted him class president, and later, student body president, which earned him the coveted corner room, with windows and sweeping views on both sides and a bigger bed. He and the other Idaho seminarians had formed a tight clique, which would be abruptly disrupted at the end of their six years of minor seminary at Mount Angel.

Bishop Sylvester Treinen of Idaho, wanting his future priests trained not as monks but rather as parish priests, split the tightknit class of Idaho seminarians geographically, with men from northern Idaho going on to major seminary at St. Thomas near Seattle and southern Idaho men attending St. Thomas in Denver, Colorado.

Wassmuth transferred to St. Thomas Seminary near Seattle, a seminary run by Sulpician priests, a French order that dedicated their lives solely toward training others. That fall of 1961, Bill was 20.

Compared to Mount Angel, St. Thomas was the Cadillac of seminaries. The brand-new 186,000-square-foot complex sat on prime real estate, several hundred acres of lush forest along the northeast shore of Lake Washington, just ten miles from downtown Seattle.

It was the golden era of American Catholicism and the church was in the middle of its post-World War II brick-and-mortar building boom. St. Thomas glittered as one of its shiny new jewels.[3]

Two years before Wassmuth arrived, architects had completed the finishing touches on the new seminary campus. More than thirty-one acres of heavily forested land had been cleared to make way for tennis courts, a baseball diamond, and a football field. The campus included a three-story classroom and library, an administrative priests' wing, a six-story dormitory block, and two-story prayer hall with a huge auditorium and stage. A large refectory dining hall was connected to a nearby convent that housed twelve sisters who, like at Mount Angel, did all the cooking and laundry.

The long driveway led through a dense forest of ferns and mossy old-growth cedars before climbing to the edge of campus. The main entrance, an impressive portico of limestone columns, was flanked on either side by mosaics and two sculptures of Jesus. Through this portico was a view of the impressive formal garden, in the center of which stood a life-size Carrara marble statue of Mary and the baby Jesus.[4]

St. Thomas's glory would be short-lived, however, as the church would sell the property in the late 1970s due to a precipitous decline in the number of seminarians. Today, the Mary and Jesus statue has been replaced by a zenlike rock fountain that welcomes students to Bastyr University, an accredited private college specializing in naturopathic medicine. Students discuss feng shui and acupuncture in halls adorned with carved wooden crosses. The forested seminary ground is now a state park. Nationwide, seminaries and religious houses that expanded during this same era now stand empty or converted to other uses—reminders of how the church celebrated itself too boldly in the gloried construction of buildings as a metaphor for the Catholic institution.

In its Catholic heyday, however, the seminarians and the priests of St. Thomas lived a rigid routine similar to Mount Angel. But compared to Mount Angel, the academic curriculum focused more rigorously on theology and philosophy, specifically the teachings of Aristotle and St. Thomas Aquinas, which were considered cornerstones of Roman Catholicism. This philosophy, called Aristotelian Thomistic or Neo-Scholasticism, is the study of Aristotle as interpreted by St. Thomas Aquinas, a thirteenth-century Dominican friar, philosopher, and theologian who was instrumental in using the works of Aristotle to explain the Catholic faith and dogma.

Aquinas believed that truth could be discovered both through faith and reason, that a conflict between the two was impossible as they both originate in God. He defended the legitimacy of reason, especially in the works of Aristotle, because he believed that reason could, in principle, lead the mind to God. Because many Catholics believed human reason also had the power to discern universally binding moral principles, they believed they could transform or reform society through the application of Catholic teachings. This background of Catholic social thought would eventually provide Wassmuth, and many other Catholics, with an intellectual rationale for working on behalf of social justice.

But the professors teaching at St. Thomas seminary were focused on the medieval philosophy of Aquinas, not on how their students would eventually utilize that knowledge in the larger society. How best to practically and properly train priests for serving in a parish—and what philosophies these young future priests should learn—was becoming an increasingly confused matter for the American Catholic seminaries in the mid-1960s.

Pope Pius XII had died in 1958 and was replaced by Pope John XXIII, who over the next decade would help usher in a tidal wave of change in church and Catholic society (along with the help of another Catholic named John—John F. Kennedy).

Between 1962 and 1965, the Catholic Church convened the Second Vatican Council (also known as Vatican II), a series of meetings that drew nearly three thousand bishops and prelates to Rome. Their discussions would eventually transform and modernize the Catholic Church, though not without alienating some of its more traditionalist followers. Among the reforms introduced were theological and ritual changes designed to make the church more relevant to the modern world. The clergy encouraged parishioners to set aside popular devotions like the rosary and instead become more active participants in the liturgies. The liturgies themselves were also changing, being adapted to different cultures and languages.

Seminary courses and masses formerly held in Latin could be held in English, or the vernacular. New theologians, some of whom touted a more open ecumenism, or unity among diverse religions, were deemed appropriate for study. These were major deviations from the way things had been, yet the priest professors at St. Thomas and other schools had little instruction on how to adjust seminarian training accordingly.

Such changes either were embraced and incorporated into daily lectures, by those who felt up to the task of interpreting the council's documents, or rejected, by those professors more loyal to the traditions of the past and who continued to teach from neo-scholastic European manuals and old Latin texts.

This schism within the seminary professorial ranks reflected a greater crisis growing within the church and its schools. As Catholics began to differ on the nature of their commitment to Church doctrine and what it meant to be Catholic, educational policy and direction also began to waver.[5] The theological foundations of the Catholic Church were shaking, yet seminary instruction remained largely cut off from this transformation until years after the council's final session closed in 1965.

As a result, Wassmuth's class of seminarians remained largely sheltered from the anxieties of the outside world. They had little knowledge of the crisis brewing within the church, much less in the whole of American society, where the sexual revolution was well underway and the groundswell of social upheaval for civil rights and against the Vietnam War had begun without them. Their isolated existence was a closely controlled life molded around prayer and discipline. There was little debate about the council's ongoing deliberations, no discussions about Martin Luther King Jr., or the growing civil rights demonstrations in the South. There was no television, little outside news, few occasions for discussing how to minister to communities being torn apart by social turmoil and cultural shifts. These were lessons each man would go on to learn on his own.

For Wassmuth, the first test would arrive in the summer of 1966, his "Deacon Summer," the term used to mark the summer before seminarians become ordained as priests. During that summer, seminarians become deacons and are given their first shot at ministering to an actual parish. Wassmuth's first assignment was to work in the migrant labor camps in Twin Falls, Idaho, a small farm town along the Snake River in the arid south-central section of the state. He drove into town and knocked on the door of the rectory. The monsignor answered, welcomed him, then pointed to the hefty housekeeper and a yappy little dog behind him. "If you get along with them, you'll get along with me." It was Wassmuth's first introduction to parish life.

He had arrived in Twin Falls with an overabundance of idealism and not enough Spanish. For weeks he ministered to poor Hispanic children who were living on the outskirts of town in a virtually uninhabitable labor camp of dilapidated old buildings and rundown military barracks. They understood little of his broken Spanish. Though he was only a deacon, the camps' residents treated him like a priest. They regarded his hallowed position highly, looked up to him, and he felt they were listening. He began a series of simple classes aimed at introducing the camp youth to the Catholic Church. It would be a few years before the church officially embraced Hispanic ministry and began more formal lobbying for social justice on behalf of immigrants and farmworkers. The pastoral plans were still being drawn up, the Spanish-speaking priests still being trained. Wassmuth had no guidance. But he was kind and he was trying.

They quickly warmed to him, and after several weeks he finally invited the group to attend church services; they promised to come. The following Sunday, not a single one stepped foot inside St. Edwards for Mass. Disappointed, Wassmuth returned to the camps to ask the youth why they had not attended. They insisted they had gone. He later discovered that indeed they had gone to church—the wrong one. They had boarded a bus sent by one of the Protestant churches and attended its services. Discouraged and humiliated, Wassmuth left Twin Falls that summer feeling as though he had failed miserably at his first parish assignment: The few Hispanic parishioners he had reached ended up attending a Protestant church. He vowed to become a better priest.

The following year, his last in seminary, he was appointed as the stenographer for a well-liked priest and professor named Father Pete. In an attempt to supplement the Latin texts with more modern, applicable teachings of the Second Vatican Council, Father Pete began to write his own courses. Father Pete's decision exemplified the kind of change that was occurring in Catholic schooling across the nation—a shift from solely institutional observances to individual ideas that reflected ongoing developments in the larger world.[6]

The council wanted Catholic teaching to be more progressive, more suited to contemporary culture. A new intellectual style emerged that opened some doctrine to interpretation. This change, referred to as the principle of the relativity of faith, gave many religious leaders and teachers a new sense of legitimacy when it came to subjectively interpreting religious truths.[7]

Father Pete modernized his courses by writing them himself rather than using standard old Latin texts. As his chief stenographer, Wassmuth listened carefully, took notes, typed them up, and distributed them to his classmates. Before long, he and the priest became known as Pete and Re-Pete. During that last year in seminary, Wassmuth became the unofficial class reporter on theology, helping his professor interpret and modernize the traditional teachings of the Catholic Church to fit the new post-Vatican Council II era. Inspired, Wassmuth felt as though the church had opened its doors to let in a breath of fresh air. Priests were being urged to adopt a more open, ecumenical attitude toward Protestants, Jews, and other non-Catholic religions. His peers and teachers were paying new importance to civil rights, religious liberty, and socially just ideals, something the council called "new humanism." The council's changes were the church's passport into a new, more modern world, and Wassmuth would be among the first to use it. Later that summer, as a newly ordained priest, Wassmuth would conduct Mass in both the traditional Latin as well as in English for three months before transitioning entirely to English. He and his classmates rode out their last year on a wave of renewed optimism about their futures. He could not wait to take his solemn vows.

In 1967, as was tradition for the year a seminarian is ordained as a priest, Wassmuth earned his first two possessions, the two most necessary for priesthood: a car and a liturgical chalice, the cup-shaped goblet he would use at Mass to contain the blood of Christ.

Wheels came first. While home for Christmas before his last months at St. Thomas, his father helped him pick out a 1967 Dodge Coronet 500 sedan with white Naugahyde seats, bronze metallic paint, and a 285 engine. He paid for it with haying money.

St. Thomas authorities prohibited seminarians from driving, but those in their last year learned that the inevitability of their pending priesthood made them invincible to most any discipline. Rarely was anyone kicked out of seminary on the eve of ordination, in their mid-20s, after a dozen years of dutiful prayer and religious study. When they could, they brought their cars nearer the seminary, slyly parking them in the driveways of neighbors, who took pity on the cloistered men and agreed to let them leave their cars. Then, when the weather warmed, they snuck out to their cars and cruised around town, comparing vehicles, venturing farther and farther from the seminary gates, sometimes even into the welcome clamor of Seattle. It was a delicious taste of freedom for men who had chosen a calling that turned its back on many of life's basic earthly pleasures.

So controlled were their lives inside the seminary that even the newly awarded right to design their own liturgical chalice symbolized a cherished act of individualism. Wassmuth, in what seemed at the time to him to be a revolutionary, avant-garde step away from the heavy ornate chalices traditional in Mass, chose an understated design of hammered white gold with a small iron cross, made in Germany. Today, it still sits on the mantel of his Ellensburg home with the following inscription: "Father Bill Wassmuth, May 23, 1967. For my parents and grandmother."

4 | The Role of Education

Teaching Tolerance

BY HIS LATE 20S, an age that most young people have either benefited from or fallen victim to their own decisions and adult experiences, Wassmuth remained under the influence of his family and his spiritual mentors. He was what his family had made of him for the first fourteen years and what his strict Catholic education had made of him for the following fourteen years. Both had made him a good man.

Though many would view Wassmuth's strict upbringing at home and school as overly rigid, it had placed priorities on important core values: honesty, integrity and fairness, the value of hard work, the strength of individuals working together in a communal fashion.

By watching his father stick up for the rights of black youth to skate at his rink, and refusing to trade alcohol for farm leases with local Nez Perce families, Bill also learned that fighting prejudice starts small, with the up front and personal.

Yet Henry Wassmuth's motto could have been "Do as I do, not as I say," given his propensity toward disparaging remarks about women and Indians. When they drove through the nearby reservation headquarters of Lapwai, Henry made offhand remarks to his sons about how "they" lived. And the strict patriarch often discriminated against women, including his wife and daughters, of whom he was convinced had no mechanical skills and relegated to household domestic chores. Wassmuth recalls his sisters going home from the fields in tears after having been sternly admonished for driving the tractor against their father's wishes—often, recalled Wassmuth, at his or his brother's urging. He learned chauvinism early, both from his father, who taught him to be a man, and from the male-dominated seminary, which taught him to be a priest. The traditional Catholic gender ideals encouraged in church and in seminary training portrayed the home as a woman's proper place, with domestic chores as her preferred activities. In Catholicism, the presumption of the more powerful male was written into canon law, forbidding women from ever holding superior positions. The requirements for ordination into the priesthood do not ask that one be smart, kind, devout, or honorable; they require only that one be *mas batizatus* (a baptized male).[1] Women were often viewed as subordinates and Catholic magazines published stories in the 1940s and 1950s that actively pushed such social roles, noting how housekeeping and childrearing (not working) gave the woman "the highest sense of fulfillment imaginable."[2] Henry Wassmuth not only limited his wife and daughters to "women's work," but genuinely believed they were incapable of handling other duties. The negative gender stereotypes that Wassmuth absorbed as a boy from his father and as a young man from his seminary training persisted, often against his wishes. Wassmuth lamented:

> Even now as an adult, when I go over to Seattle and get on a city bus and look up and see it's a woman driver my immediate reaction is, "She can't drive this thing." My father would have been absolutely convinced of that. Then my head takes over and I think, "Sure she can drive this bus, that's silly, she's probably as good or better driver than a guy." I know where it comes from, but that feeling in my gut is still there. I have to think my way around it. If I somehow delude myself into thinking it isn't there, then it surfaces in my actions without my knowing it, by means of inadvertently mistreating people.

The development of prejudice can be traced to home and parental influence, especially during a child's formative years. According to the Leadership Conference Education Fund, children are already aware of racial differences by the age of three.

However, schools and other social institutions where children spend most hours of the day also contribute to their socialization. Where families fail, Wassmuth believed schools should step up.

Ideally, of course, children arrive at their classrooms with well-formed values and a solid character, allowing them to soak up basic skills and information. But many children arrive at the school gate with a serious deficit of values due to families that have been torn apart, parents that are overworked, undereducated, or simply not paying enough attention to raising their children. Wassmuth:

I don't think people automatically know how to be parents or automatically know how to raise kids well. There are five years that children learn family values before they are introduced into the educational system. . . . the prime time to help children formulate ideas about fairness and diversity are in the pre-school years when the child begins recognizing differences between himself and others. Those differences can either be portrayed as something that is threatening to them, or enriching to them, and that initial portrayal will be carried with them as they go through life.

Communities need to offer good solid parenting skills, in the hospitals, schools, at birthing classes, for example. Here I am, a non-parent advising parents, but on the other hand, more kids called me Father than anybody else in northern Idaho. Perhaps because I am not a parent, I can see the things that parents do that are counterproductive. In fact many parents create a whole lot tougher world for themselves and for their kids by failing to teach tolerance.

While schools are where students are expected to learn the fundamentals such as reading, writing, science, and math, schools are also where young people learn to think with purpose, to test out the standards of their societies, and assume responsibilities toward other students, their families, and the larger community. Society benefits when children read, write, and compute well, but also when those same children learn to cooperate, solve problems peacefully, and treat one another with respect. Wassmuth believed schools should be prepared to teach basic values such as honesty, self-discipline, tolerance, and fairness, to make up for any deficit of parental education.

By age twelve, many children already have learned stereotypes about ethnic and religious groups. These stereotypes often underlie and foment hate crimes, half of which are committed by young men under age twenty.[3] Schools and colleges are ideal for countering prejudice because they provide a structured environment for youths of different backgrounds to mix, interact one-on-one, and form direct human relationships. The U.S. military has played a similar role for adults. Because schools are so key to shaping the behaviors of future citizens, a basic understanding of human rights should be a key part of students' education. Some European countries have already taken formal steps to adapt their curriculums with this in mind. In Sweden, for example, teaching about human rights has been a basic principle for education at all levels since 1962. Despite an exploding worldwide interest in human rights education in the last fifteen years, the U.S. federal and state governments have yet to come up with a comprehensive plan for introducing human rights education into the American curriculum.

Most of the human rights education that is happening in the United States is by individual teachers and nongovernmental organizations. For example, pilot programs with school and community-based human rights education were developed between 1997–1999 in four American cities: Atlanta, Georgia; Minneapolis/St. Paul, Minnesota; St. Louis, Missouri; and San Antonio, Texas. The program used a human rights framework to determine and analyze local problems, develop solutions, and work for change through networking and cooperation.[4]

Human rights education is within the state-mandated curriculum in some form in twenty of the fifty states, but the only states mandating implementation are Georgia, Kentucky, Louisiana, Massachusetts, Maryland, Minnesota, New Jersey, New York, Ohio, South Dakota, and Texas. No state requires teacher training in human rights education, however.[5]

Embracing a commitment to academic excellence, as well as high standards of civility, some U.S. schools have adapted Teaching Tolerance, a program of the Southern Poverty Law Center aimed at improving diversity education from pre-school through college.[6]

Even when outside resources are available, primary responsibility falls on the shoulders of individual teachers who are dealing all day long with matters that contain lessons on human rights—order and justice, maintaining personal dignity, individuality, and objectivity.

In fact, many teachers incorporate such value lessons into the classroom setting everyday. But mention more formal character education or moral education and most school board members run the other direction. Which morals does one teach? Won't discussing moral questions in the schools result in censorship disputes or other controversies that school administrators would rather avoid? Not if moral education is limited to the basic values shared by all people of a community: rejection of violence, treating others with dignity, and the importance of honesty and tolerance.

There are pressing and pragmatic reasons for schools to take proactive steps to combat intolerance: Hate groups are increasingly targeting school-age youth and disseminating racist literature on school grounds. In the South, Ku Klux Klan (KKK) literature has circulated in the schools since 1979, according to watchdog groups. State education officials in the five Northwest states have reported similar activity aimed at public school students. Crosses have been burned during football games in North Carolina, Indiana, and on campuses in California.[7] After the Aryan Nations located its headquarters in North Idaho in 1973, local high schools and college campuses were more frequently the recipients of racist literature.

"Post Falls (Idaho) Detective Rod Plank returned my call," read the memo from one North Idaho citizen to Wassmuth and the Northwest Coalition Against Malicious Harassment. "He said there has been a constant flood of hate literature being dropped in Post Falls for months now. . . . He said there's been an increasing number of local youth aged about 17 to early 20s involved with the Aryan Nations and they know many of the young people who are doing the leafleting, however there's not much they can do about it."[8]

The material described in this memo included a racist newspaper called *Thunderbolt*, published in Marietta, Georgia; a flyer featuring a picture of a black man kicking a white man with the message that "this was the world" that Bill Wassmuth and other human rights activists wanted; an anti-Semitic paper on communism and Jews; and a leaflet that had been left on the windshields of cars at the local high school titled "Attention White Students."

This particular flyer, aimed specifically at students, included ten questions such as: "Does your school try to teach you that all the races are equal? Did you know that the government has instilled a plan to integrate all schools with people not of the White race thru forced bussing? Does the school you attend teach and promote racial mixing and even worse that it's all right to marry or date someone from a different race? Does your school try to teach you that Martin Luther King Jr., is someone that should be honored by the White Race? . . . If any of these questions have interested you or you have asked them before and no one has given you the correct answers you seek, Aryan Nations can help."

At the bottom of the flyer was an Aryan Nations P.O. box address and a phone number.[9]

Attempts to use public schools to spread hate are sometimes much more subtle. Racist groups try holding meetings or forums at public school facilities under the thinly veiled guise of intellectual freedom. They may enter into busing disputes, or take up the cause of a white student disciplined for a racial fight or epithet.

When four Hispanic students in Sunnyside, Washington, were accused of sexually assaulting a white wrestler in 1992, the Aryan Nations jumped at the hazing incident as an opportunity to fan racial hatred. They sent flyers to parents with a photocopy of a story that ran in the *Spokesman-Review* along with this message that read: "You can have EDUCATION and SPORTSMANSHIP . . . Or you can have NON-WHITES, BUT YOU CAN'T HAVE BOTH! Join Aryan Nations."[10]

That same year, American Front, a neo-Nazi skinhead organization, responded to a series of racist incidents at the local high school in Albany, Oregon, by targeting junior and senior high-school students with a mass mailing of neo-Nazi literature to their home addresses.

Higher education institutions throughout the Northwest and Midwest have been similarly targeted. Racist groups look to college and university campuses to attract young followers who can spread hate messages by recruiting among their peers and sponsoring racist activities and speakers under the guise of academic debate. Ill-conceived campus speech codes have been regularly shot down as contrary to the

First Amendment, leaving many colleges and universities without suitable policies for responding to the kind of protected hate speech that can incite others to act out violently. Instead of trying to ban such activities, colleges and universities should set up a framework for a counterresponse that makes clear the institution's support for human rights. As hate groups increased the use of educational institutions to disseminate racist materials, Wassmuth urged public schools to take equally aggressive steps to counter the impact of such destructive messages.

Recognizing the key role that education plays in fighting hate, human rights organizations have made education, not only among school-aged children but also in the broader community, a core element of their efforts. Idaho human rights organizers enlisted the help of school children to build the nation's first permanent memorial to Anne Frank and the cause of human rights, for example. The memorial was dedicated in August 2002 in the state capital, Boise, on land donated by the city. Idaho residents and teachers set out to create a permanent memorial after a traveling Anne Frank exhibit inspired Idaho school children in 1995. Children statewide saved up coins, and forty-four schools eventually contributed $40,000 toward purchasing the statue.

The Northwest Coalition Against Malicious Harassment, a multistate nonprofit watchdog group that Wassmuth helped establish in the late 1980s, had as its primary focus the task of promoting public awareness about prejudice and racism. It sent out newsletters and published reports detailing bias-crime incidents across the region and provided pertinent advice on how communities can prevent and confront them.

Coeur d'Alene human rights activists more recently founded a Human Rights Education Foundation, which awards scholarships to minority students, such as members of the local Coeur d'Alene Tribe. With a generous million-dollar donation from Idaho philanthropist Greg Carr in 2001, the foundation began planning construction of a new state-of-the-art Human Rights Education Center in Coeur d'Alene. Longtime Northwest human rights activist Tony Stewart, a North Idaho College Professor and Foundation member, is hoping the center, once completed, will match the scale of other national civil rights centers such as the Rosa Parks Library and Museum in Birmingham, Alabama, or the Simon Wiesenthal Center in Los Angeles.[11] Each of these centers has a strong emphasis on education. Like them, Coeur d'Alene's Human Rights Center will provide educational programs that teach tolerance in partnerships with local school districts, colleges, and universities. Educators, elected officials, law enforcement personnel, community leaders, business owners, and visitors will also benefit from the educational programs. The center will tell the story of Coeur d'Alene's epic two-decade battle against the Aryan Nations, but primarily will be used as an educational tool. Foundation board members are recommending that 25 percent of the budget be spent on adult programs, versus approximately 75 percent for youth programs.[12]

Such tactics mirror researchers' belief that it is during the early, formative years of children's lives that they begin to distinguish differences and make judgments about whether those differences are "bad" or "good." The elementary years are also the time young children learn to live and work in a group, to share, observe rules, and acquire new skills working and playing together.

But human rights education is often limited to the "Heroes and Holidays" method of teaching about famous persons of color or diverse holidays, such as Martin Luther King, Hanukkah, or Kwanzaa. While these are important, students could also benefit from everyday classroom activities that promote tolerance in a more personal way and in a method more integrated in the basic general curriculum.

In Guna Svendsen's high-school Spanish class in Needham, Massachusetts, students are asked to talk in Spanish about where their families are from, then place yellow Post-it notes on large maps of the world, pinpointing the country of their ancestors. At the end of the exercise, the sticky yellow flags usually cover a large portion of the map. Svendsen uses the simple and nonthreatening exercise to help reveal to students that American culture actually has its roots in a rich array of diverse cultures.[13]

When white supremacist Chevie Kehoe was arrested after a shootout with Ohio police officers during a traffic stop, teachers at his hometown high school in Colville, Washington, recognized an opportunity to teach tolerance. Kehoe was convicted of counts of murder, conspiracy, and racketeering in 1999 and sentenced to life in prison. He had attended Colville High School, which made the news particularly relevant for a discussion of white supremacism and human rights issues in the class.

"It's hatred. It's wrong. I teach it as very un-American," said one Colville High School teacher when interviewed by the regional newspaper in Spokane for a series on race relations. "I tell my kids, 'If you're made of the right stuff, you're not going to treat other people like that.'"[14]

Indeed, children learn about human rights best through everyday experiences: their families, the life of the school, the social dynamic of the classroom, extracurricular activities, and relations between students as well as teachers, who are often their role models.

Teachers need adequate training to recognize and respond to racism when it surfaces. With that in mind, states and local school districts should equip teachers and staff with the necessary moral backing and academic resources. In a survey that Wassmuth helped commission, teachers in four Northwest states expressed a need for tolerance curricula, programs, and resources. Both regional and national organizations make resources available to schools and communities that are fighting hate and prejudice. Notably, the Southern Poverty Law Center offers the useful and free *Ten Ways To Fight Hate* publication, as well as "Teaching Tolerance" kits for teachers.[15]

Schools can also offer services for victims of bias-motivated violence and create student-led conflict mediation teams (approximately 300,000 high-school students are physically attacked each month, according to the National Institute of Education). In some schools, internal faculty human relations committees offer suggestions for diverse resources and improve in-service training for teachers, administrators, and other personnel working with children.[16]

Both schools and students will be intellectually richer if the perspectives of those voices silenced or excluded from male-dominated Eurocentric history are woven into their educational fabric.

When Bill was attending school in Greencreek, the contribution of the region's significant Nez Perce and Chinese populations was ignored completely in local history discussions.[17] Idaho was built on the backs of diverse peoples who came to work the state's mines, timber mills, and railroads. Wassmuth noted:

> But when I went to grade school in Idaho, I never knew about any of that, and I'm not certain much of it is taught now. We choose to ignore that the Chinese built the railroads, or that the Native American cultures were decimated. It's a matter of the victors writing the history. If you drive up and down Idaho and stop and look at the historical markers along the road, they mark a battle between the Indians and the pony soldiers. If the Indians won, it is labeled a massacre. If the pony soldiers won, it's labeled a victory. It's the coloring of history to suit the ones who won and a failure to recognize that the Indian people were fighting to defend their homes. Those doing the invading and massacring were the pony soldiers. We need to get history right. Critics may call that political correctness, to them I say that's absolutely right. Political correctness to me is a positive, not a negative. If it means treating other people better and getting history right, then I would hope I am being politically correct; it's fine by me.

The public school system has always been an evolving institution that changed in relation to the nation's economic needs and cultural values. Public schools were first developed at a time in American history when child labor and slavery were still legal.[18] In the 1950s and '60s, education issues such as desegregation reflected wider social and political concerns.

Today, students need to be prepared for life in an ever-more globally interconnected society. The multi-ethnic configurations of communities is changing and creating interdependence between diverse nations. In 1970, foreign trade made up just 13 percent of the American gross domestic product. Today it is nearly 30 percent of the GDP.[19]

Because globalization is a trade-driven phenomenon, doing business in the current climate is dependent on cultural awareness and tolerance, especially in the Pacific Northwest where exports of timber, apples, wheat, and other agricultural products account for an increasing percentage of economic growth. A multicultural academic environment is key for preparing the nation's future citizens, and it can create a solid foundation for being a good citizen and living peacefully in an increasingly complex and interconnected world. Knowledge and understanding about foreign countries and an acceptance of people from different races, religions, cultures, and nationality is a necessary part of American education because it is not only key to understanding American history, but also to understanding the nation's foreseeable future. Wassmuth believed globalization, which requires an education that prepares youth to succeed in an international climate, was an issue that resonates in small communities, where sons and daughters increasingly leave for college or jobs in the regional urban centers. Parents want the education that will successfully prepare their children for adulthood. Wassmuth believed:

> Even a bigoted parent can be moved along the lines of, "Look, when your kid moves out of Jonesville, Idaho, and goes to Seattle and starts working for Microsoft, he or she could well end up working for a lesbian person of color as his or her boss. Now, how are you going to prepare your son or daughter to work productively in that environment if you do nothing in this community to prepare them for encountering diversity at that level? Your bigotry just limits the options for your kid."

As Wassmuth points out, one of the simplest and most common ways to challenge prejudices and unfair stereotypes is interaction with people from different backgrounds—sometimes difficult in relatively homogenous regions like the interior Pacific Northwest. In this sense, foreign exchange programs are an important tradition in American schools as they provide opportunities for students who have never before been exposed to cultures other than their own to interact one-on-one with someone different from themselves. Pen-pal programs that allow students to get in touch with people in other parts of the country or world can also be a simple tool for teaching tolerance. American schools are poised to take advantage of tolerance education precisely because the United States, as a result of mass immigration, is a land of a variety of ancestors, languages, religions, manners, and customs. It is different from the relative homogeneity of some nation states in Europe, Japan, or China, where regardless of regional differences, the majority of citizens share a single ethnic identity and common history.

For older students who know enough about other countries to understand the reasons behind differences in social customs and cultures, it may be effective to study past and present human rights struggles in courses such as history, geography and social studies, or literature. But systematic instruction in human rights, no matter how seamlessly it is woven into interdisciplinary subjects, will not necessarily ensure that students learn how to be tolerant themselves. This is where extracurricular activities can make a difference. The most effective education takes the form of actual experiences, and in American schools, students' experiences often include influential coaches, assistants, volunteers, and others who help support their extracurricular programs.

Extracurricular activities such as band, drama, debate, and other clubs provide poignant opportunities for teaching tolerance. In Boise, Idaho, for example, high school drama students wrote, produced, and performed a play entitled *Not That I'm Prejudiced or Anything,* a story about a family of clowns (Harlequin-Americans) who are discriminated against as newcomers in a small rural town. The students later donated profits from the play to the Anne Frank Human Rights Memorial. Sports has also proven a powerful force in bridging racial gaps and fostering shared culture, especially in rural areas where sports teams are one of the primary activities where students from different backgrounds are asked to work together as a team. Idaho's World Sports Humanitarian Hall of Fame makes a point of honoring the humanitarian achievements of diverse professional athletes, including Chi Chi Rodriguez, Arthur Ashe, and Jackie Joyner-Kersee, for example. But schools and universities cannot rely only on extracurricular activities, sports, or toothless "diversity resolutions" to improve the cultural climate on campus. Working class people, people of color, women in nontraditional fields, and others who are marginalized need better and more affordable access to higher education. And Wassmuth was in favor of teacher training on college campuses that would require classwork in ethnic and cultural literacy, so they will be able to include information about the history and the contributions of groups traditionally left out of the curriculum.

Northwest public universities have dedicated significantly more resources to multicultural aims in recent years, adding new cultural studies programs, hiring diversity directors, and slowly building minority enrollments. But the universities' efforts will continue to be viewed as mostly symbolic until the makeup of their administrations and student bodies better reflect the diversity they claim to support.

Private schools carry similar responsibilities. Leading the way in the Inland Northwest is Gonzaga University, a private, Jesuit-run school. Inspired and aided by Bill Wassmuth's efforts to combat hate in the Northwest, the school in 1997 founded the Gonzaga University Institute for Action Against Hate. The institute's purpose is to use academic and scholarly resources in a focused way to combat hate. A professor within the program recently published one of the most extensive bibliographies of hate studies materials available to researchers. It is included in the institute's first issue of *The Journal of Hate Studies*. The annual publication prints interdisciplinary ideas and research about the study of what hate is, where it comes from, and how to combat it.

The inaugural issue is dedicated to Bill Wassmuth.

5 | Boise and Beyond

1967–1979

WASSMUTH drove away from St. Thomas Seminary with his suitcase and a smile on a warm spring day in May of 1967. The white Naugahyde seats in his Dodge Coronet still carried that new car smell. He rolled down the windows, turned up the music, and relished the trip back to Greencreek. He was headed home for ordination, a proud day he had been looking forward to for twelve years.

Ordinations and weddings in Greencreek have two things in common: First, there is no need for invitations because everyone just comes. Second, both are a three-day affair involving a day of preparation, a day of celebration, and a day of cleaning up afterward. When he arrived, the town already hummed with the anticipation of a favorite tradition.

Greencreek produced so many priests, its residents pulled together ordination celebrations almost on autopilot. Pies and casseroles went into the oven. The church was spruced up. Arrangements were made for who would host the guest priests and Bishop Bernard Topel of Spokane, who would perform the ceremony. The morning of the ordination, Wassmuth's mother, Isabelle, did up her red hair in rollers, manicured her nails, and dressed in her best hat, fancy white purse and shoes, pearls, and a suit. Henry Wassmuth shined his dress shoes twice, slicked back his hair, and traded in his farm duds for a suit and tie, complete with a tie clip and carnation in his lapel. Priests from around the region and nuns from the nearby St. Gertrude's convent filed into the Greencreek church, where ten members of Wassmuth's immediate family filled the front pews.

Wassmuth, bedecked in white and silver robes, strode slowly into the church and lowered himself down onto his stomach in front of the altar. He lay there, face down on the floor, while a long list of saints was invoked. This act, to "lie prostrate," symbolized his recognition of being unworthy of the office, of his dependence on God and the prayers of his Christian community.

Quiet settled over the pews as the bishop began the essential ordination rite, the laying on of hands and prayer of consecration, a ritual intended to invoke the Holy Spirit to come down upon the man being ordained, giving him a sacred character and setting him apart for the priesthood.

Wassmuth accepted his vestments, the religious garments that priests and bishops wear when celebrating Mass or performing other priestly duties. The bishop gave him a chasuble, a rich gold brocade robe trimmed in crimson, and a stole, a scarflike piece of rich red fabric that hung from around his neck to reflect the scripture of Matthew 11:30, "For my yoke is easy and my burden light."

Wassmuth knelt down before several priests, who bound his hands in white cloth. The bishop anointed them with sacred oil and blessed them with prayer.

Like all diocesan priests, Wassmuth made two crucial promises as part of the ordination ceremony: celibacy and obedience. At such a peak moment of spiritual strength, he was sure he could keep both. After the pledge, he gave God's blessing to those in attendance, starting with his parents. They kneeled before him at the front of the church, their hands clasped, heads tilted upward to receive the communion from their second son. First he fed them the bread representing the body of Christ. Then he gave them a sip of liturgical wine representing the blood of Christ. They swallowed with solemn pride as the congregation watched in silence. There had been communion. But there had been something else: a silent but significant exchange of respect between Wassmuth and his father. The next day, on Sunday, Wassmuth gave his first High Mass in Greencreek, and it was official: He was Father Bill.

Before he had even unpacked his suitcase back at the farm in Green-creek he was called to service. The Boise-based Idaho diocese needed him to fill in for a priest in south Boise who was headed to Ireland for the summer. Wassmuth quickly said his good-byes and set off down the state's only north-south highway, a narrow, dangerous road that snakes along the river canyons of Idaho's rugged central wilderness. The trip took him half a day. He spent the other half of the day with the Irish priest he had come to replace. But it was not enough training time for Wassmuth, a newly ordained neophyte who struggled with even the simplest tasks. The first Sunday after the priest had left, Wassmuth forgot to turn on the lights during Mass. He ran out of communion wafers. In Sunday school, a second grader baffled him with a question about the meaning of nothing, so as to better understand how exactly God could have created the world out of nothing. He kept forgetting things and saying "oops."

But his patient Boise parishioners forgave his mistakes and helped when they could. They gave him his first wedding, his first funeral, his first communion.

At the summer's end he transferred to St. Mary's parish in the small agricultural town of Caldwell, just outside of Boise. With his seminary Spanish, the diocese was counting on him to reach the community's growing Hispanic population. He was appointed as the associate pastor to another Irish priest, this one a notoriously domineering man named Father Quinn, who went through associate pastors faster than communion wine.

Though Wassmuth did not know it, the bishop of Idaho had already come to the conclusion that Wassmuth was Father Quinn's last chance. If the surly priest could not get along with the nice, hard-working farmboy from Greencreek, he would be transferred to a parish without an associate pastor. The first year went smoothly enough, but Father Quinn controlled Wassmuth's every move, assigning him only the most menial administrative tasks, despite his hunger for a more social, spiritual role. He was eventually, grudgingly, given the youth and Hispanic outreach task. In the late 1960s, Caldwell's Hispanic population lived primarily in migrant camps in small rural farm towns on the outskirts of town. Mexican workers had been hired in the region as early as the 1880s to help lay the Oregon Short Line Railroad, around which towns like Caldwell, Nampa, and Pocatello sprang up.[1] New waves of migrant laborers arrived to work the region's farms and ranches, harvesting sugar beets, sweet corn seed, and onions. Most laborers lived largely segregated from the rest of society, in makeshift camps that often lacked running water and basic sanitation.

Wassmuth drove slowly through the camps each day, asking about workers' spiritual needs. He began performing marriages, funerals, and masses in broken Spanish. He tried, often in vain, to transform what was primarily cultural Catholicism into something more meaningful, spiritual, and conscious. The conditions in the camps were deplorable, worse than he had seen during his deacon summer in Twin Falls, but Wassmuth had not yet developed the sense of social justice that would have compelled him in his later years to do something about it. Elsewhere across the nation, Catholics were increasingly involved in social justice movements, notably in support of the civil rights, peace, and farmworkers movements. A national office had been opened in Washington, D.C., for Spanish-speaking Catholics and regional offices were opening across the country to encourage Hispanic ministry and to lobby for better healthcare, education, and working conditions for the migrant population. But this sea of change had not yet penetrated isolated Idaho, and Wassmuth did not push for change. He just quietly performed his spiritual duties, relying on what he had been taught in seminary: that religion existed to help one accept one's lot in life no matter what, even if it was impoverished and unfair. Yet each time he returned to the rundown camps to find conditions worse or no better than before, he began questioning what difference his spiritual counsel was making and contemplating what more he could do.

Meanwhile, the Caldwell church's established parishioners, concerned over the unusually high turnover of associate pastors under the overbearing priest, took turns inviting Wassmuth to their homes for dinner to relieve him from the oppressive presence of Father Quinn. In pursuit of his childhood dream, Wassmuth started flying lessons with another Boise priest on their days off. He earned his pilot's license that year.

But on the ground, his spiritual aspirations fell flat, despite his first big break. When Father Quinn left for Ireland that summer, he left Wassmuth in charge of the parish. Drawing on all his seminary theology, Wassmuth delivered polished traditional Masses, one after another. He heard confession and responded as he had been taught. He followed every rule, but still he felt a nagging sense that something was not working. Parishioners seemed unmoved, despite his enthusiasm for the scripture and charismatic delivery. The theology all made sense to Wassmuth, who had been studying it, devouring it, for more than a dozen years within the institution of the Catholic Church. But his liturgies were not connecting to parishioners' real lives, and though it rubbed him wrong, he knew no other way.

In the evenings, Wassmuth retired to the priest's quarters to relax. Father Quinn had a private sitting room that, up until his departure for Ireland, had been by invitation only to Wassmuth. In it, Quinn kept a large state-of-the-art color television that was off-limits to everyone but the priest himself. Before leaving, Quinn had fastened a large blanket over the television with masking tape so Wassmuth could not watch it. As soon as he had left, Wassmuth had several priest friends over for a "Thank God He's Gone" party in the priest's sitting room. Someone pulled off the masking-taped blanket and flipped the television switch on. Convinced by Quinn that parish spies would discover any misstep Wassmuth made while he was away, Wassmuth begged his friends to cover the television back up. When they departed, Wassmuth carefully retaped the blanket over the forbidden box.

Like some parishioners, and most associate pastors at St. Mary's before him, Wassmuth feared Quinn. But after a few nights alone in the rectory, boredom overcame paranoia. Soon he was sneaking regular peaks at the off-limits television late at night: not risqué for the average man in his late 20s, but an act of defiance for Wassmuth. When Quinn returned from Ireland, as many in the parish had predicted and feared, things rapidly deteriorated. Wassmuth was stripped of nearly all the responsibilities he had taken on over the summer and relegated again to minor tasks and a few Masses. Worse yet, parishioners had begun calling to ask which liturgy Wassmuth would be leading and which liturgy Quinn would be leading.

Increasingly worried that the split might be dividing the congregation, Wassmuth called the bishop. The bishop moved Wassmuth first, and a few months later reassigned Quinn to a small parish where he worked alone.

Wassmuth's new post was as priest of the Lady of the Lake parish in the scenic central Idaho mountain town of McCall. For a priest from Idaho, it did not get much better.

It was 1969, the year astronauts walked on the moon and Woodstock rocked a generation. Wassmuth lived in an A-frame cabin that was practically a snowball's throw from the ski hill. He performed pastoral visits on a powerboat on Lake Payette. Because Boise's wealthy residents flocked to nearby McCall to ski, boat, and otherwise play—but not to attend Mass—Father Bill's services were not in high demand. When his phone line went dead for four days, no one noticed. Parishioners' biggest complaint was that he did not spend enough time gabbing at the coffee klatch room downtown. He joined the local flying club and practiced landing a little tail dragger single-engine plane on a runway flanked by high snow banks. When summer arrived he planned to fly to the isolated, rural missions he was responsible for in a rugged 200-mile radius: St. John the Baptist Station in mountainous Cascade, St. Jude the Apostle Station in Council, and St. Jerome's in Riggins, along the Salmon River, known ominously as the River of No Return.

He would never have the chance. His dream job was cut short by a call from the bishop offering him a promotion to the church's main office in Boise. The bishop wanted him to move to the state capital to work in the religious education office on behalf of the entire Idaho diocese. It was a big promotion, but Wassmuth was reticent. He had been content in McCall. Life was good there. He told the bishop he was flattered, but he did not think he had proper experience for the job. The bishop said not to worry, he thought of that and already signed Wassmuth up for a three-year summer school program at Seattle University to get his master's degree in religious education. Wassmuth could not decline.

The summer of 1970, Wassmuth packed up his things and locked the A-frame's door behind him. A few weeks later he was living in a Seattle University dormitory with approximately 150 priests, nuns, and laypeople from all over the country, attending SU's summer school. SU had started the master's program the year before Wassmuth enrolled. In Seattle, in the early 1970s, even a Catholic campus had a hint of revolution. SU's faculty included a number of Jesuit professors who had worked in Latin America and been inspired by an emerging school of thought called Liberation Theology, which urged the church to focus on liberating people from poverty and oppression. Liberation theologians argued that the scripture required Christians to improve social and economic justice for all people. The theory had roots in the religious and social movement that swept over the Latin American continent in the 1950s and '60s in response to the abject poverty in which a majority of the population lived. SU professors emphasized social justice and encouraged students to pay attention to current events, an awakening for many of the nuns and priests who had up until then been sheltered in isolated seminaries, convents, and parish houses.

Here, however, the students shared rooms, meals, and secrets. They grew close. Wassmuth experienced for the first time what many college students everywhere do: a sense of belonging, what it feels like to get drunk, the rush of falling in love. The major difference was that he was twenty-nine, not eighteen, though his giddy behavior belied his age. One night, Wassmuth, a priest from Iowa, and two nuns bought several bottles of hard liquor, went up to his room, plugged in eight-track music tapes, and drank just to see how wasted they could get. Students kept a keg of beer on tap in the dorm recreation room. Wassmuth had never been in an atmosphere with so few rules. But it was no accident. The whole program, Wassmuth discovered, was about freedom from restriction, about transforming priests and nuns from textbook-trained institutional ministers into real people, with real experiences.

He had been Seminarian Bill, then Deacon Bill, then Father Bill. Here he was just Bill, and he was expected to figure out just who that really was.

In seminary, he had learned institutionalized theology based on Aristotle and St. Thomas Aquinas, with most of the instruction in Latin. Summer school convinced Wassmuth that the traditional theology, religious dogma, and abstract concepts he had been preaching did not have enough relevance to parishioners' real lives. As called for in Vatican II reforms, SU professors were teaching a more pastoral approach. Instead of directing people into the church's mold, priests were encouraged to fit the church message to the people, in part to reach out to the disenfranchised.

After Vatican II, the church had committed itself to more actively promoting justice and human rights, which inspired many American Catholics to get involved with the civil rights, women's rights, labor, and peace movements. Bishops elsewhere in the world—especially in Latin America, Asia, and Africa—began heeding the church's call by more loudly denouncing political disappearances, torture, exploitation, and racism in their countries.

What Wassmuth was learning at Seattle University was part of this new, more public focus on social justice that was developing within the American Catholic Church, which issued nearly two hundred official statements and letters on behalf of social justice in the two decades following Vatican II.[2]

But liberation theology had come under attack by more traditional church leaders as being tied to Marxism and revolutionary socialist movements in Latin America, an accusation its advocates strongly denounced. A Brazilian archbishop lamented, "When you give food to the poor, they call you a saint. When you ask why the poor have no food, they call you a communist."

He did not know just how controversial the post-Vatican II changes were within the church's ranks, but he realized the new religious education tools he was learning were a 180-degree turn from what he had been taught before. Wassmuth welcomed the change. He felt as though the old ways had failed him in Twin Falls, Caldwell, and

McCall. This new approach made sense: If he knew himself better, maybe he would be a better minister and teach others to minister better. Maybe he could better address the problems of the people to whom he was preaching. Religion meant really working with the people, not just reading Latin from some old Bible. Religion now had a face, the face of parishioners he had not inspired, the face of migrant workers he had not helped.

Before summer school, Wassmuth had always believed in a kind of religious duality: that God's world was separate from the human world and if he concentrated too much on being a person, he risked veering off the spiritual track in some false direction. He had been taught that he should first get his relationship straight with God, and if there was any time left over, then work on relationships with fellow human beings. Now he was beginning to believe that God's world and the world of humans were intertwined, that only by dealing successfully in the human world could he thrive in God's world. If that is the case, he thought, he could not successfully work on his relationship with God unless at the same time he was working on his relationship with other people. This spiritual epiphany moved social justice issues from the fringe to the heart of Wassmuth's gospel.

Wassmuth found support for the concept in the scriptures. In Matthew 5:23, the Lord says if you are bringing your gift to the altar and you have something against your brother, go first and get squared away with your brother and then return to the altar. In the parable of the Good Samaritan, Jesus tells of a traveler on the road who took pity on a severely beaten and wounded stranger as an example of how dedication to God is linked to one's love of neighbor.

For the first time, Wassmuth understood the theology behind Martin Luther King's call to liberate "oppressed and dependent peoples."[3] And he realized that fighting for social justice was not only a Catholic concern, or even just a Christian one, but rather a broader movement galvanizing the nation.

While SU's classes transformed Wassmuth's spiritual life, he struggled to reconcile the new ideas with the old ones he had learned at Mount Angel and St. Thomas. He took weekend trips to the Pacific

Ocean just south of the Quinault Indian Reservation to clear his head. He parked his car above the rocky cliff and scrambled down a steep embankment with his sleeping bag and knapsack to camp on his favorite spot of beach. He built a driftwood fire, cooked a steak over it, drank a bottle of wine, talked to God, and pulled himself together. It was a ritual he performed often during his summers at SU.

Campus life transformed him socially, as well. For the first time, Wassmuth formed friendships with several women. Before, close relationships with women had been considered "occasions of sin" for the celibate priest. But now, Wassmuth and most of the other college students around him felt the church was on the verge of some major institutional changes, specifically, optional celibacy, giving priests the right to marry. Wassmuth never believed he would spend his whole life alone, but until the church made optional celibacy official, he guarded carefully against letting his friendships develop into something more. To him, celibacy meant abstaining from sexual intercourse, but that did not prevent him from falling in love.

His first crush, a Boise woman, often came to Seattle to visit during those summers at SU. One hot afternoon he took her to a favorite stretch of Pacific sand. They lay on the beach all day, talking, laughing, their inhibitions melting slowly away under the July sun. That afternoon Wassmuth felt something new happening to his body that he felt certain was wrong, something he had spent years learning how to control and deny: a sudden and strong sexual urge. Confused, unable to face his friend, and unsure what else to do, he got up from the blanket and started running down the beach. The athletic brunette jumped to her feet and ran after him. His sexuality, his vow of celibacy, these were things they could talk about, she insisted when she caught up to him. They could do something about how he was feeling, or they could not. But don't run away, she admonished. You cannot always run away from women.

Despite his vulnerability at that moment, Wassmuth remained absolute about maintaining his vow of celibacy, and as a result their relationship stayed chronically platonic. Eventually, she began dating someone else, though they remained friends. After that summer, and particularly after that day on the beach, Wassmuth was no longer naive about the potency of human sexual desire.

The last year of his SU master's program, 1973, the graduating class chose the song "Age of Aquarius" as their processional music. For Wassmuth it was the dawning of a new religious identity. He had become a human being who was working as a priest, rather than a priest disguised as a human being. He could live openly, though alone, fight for what he believed was right, and still find solace in the scripture and official church teachings. From 1973 on, social justice became one of the defining elements of his spiritual message.

After SU graduation he returned to Idaho to begin his work in the diocese education office. His first assignment was to write the guidelines for all the religious education programs for Idaho's nearly sixty parishes. In consultation with other religious educators statewide, Wassmuth authored The Idaho Plan, a guideline for religious education, with social justice issues at its core. As he wrote, he kept his favorite motto tacked up at his desk: "If you want peace, pursue justice." For the next five years he traveled across the state training teachers to implement the plan. He was among the first Catholic priests to make social justice an official statewide priority. He was promoted to director of religious education for the diocese. More career advancements would follow.

When officials in the U.S. Catholic Church decided the nationwide catechetical guidelines needed updating, they chose Wassmuth because of his Idaho Plan. He was asked to represent the rural West on a national, twelve-member committee and charged with drafting the new catechism guidelines.

The committee, Wassmuth recalled, was a new exercise in democracy for the U.S. Catholic Church. The committee pointed to church documents such as Lumen Gentium, which described a more social and biblical concept of church, giving more attention and responsibility to the role of the laity. Before this time, the clergy had been solidly at the helm, while the congregations were left to "pay, pray, and obey."[4] But the collaborative atmosphere surrounding Vatican II had begun to democratize the church, making cooperation and consultation between clergy and congregation at the parish level more common than before. Wassmuth was among those pushing for such democratization. Before drafting the catechism guidelines, Wassmuth and his committee sent out questionnaires asking for parishioner input across the country. The parishes sent back thousands of comments, which the committee then used to create a first draft of "Sharing the Light of Faith: National Catechetical Directory for Catholics of the United States."

Wassmuth, chairman of the committee, began working closely with an African American priest from Detroit, who went on to become an archbishop, to weave social justice into the heart of the document. He would later perm his straight hair into an afro like the one worn by the colleague from the Midwest, whom he admired for his outspoken support for civil rights and social justice.

Wassmuth flew across the country in 1976 and 1977 to meet with priests in different states and church officials in Washington, D.C. The National Association of Diocese Directors of Religious Education asked him to serve as president. He was rapidly becoming one of the national church leaders in the field, the kind of successful, active priest destined to become a bishop someday.

The committee's catechism guidelines, however, underwent a grueling editing process before the National Conference of Catholic Bishops approved them in 1977. Wassmuth was dismayed to see the document he had proudly penned, chopped up and watered down by the bishops. Even worse, the guidelines were essentially shelved after their approval and not widely circulated. Wassmuth grew disenchanted. The catechism guidelines process had begun under Pope Paul VI, the Bishop of Rome from 1963 to 1978, who had instigated and carried out the Vatican II reforms and was a vocal supporter of social justice. But the project bogged down in 1978, which was a year of tumult for the Catholic hierarchy and was known by many Catholics as the year of three popes. Pope Paul VI died unexpectedly, and the Italian appointed to be Pope after him died suddenly of a heart attack after serving only thirty-three days in the position, a development that has spawned numerous conspiracy theories over the years. John Paul II, known for his doctrinaire conservatism, was appointed three days later. The direction of the church shifted significantly on a number of issues that year, and Wassmuth felt his socially progressive catechism guidelines had fallen victim to the transition. He kept his growing sense of trepidation about high-level church politics to himself. That year, several priest friends mentioned that his name was coming up in talks with Rome about nominations for new bishops. He was on the short list. The murmurings disturbed him, as he would not be able to say no, as had been the case with every church promotion thus far. Wassmuth worried his own convictions would conflict with the church's if he continued up the chain of church politics.

He was also wearying of the constant travel and politics of his job as religious education director for Idaho and the national association. Each time he flew from Washington, D.C., to Boise, he swore he would never live anywhere that the newspaper would not crinkle when opened because the humidity was so high. He began having a few drinks in the evenings to take the edge off the stress. An idea hit him mid-martini while flying into the sunset on his way back home to Boise. He asked the flight attendant for paper and a pen. He wrote the following letter: "Dear Apostolic Delegate, I'm writing to express my belief in and support for optional celibacy for clergy and the ordination of women as priests. Sincerely, Bill Wassmuth."

The apostolic delegate was in charge of making bishop nominations to Rome. Every letter Wassmuth wrote to the apostolic delegate went into a file with his name on it. Wassmuth calculated that if he ever was nominated for bishop, they would pull the file, see the letters, and say "forget it." He wrote many. The bishop nomination never materialized.

That year he was offered several jobs with various Washington, D.C., Catholic-affiliated organizations. Tired of working with the people who were working on behalf of the multitudes, he turned them all down.

In 1979, a decade after leaving quiet McCall for the fast-paced lifestyle of lobbying, networking, and church business in Boise and beyond, he called the Idaho bishop and asked to return to the parish. He had moved up the church ranks over the course of a decade. He held influential positions and spent weeks at a time in Washington, D.C., and other metropolitan hubs. He devoted himself to weaving social justice into the everyday fabric of Catholic doctrine. But after ten years, and a stinging run-in with the hierarchy, he was ready to be a priest again. Bishop Treinen, a close confidant, sympathized and said he would take Wassmuth's request into consideration.

Nearly certain he would be assigned to a vacant parish in predominantly Mormon, conservative southeastern Idaho, Wassmuth could barely hold back his glee when offered a post at St. Pius X in Coeur d'Alene, Idaho. The scenic lakeside resort town was in the state's northern panhandle, just a half day's drive of his Greencreek home. He envisioned a lifestyle not unlike that in McCall—waterskiing on the lake in the summer, hitting the slopes in the winter. He decided that before accepting the position outright he would ask the local Coeur d'Alene parish council what they thought. Wassmuth walked into the meeting wearing a leather jacket and cowboy boots. His permed hair was combed, but unruly. He sported a beard and wore a ring. He was the most unconventional priest Coeur d'Alene had ever seen.

Part of a new breed of clergy, he was among the many nuns and priests who, after Vatican II, began abandoning the identifying religious attire and trying experimental liturgies that would be more meaningful to the secular world. His unconventional ways—that he did not always wear his collar, that he permed his hair, that he sometimes wore jewelry—particularly troubled his father, who every time Wassmuth went home pleaded with him to be more traditional.

But Wassmuth was part of a broader movement of institutionalized dissent that developed in the 1970s among members of the Catholic clergy (especially those who had become priests after Vatican II) in response to the social movements within contemporary society. Many embraced a new kind of collaboration with the laity, allowing parish representatives to play a larger role in governing the local churches—something unheard of with the more hierarchical pastors of generations past. Priests and nuns also increasingly balked at toeing the church's party line on premarital sex, divorce, contraception, or politics.[5]

If they came up at all, these differences did not bother Coeur d'Alene's parish council, however. They asked Wassmuth only if he would be willing to trim his hair and beard. Usually in the Catholic Church, the people do not choose their pastor, the bishop does. But Wassmuth, convinced the parish voice should be heard in all major church decisions, told the Coeur d'Alene parish council that if they felt he was not a good fit he would refuse to accept the position, thereby allowing their wishes to be carried out. Flattered by Wassmuth's deference, the council asked him to accept the post. He trimmed his hair and moved there in 1979. It was the beginning of an invincible bond of mutual—even familial—affection between Wassmuth and the St. Pius X parish that would carry them through one of the city's most tumultuous decades.

6 The Role of Religion

Confronting Theologies of Hate

WASSMUTH relished the idea of stepping back into the role he loved most—that of a parish priest. In the decade that he had worked in Boise and commuted for church business to major American cities, he had become much more aware of the nation's pressing social ills—poverty, discrimination, discontent. He also knew, from his bishop's warnings, that the community he would be serving was home to the Aryan Nations, a racist sect that had moved its headquarters from California to Idaho in the early 1970s. The combination of Wassmuth's new social awareness and his renewed longing to work again as a community priest, poised him to use his pulpit to address the brewing racial tensions in Idaho. When his parishioners complained about receiving anti-Semitic Aryan Nations pamphlets, he drafted sermons about the virtues of tolerance and loving one's neighbor, then joined the twenty-seven other religious leaders in denouncing the racist handouts for distorting and corrupting "both Scripture and history." While the denunciation acknowledged the free speech right of the Aryan Nations to preach their own version of Christianity, more important, it inspired the community to voice their outrage at the use of "hate tactics and coercive intimidation," which most of the region's pastors believed to be contrary to the Gospel.[1] This bold move by the community's religious leaders was the first spark to ignite North Idaho's tenacious grassroots community movement in support of human rights. Because of pivotal experiences that would unfold over the next decade while fighting the Aryan Nations in Coeur d'Alene, Wassmuth grew to believe that clergy and mainstream faith communities had a moral duty to counter racist

movements that were using theo-political reasoning to justify violence. He was convinced that churches played a key role in community
cohesiveness, especially in rural areas. As racist fringe groups began re-
vealing the religious convictions behind their views in the early 1980s,
Wassmuth maintained that church leaders from across the ideological
spectrum must be prepared, willing, and ready to respond with sound
theological perspectives.

Wassmuth explained:

> I think the faith community needs to establish the moral plan of the
> community, help frame the moral parameters of the community, and I
> do not mean moral in the sense of sexual behavior, but moral in the
> sense of how we treat our neighbor and how we interact with each other.
>
> I think faith communities exist to be a leaven in the larger com-
> munity. Take a Catholic parish, for example; I think that if it is doing
> what it is supposed to be doing, it exists not for the sake of its own
> members or increasing its own membership, but for providing a com-
> munity with a context from which they can individually and collectively
> live their lives in a manner that will affect positive change in the lives of
> their greater communities.

Wassmuth began formulating his notions about faith communities
as leavens for affecting social change in the mid-1970s while pursuing
his master's degree in religious education. At the time, the global
struggles of the poor and oppressed were getting more attention from
Catholic leadership and had become a regular part of the graduate curriculum at Seattle University. Wassmuth became convinced that religious faith and social justice activism went hand in hand.

> I didn't believe you could do what we were called to do as Christian
> people without being called to social justice. There were many others al-
> ready on that same track, certainly Martin Luther King, and Gandhi
> from the Hindu point of view.

From the day he accepted the priesthood position in Coeur d'Alene
in 1979, he used his faith as a tool for bettering his community. He helped form a hospice to nurse the dying. He volunteered at the YMCA

and soup kitchens. He opened his parish doors to a newly formed group of concerned residents who were worried about a surge of activity at a nearby white supremacist compound and a series of racist threats, which residents believed were linked to it.

It was the ministers in town, led by a Protestant pastor, who first spoke out against the Aryan Nations in Coeur d'Alene. They felt the Aryan Nations was doing an injustice in the name of Christianity. They were saying "Hey folks, the Christian message is being distorted here, distorted to try to destroy people rather than help them."

For most everyday church-going folks, it is hard to imagine that someone calling himself a minister would set fire to a cross, or that a church that considers itself Christian would erect swastika flags, hang pictures of Hitler on the walls, or instead of saints, display portraits of men like Robert Mathews who have broken the commandments against murder and theft.

For those who attend Sunday services seeking the kind of spiritual inspiration that values fairness and kindness, it is hard to believe that mass acts of fatal terror, like Oklahoma City and Waco, could be inspired by religion; that regular individuals, such as a Jewish talk show host in Denver, an affluent lawyer and his family in Seattle, and a Filipino postman in Los Angeles, could be murdered in cold blood as the result of some twisted interpretation of God's will.

But these acts of violence, and many others, have specific links to religions that teach hate: churches with innocuous-sounding names like Church of the Creator, Church of Jesus Christ Christian or Scriptures for America. They are Christian Identity, a growing network of supposedly faith-based white supremacist movements that rely on interpretations of the Bible so twisted, so far from the basic teaching of Jesus that many pastors agree it renders the basic Christian tenets virtually unrecognizable. Wassmuth stated:

Christian Identity is a distortion of Christian theology that is used to validate racism. It offers white supremacists justification in God's name for their bigotry.

Because of their familiarity with Christian doctrine and the Bible, Wassmuth pointed out that religious leaders have both the expertise and the moral authority needed to fight the increasingly theological claims of racists who have traded in their old white hoods for Bibles. For example, Numbers 25 has been used by extremists in the Christian Identity movement (such as the Phineas Priesthood) as religious justification for violence against interracial couples.[2] In one part of the Old Testament, God was angry about Israelites mingling with foreign tribes and worshiping foreign gods. When an Israelite man brought home a woman from another tribe, another Israelite named Phinehas killed them both. In Numbers 25, God praises Phinehas for being zealous for his God. Christian Identity groups interpret the scripture racially, when the real point of the scripture, say other Christians, is to discourage the worship of foreign gods. Unless clergy and congregation from mainstream denominations rally against such misuse of the gospel, Wassmuth worried that Christian Identity's brand of religious hate would continue to inspire violence.

Christian Identity is based largely on the notion that the white race is the "seed of Adam" and the biblical Israel chosen by God. Followers believe white Anglo-Saxons are God's chosen people, while Jews are the biological offspring of a sexual coupling between Satan and Eve in the Garden of Eden, and people of color are subhuman animal-like beasts of the field. Identity pastors attempt to provide theological justification for racist violence, most of which stems from narrow and, according to religious experts and clergy, horribly misguided interpretations of the creation accounts in the book of Genesis.

Equally disturbing is the potential volatility of the apocalyptic end game many Identity leaders espouse: that the world is on the verge of a final, epic struggle between good and evil, in which the white race will be pitted against the Jewish conspiracy and its associates in order to redeem or reclaim the world.

Through its antigovernment conspiracy theories and hatred for people of color and Jews, Christian Identity slowly became the spiritual umbrella under which several divergent extremist groups began to unify. Before Identity, many of these groups existed as estranged fringes of the radical right, each obsessed with its own causes: the anti-Semitism of the Posse Comitatus or the anti-Catholicism and racial hatred of the Ku Klux Klan, for example.

Most experts agree that the Identity movement began as British-Israelism, a bizarre racialist religious movement that originated in Britain in the 1700s. After it was used to justify colonizing the vast lands under British rule, the movement fizzled. It is thought to have jumped the Atlantic in the late nineteenth century, spreading into California and the Pacific Northwest alongside the Ku Klux Klan movement in the 1920s. Its adherents were mostly individual lecturers and eccentrics, most notably a military science instructor at Yale, a New England lawyer, and the editor and publicist for automobile manufacturer Henry Ford.[3] The decision to publish a series of anti-Semitic articles in Ford's weekly *Dearborn Independent* was a significant step forward for Christian Identity. A series entitled "The International Jew: The World's Foremost Problem," was distributed to Ford dealerships nationwide during the 1920s, making racist arguments available to a large U.S. audience.[4] The series urged Americans to study "The Protocols of the Learned Elders of Zion," a fraudulent and virulently anti-Semitic turn-of-the-century document supposedly proving alleged plans for a Jewish-Masonic world takeover.

Christian Identity's West Coast hotspots were Vancouver, B.C., and southern California, especially Los Angeles. The small group of British émigrés that formed a congregation of Anglo-Israelites in Hollywood had beliefs that largely emerged from one of nineteenth-century Britain's most pressing intellectual problems: how to justify continued colonialism.[5] In the 1940s, the congregation met with Wesley Swift, who had originally been ordained as a Methodist minister but had become one of the major West Coast supporters of anti-Semitic populist Gerald L.K. Smith. He combined Christian Identity with Aryan philosophy and political extremism and thus founded the Church of Jesus Christ Christian. Listening to Swift preach, Richard Butler found the inspiration to eventually move to Idaho and found his Aryan Nations compound.

Butler had racist leanings long before hearing Swift preach, however. He once told a reporter for the *Los Angeles Times* that ideas began taking root while working in India, where he had been sent by an aircraft company contractor to overhaul planes for the Royal Indian Air Force. He became fascinated with the caste system. Though he later enlisted in the Army Air Corps and taught aircraft hydraulics in the China-Burma theater during World War II, he disagreed with fighting Germany. His admiration for Hitler grew during the war, even while his compatriots were fighting against him in Europe. When he returned to the United States, Butler latched onto Senator Joe McCarthy's anti-communist witchhunt, joining a signature campaign to expose communist teachers. It was there, he told reporters, that he met those who introduced him to Swift.[6] One of the last straws was the announcement by his Presbyterian pastor that he would be extending the church's welcome to more minorities. And later, a federal loan obtained by his employer Lockheed Martin required the hiring of more minorities at the plant where Butler worked as an aeronautics engineer. His resentment of minorities only grew.[7] It was with Swift that Butler claims to have had the life-changing religious epiphanies that prompted him to take over the helm of the Church of Jesus Christ Christian (Aryan Nations) after Swift died. He moved it to Idaho (one of his favorite vacation and fishing spots) in 1973.

First, Butler did a stint as leader in Kootenai County of the Posse Comitatus, a group that rejected any governmental authority above the county sheriff.[8] But after the posse fell apart, he turned his attention toward building the Aryan Nations compound. The twenty-acre spread, with its guardtower, German shepherds, swastika-adorned pulpit, and uniformed guards, would later become the most well-known chapter of the Christian Identity church and a magnet for its followers.[9]

The subsequent rise of Christian Identity's popularity roughly coincided with the farm crisis in the late 1970s and early '80s, when low crop prices, high interest rates, and foreclosures bred desperation, mistrust, and hatred of the federal government, especially in the rural Midwest, which was losing multiple farms every day. Butler and his followers capitalized on this discontent at his annual World Aryan Congress meetings, which provided a gathering place for the growing number of hate groups who attached themselves to Identity doctrine. Butler's Idaho compound gained national notoriety after members of the white supremacist group The Order (who had often been guests at Butler's compound) were arrested for a series of holdups, counterfeiting operations, bombings, attacks on synagogues, and eventually the murder of Denver talk show host Alan Berg in 1984. In 1986, a second group calling itself The Order II committed a series of bombings in Coeur d'Alene, including one originally intended to kill Bill Wassmuth. That act ultimately did more harm to the Aryan Nations itself than it did to Wassmuth, whose response to the incident helped galvanize the community and marked a turning point in the battle against the unwanted white supremacist group.

Domestic terror waned after the aggressive law enforcement crackdown of the mid-1980s that busted The Order. But in the early 1990s, the popularity of Christian Identity surged again with the emergence of the militia movement. The government's botched siege at Ruby Ridge in northern Idaho, which killed the wife and son of Randy Weaver as well as a federal agent, aggravated an already tense atmosphere. Two months after the fatal events at Ruby Ridge in 1992, Colorado Christian Identity leader Pete Peters invited more than 150 white supremacists, tax protestors, Freemen, Klansmen, neo-Nazis, militia leaders, and various other extremists to discuss how to respond to the Weaver debacle. This would prove to be a seminal event, forging an important link between the religious Identity movement and the growing militia and Christian Patriot movements.

Over the years, Christian Identity retreats have sheltered their share of terrorist martyrs. When Posse Comitatus leader Gordon Kahl was on the lam, he holed up with Christian Identity followers in the South. He later died in a shootout with federal marshals in 1983, providing the movement with one of its first martyrs. When federal law enforcement officials were closing in on The Order, some members sought refuge in a Christian Identity religious enclave called Covenant, Sword & Arm of the Lord in Arkansas. The Phineas Priesthood followers who set off bombs at a bank, newspaper office, and health clinic in Spokane, Washington, in 1996 were exposed as part of a violent faction that had met at an Identity church in northern Idaho called America's Promise Ministries.

The Montana Freemen, Oklahoma City bomber Timothy McVeigh, Olympic bombing suspect Eric Rudolph, and Buford Furrow, accused of murder and an attack on a Jewish community center in 1999, all were discovered to have Christian Identity ties.[10]

Law enforcement officials also found Christian Identity literature, as well as literature from the Illinois-based World Church of Creator extremist group, in the home of the Williams brothers, charged with burning three synagogues in 1999 near Sacramento and the murder of a gay couple near Redding, California.

Yet despite the clear, multidecade link between Christian Identity and racially motivated terrorism, mainstream Christian denominations have failed to out-Bible Identity's hate-based theologies. Wassmuth:

> All of the major denominations have social justice issues at the heart of their messages. It's just a matter of whether or not it is pushed to the surface. If the mayor of Jonesville, Idaho, belongs to the UCC church and that pastor is preaching a message of respect for diversity, that mayor is going to have to sit down and listen on Sundays and it's going to reinforce his action when somebody comes around to him and says we need to do something because the Hispanic population or the Native American community is being mistreated. Now he's got a moral imperative from his faith community and that helps move it along down the line. Too often, [tolerance] is an ideologically held value, but not implemented in their daily lives. It needs to be a keystone of their pastoral ministry.

But many pastors struggle, as Wassmuth himself did, with striking the right balance between speaking out against hateful ideologies and remaining tolerant toward religious ideas that differ from their own. Regardless of who defines whom as Christian, the U.S. constitution protects freedom of religion as a deeply held value. Wassmuth:

> No group should be persecuted for its religious beliefs. . . . but it can be very challenging to have a really strong faith and be able to look at some-

body else with a different faith and say, "Your faith has just as much right to be right as mine. Yet I disagree with your interpretations of the Bible."

And more conservative church leaders worry that by speaking out against Christian Identity racism they may alienate parishioners who agree on other crossover issues, such as abortion, taxes, gun rights, home schooling, and the overreaching federal government. Bigoted extremist groups have managed to co-opt many of the more mainstream political issues important to the broader Christian right, making it considerably more difficult for mainstream Christian denominations (especially more conservative churches) to oppose them.

The violent acts linked to Christian Identity followers are rarely openly advocated by Identity preachers. More often, their bigotry is less overtly displayed than with white hoods, cross burnings, or other white supremacist symbols of the past. Instead their hatred is masked within the trappings of mainstream religion. They leave violent acts to "lone wolves," those who act alone to avoid drawing the attention of law enforcement to the Christian Identity groups they are often loosely identified with. This tactic, called "leaderless resistance," a phrase coined by ex-Ku Klux Klan Grand Dragon Louis Beam, encourages action by small cells of less than eight persons. Domestic terrorist groups are downsizing their operations into small cells, making infiltration and surveillance by law enforcement much harder. Additionally, if a leader of one of these cells gets in trouble, an entire organization is not compromised. As a faction of the Aryan Nations boasts on its Pennsylvania-based website: "We are everywhere, we are nowhere."

As the influence of white supremacist leaders such as William Pierce (who died in July 2002) and Richard Butler (whose ailing health has limited his leadership abilities) wanes, a new, more radicalized generation of Christian Identity leaders are stepping forward. As links on the Aryan Nations website reveals, this generation claims to be Christian but at the same time "not a nonviolent organization." These days, white supremacy leaders are touting White Power concerts featuring bands like Fueled by Hate or Intimidation One to rally younger members with music and new media. Since September 11, 2001, the Aryan Nations has even developed an Islamic Ministry Outreach, whose website features pictures glorifying suicide bombers, and calls John Walker, the young American captured while fighting alongside the Taliban, an Aryan Muslim Warrior. This unification of foreign and domestic racially based terrorism is a troubling new threat to human rights.

Meanwhile, the less radical Christian Identity churches that feed and protect their more extremist comrades, continue to function transparently. Followers hold Bible conferences at mainstream hotel conference centers or host home fellowships and feast celebrations.[11] The religion's flagship publication is the *Jubilee,* a bi-monthly tabloid newspaper innocuously (and often anonymously) slipped into news-stands at rural gas stations and other small locally owned businesses throughout the Northwest, despite its racist overtones.

In fact, what makes Christian Identity so insidious is exactly how common it seems, sometimes indistinguishable from mainstream Sunday morning worships. For example, witness the racism and anti-Semitism emanating from the religious messages of pastor Ray Barker, who operated his small Christian Israel Covenant Church just outside of Gig Harbor, Washington:

"Judeo-Christianity is a lie from the pit of Babylonian Hell. . . . Judeo Christianity is an oxymoron. You can't link two absolute opposites together with a hyphen and create a new entity. . . . Judaism is the pinnacle of filth, occultism, and everything that's evil. You are either a Christian following Christ or a Jew following the Satanic religion of Judaism."[12]

Such tenets are so extreme, it is easy to dismiss the ideology as whacko and not take it seriously. But in reality, some of the racist beliefs that form the kernel of Christian Identity also have roots in the histories of Christian mainstream religions. Wassmuth:

[Idaho State University Professor] James Aho found, for example, that one reason that some white supremacists came from Catholic backgrounds was because the authoritarian structure of the church allowed them to shift into the authoritarian structure of white supremacy with some ease. I began looking at the Catholic Church with a little more open eyes. . . . The Crusades, the witch hunts, the Inquisition. The structures of religious institutions can play a role. Some of the greatest attacks on human rights have been faith-based, but some of the greatest movements toward humanity have also been faith-based, like the civil rights movement, so there's an obligation there.

Wassmuth believed mainstream denominations have a pressing moral duty, because of their histories, to speak out now against the racist ghosts of their pasts: For centuries, wars have been fought, people and communities hated, banned, tortured, and executed in the name of religion. Marking Jewish clothes with a badge was a church decree by the Fourth Lateral Council in 1215 and was revived by the Roman Catholic Church in Italy in the sixteenth century, several hundred years before Hitler required a yellow star for German Jews in 1939. The Talmud and other Jewish books were burned during the Inquisitions in thirteenth-century Paris, some seven hundred years before Hitler set fire to a pile of books and art in a public square in Berlin.[13] Anti-Semitism has been a stain on theology for centuries, by Catholics, Protestants, Christian evangelists, and even Black Muslims.

In early America, the English colonists who settled the New World brought with them a vitriol for Catholics that stemmed back to the Protestant Reformation. During the nineteenth century, mobs assaulted nuns and priests, Catholic churches were burned, and Protestant preachers warned that the Catholic emigration from Europe was the Armageddon described in the New Testament Book of Revelation. Because many of the immigrants to America were Catholic, anti-Catholic rhetoric quickly became intertwined with racist anti-immigrant sentiment.

White Christian leaders throughout U.S. history have also twisted interpretations of the Bible to justify slavery, torture, and murder of African Americans and Native Americans.

Mainstream churches are feeling the press of moral duty to speak out publicly, however. Increasingly they are acknowledging their own racist ghosts and reminding their congregations that hate and theology often have been allied at the expense of what most Christians believe Jesus actually taught: compassion, justice, loving your enemies, and telling the truth.

In 1994, the Lutherans published "The Declaration of the Evangelical Lutheran Church in America to the Jewish Community," and in 1998, the Roman Catholic Church followed by publishing "We Remember: A Reflection on the Shoah." In 1999, the Washington and Montana Association of Churches began a courageous regional project to raise awareness about hate groups that use Christian scripture to justify bigotry. The project, When Religions Teach Hate, drew representatives to Los Angeles in March 2000 from ecumenical and interfaith organizations in ten western states. The groups met to develop strategies for confronting hate groups in the West and began funding seed grants in Arizona, California, Colorado, Idaho, Montana, New Mexico, Oregon, Utah, Washington, and Wyoming. Wassmuth was closely involved with such projects, which helped motivate faith communities to organize against religiously motivated bigotry.

In an article written in 2002 for the *Journal of Hate Studies,* United Church of Christ Minister David Ostendorf even called on faith leaders across the nation to point out what he says Christian Identity really is: heresy.[14]

"Though the Christian faith has multiple and varied forms, traditions, denominations and doctrinal differences, there are certain categorical truths that bind its manifestations: Christian Identity's notion of salvation by race is not one of them," wrote Ostendorf, who helped fight the Posse Comitatus in the 1980s and later served as director of the Chicago-based Center for New Community, which urges faith-based organizing initiatives. "Identity is so far afield from the foundational tenets of Christian teachings as to be unrecognizable. It is so removed from the basic teachings of Jesus as to be a caricature of his way of life and his admonitions about living justly and righteously. It is so intent on appropriating the story of the ancient Israelites that its interpretation of that story is simply preposterous. It is so certain of its own convoluted 'truths' about race that it advocates violence as a means to secure white supremacy and to achieve racial purity. Christian Identity defines the word heresy. American religious leaders must take this heresy seriously. . . . Christian Identity must be exposed for what it is—a racist, anti-Semitic ideology that foments hate and advances a pseudo-theological rationale for white superiority. It is also, indeed, the glue that binds the white supremacist movement in America."[15]

Many churches are actively learning the tools for combating racist groups in their communities, and pastors are playing a larger role in turning the tide against this kind of prejudice. In Coeur d'Alene, Bill Wassmuth's outspoken declarations against the hateful ideologies of the Aryan Nations helped rally community opposition so strong it out-witted and outlasted the group it formed to combat.

In Montana, during the eighty-one-day standoff between federal law enforcement agents and the Freemen in 1996, Pastor Jerome Walters not only preached against hate to his Lutheran congregation but also published a three-part series of articles exposing the biblical agenda of the Freemen in the local newspaper. Walters hung a banner from the exterior brick wall of his church that read "One Lord of All" and extended a welcome in seven languages. He spoke publicly about the appropriate Christian responses to such rhetoric and proposals for community life, then published "One Aryan Nation Under God," a book analyzing how religious extremists use the Bible to justify their actions, and called for church leaders to play a bigger role in countering them.

"Public ministers have a unique calling to respond to racial extremism," wrote Walters, now a Lutheran pastor in Washington State. "They are given the vocation of going public with the gospel. . . . The use of sermon illustrations, Bible studies, prayers, and pastoral care addressing racial extremism with both the law and the gospel will serve congregations well. What also needs to be emphasized is the pastor's responsibility to bring the Word of God to bear in the larger community outside the walls of the meeting place of the congregation."[16]

In Noxon, Montana, a small town with headquarters of the Militia of Montana, members of the Noxon United Methodist Church issued a public statement called "A Christian Response to the Militia," condemning "selective love and vengeful hate" and pointed to biblical concepts of "redemptive love and sacrificial service, even to those, yes, especially to those who we call our enemy." It also warned against using fear, suspicion, and scapegoating as "social tools for organizing movements and seeking change."[17]

Similar ecumenical statements have been drafted, signed, and published by mainstream denominations throughout the Northwest in response to racist groups in their communities.

Small-town church leaders and their congregations can play a crucial role in battling prejudice by speaking out boldly and publicly against the misuse of Christian gospel to foment hate. Wassmuth emphasized:

> Many of these smaller rural community people are very entrenched in their little rural churches, and for so many people their faith is what forms the basis for their decisions. The faith community absolutely needs to push on this issue.

7 | Coeur d'Alene
1979~1988

WHEN WASSMUTH decided to return to parish work in 1979, few posts seemed as attractive as the central Idaho mountain town of McCall, where he previously served as a priest. Coeur d'Alene, however, had rival potential.

Settled aside a stunning woodland lake in the Rocky Mountain foothills a few hours south of the Canadian border, Coeur d'Alene was considered one of the state's gems. Sustained by mining, logging, and tourism, the city was small, with a population of about 20,000, but conveniently located only thirty-five miles east of the regional metropolitan hub at Spokane, Washington.

Through the church grapevine, Wassmuth knew that the city's parish had strong, progressive leadership who would appreciate his concern for the poor, sick, elderly, and disenfranchised. He had hardly unpacked his Bible before he and other community members started a hospice program in the local hospital to comfort the dying and their families. In fact, Coeur d'Alene's St. Pius X parishioners were all he had hoped for: down-to-earth, faithful, and compassionate. They understood and appreciated his salt-of-the-earth grit. He was one of them: devoted to God, educated in the gospel, yet not averse to drinking, smoking, and playing dice. He wore his collar when he needed to and cowboy boots when he needed those. He waterskiied and rode mechanical bulls. The congregation loved him.

He opened the parish doors to any group in need of a place to meet, from Alcoholics Anonymous to a small group of ministers and town residents concerned about recent racist attacks in the city. Wassmuth made it clear: his church welcomed everyone.

"Someone on trial for murder, or a convicted sex offender, has a right to be there," he told the *Spokesman-Review* in an interview.[1] "The church is a place for healing."

Wassmuth set out to remedy the community's ills on a personal level. He counseled young pregnant girls, stayed up nights with sick children, helped drunks get sober, and, in what would mark the beginning of a lifelong battle against extremists, he answered Barbara Strakel's phone call.

Strakel, a Coeur d'Alene teacher, had befriended a group of outcast teens who had fled a local religious cult and had been gathering at a restaurant where her husband worked, the Third Street Cantina. Isolated from their families and convinced they would burn in hell for leaving the fundamentalist Catholic sect, the teens desperately needed counsel. Strakel tried, but soon realized what they really needed was a priest, someone schooled in Catholic theology and doctrine. She looked up St. Pius X in the phone book and found Father Bill, as he was affectionately known around town.

Wassmuth had been warned by his bishop about the growing number of extremists, Catholic and non, moving to North Idaho. Specifically, he had been briefed about two groups—the relatively small Aryan Nations and a rapidly growing schismatic sect operated by Francis Konrad Schuckardt, a charismatic religious leader who moved to North Idaho in the late 1960s to found a community of apocalyptic survivalist Catholic separatists. Because of the seriousness of abuse allegations he was hearing firsthand from children and families attempting to leave the sect, and perhaps to a lesser extent because of his Catholic loyalties, Wassmuth trained his sights first on combating Schuckardt. It was a struggle that would unwittingly prepare him for an even bigger battle later against the Aryan Nations, whose leader Richard Butler moved to North Idaho to found an extremist sect.

Schuckardt, a Seattle native, was among the first sedevacantists, a group of traditional Catholics who believe that the Roman Catholic Church is without a true pope because since Vatican II, the popes were teaching heresies and had therefore lost their authority. *Sede vacante* is Latin for "the chair is empty," in reference to the Chair of St. Peter. Schuckardt was not only one of the first sedevacantists, but he would prove to be one of the movement's most embarrassing figures. His church was characterized by a mix of survivalism, paranoid conspiracy theories, and controlling Catholic dogmatism. Calling Vatican II a demonic conspiracy, Schuckardt warned his followers about shadowy anti-Semitic conspiracies, claiming Jews and Freemasons had infiltrated the Catholic Church and were planning its downfall in pursuit of a one-world government.[2]

Wassmuth had a bad intuitive feeling about Schuckardt, who claimed to be Catholic but was the antithesis of much that Wassmuth believed and had been trained in. Ironically, Schuckardt and Wassmuth studied Catholicism in the same halls. Both attended the Jesuit-founded Seattle University, but Wassmuth's religious schooling, more than a decade after Schuckardt's, would lead him down a vastly different spiritual path.

Schuckardt earned a degree in education and linguistics from Seattle University in 1959, just before Vatican II convened. After graduating, he joined the Blue Army, a mainstream Catholic organization affiliated with the Marian order, but in 1961 fell ill with typhoid, which doctors predicted would kill him. His surprise recovery was considered a miracle by Blue Army followers. Afterward, he rose quickly through their ranks into a top position but was dismissed in 1967 for publicly condemning Vatican II and its proposed reforms. The next year, in 1968, he moved to Idaho and founded a militant traditionalist community called the Fatima Crusade, whose few dozen followers met in a dilapidated two-story house in Coeur d'Alene.

Schuckardt's disdain for the Vatican II reforms—especially the shift from Latin Mass to the vernacular—prompted him to rename his group the Tridentine Latin Rite Church. Three years later he was ordained as a priest and consecrated as a bishop (all within a three-week period) by an ousted bishop named Daniel Q. Brown, who was connected to the North American Old Roman Catholic Church, a sect founded in Holland that broke away from Rome in 1723. Buoyed by his spurious new credentials, Schuckardt immediately ordained several priests of his own, helping elevate his church to one of the nation's most rapidly growing and influential Catholic separatist groups.

Throughout the 1970s, Schuckardt traveled extensively across the West and Midwest, recruiting and lecturing to groups of disillusioned Catholics about the evils of Vatican II reforms—changes Bill Wassmuth was at the same time embracing with zeal. Schuckardt's charismatic speaking ability drew families from across the country, particularly California and Illinois. By 1978, Schuckardt had moved the church's headquarters from Coeur d'Alene to nearby Spokane, Washington, and by the early 1980s, claimed his group had grown to five thousand members, with eight hundred living in the Coeur d'Alene-Spokane region.[3] The church began purchasing significant landholdings, including a massive former Jesuit school called Mt. St. Michael's Scholasticate in Spokane.[4] Meanwhile, Schuckardt continued recruiting in Idaho and the region, espousing anti-Semitic and antigovernment conspiracies just shades different than some of the rhetoric and literature that nearby Aryan Nations leaders were using to recruit families.

Schuckardt always maintained that his views on Jews were his private opinions and not his movement's official teachings. However, tapes of Schuckardt teaching teenagers at church seminars in the mid-1970s reveal that he taught that modern Jews were not the same lineage as Old Testament Jews, and that a powerful group of Jews, called Zionists, were a sect intent on destroying Christianity and taking over the world. As proof, Schuckardt claimed that Zionists started the Bolshevik Revolution and World War II as part of their strategy to form a world Jewish state.[5] Like Aryan Nations leader Richard Butler, Schuckardt had been influenced by the infamously racist Protocols of the Elders of Zion.[6]

In 1980, ex-members of Schuckardt's church alleged publicly that anti-Jewish and anti-American philosophies were required reading in his church.[7] Specifically, members reported Schuckardt taught that America was a Freemasonic Republic and that it was anti-Catholic to support the U.S. government or to honor the American flag.[8]

While Schuckardt did not have a compound, per se, his group did start a satellite community called the City of Mary in nearby Rathdrum, a small town approximately fifteen miles outside of Coeur d'Alene. A member of one Southern California family who had moved there in 1970 once confided that he was so sure the Vatican II was a Judeo-Masonic plot to undermine the church that he had considered joining a Catholic militia to defend his religion against the government.[9]

But Schuckardt's paranoid, heavy-handed leadership was not for everyone. While people arrived to join Schuckardt's church, there were others who wanted out. To provide a safe harbor for the former members, as well as to monitor and pressure Schuckardt and other fringe groups in the region, Wassmuth helped found a Cult Awareness Center in Coeur d'Alene. The controversial center drew both praise and criticism for "blacklisting" up to sixteen local groups determined to be destructive cults. Several out-of-the-mainstream churches, including Scientology, complained publicly about being on the list. Others called to ask why Mormons, Jehovah's Witnesses, and other religions were not on the list. Critics charged that nearly all religions would fall under the definition of a mind-control cult. One Episcopalian even accused the center of "promoting bigotry,"[10] an ironic charge given what was yet to unfold in Coeur d'Alene. Wassmuth's sense that Schuckardt's church was more menacing than its leaders claimed would prove correct. But Wassmuth would not get to say "I told you so" until five years after he had arrived—in 1984, when Schuckardt was exposed in a wave of sex and drug scandals. Local newspapers reported on allegations of psychological and sexual abuse, with families claiming in court and to the media that they had been pressured and torn apart, their children paddled with sticks and forced to crawl across cement on their knees, bloodied from hours of prayer.[11] Former members testified they were deprived of sleep, food, and drink for days at a time, and prohibited from watching television, reading books, or visiting outsiders without church consent.[12]

As serious charges against Schuckardt were lobbed into the public spotlight, his followers were splitting into two factions, one that supported him, and another that supported his second-in-command. Church opponents alleged publicly that he was addicted to painkilling drugs, which he was taking for a variety of illnesses.[13] Soon after, there were charges that Schuckardt sexually abused some of the young men working as medical aides for him. Schuckardt denied the allegations, claiming they were a plot by his rival to seize control of the church. Yet at the same time, across the border in Idaho, a number of different children, both male and female, complained to Wassmuth that they had been sexually harassed by Schuckardt. Independently, several children told Wassmuth the same story about Schuckardt, allegedly requiring them to disrobe and stand naked in front of him as they exited the swimming pool.

Acting behind the scenes, Wassmuth counseled victims and urged them to share their traumatic experiences, ultimately helping to expose the embattled cult leader. In June 1984, Schuckardt fled the region, with allegations mounting on both sides of the Washington–Idaho border. The power struggle between his warring church factions came to a head with shots being fired; Schuckardt and his followers fled after stripping his plush Spokane mansion of $250,000 in cash and property, which a judge eventually ordered returned. He gave nothing back, however, instead he founded another school and priory in Greenville, California, one hundred miles north of Reno, Nevada. His racist ideas would eventually run into opposition there, too, with parents complaining that his school was "perpetrating a fraud" by teaching that the Jewish Holocaust in World War II never happened.[14]

The law would catch up to Schuckardt three years later when SWAT teams raided his California priory, arresting him and nearly a dozen followers on drug and stolen property charges, some of which stemmed back to the Spokane case. Authorities seized Demerol, morphine, Dilaudid, Percodan, and a quarter-pound bag of marijuana labeled tea,[15] as well as gold coins, silver bars, and German and Swiss currency. And there, among the church statues, rifles, handguns, religious books, and video equipment, was a telling piece of propaganda: a pamphlet titled *Death to the Racemixers*.[16]

It was proof that Wassmuth had indeed been fighting a hate group, not just a religious cult, even though he may not have recognized it as such at the time. Had he known, it might have been less of a surprise when an Aryan Nations skinhead walked into the Cult Awareness Center to ask if they considered his group, the Church of Jesus Christ-Christian, a cult. But Wassmuth had been too consumed with Schuckardt to realize that the youth's arrival at his doorstep forewarned a dangerous new development in his efforts to battle extremist groups in the region.

Aside from the ongoing Schuckardt drama, Wassmuth was comforted to be back in North Idaho, out of the sagebrush plains and potato fields of the south, and close enough to his aging parents that he could drive home to Greencreek to visit on weekends. And, almost equally important to Wassmuth, it was a paradise of mountains and national forests, with countless rivers, freshwater lakes, blue-ribbon trout streams, and ski areas—all within a fifty-mile radius.

In Boise, he had lived for years in a sad little prefab house tucked behind the Our Lady of the Rosary, his base of operations for educational work within the Idaho Catholic diocese. On days off, he would search out snow in the Wasatch range near Salt Lake City, or ski at Bogus Basin, a local ski resort above Boise's foothills that, for a native North Idahoan spoiled by long runs and a reliable snowpack, matched its name.

Wassmuth had long known what a great place Coeur d'Alene was, but the rest of the country was just discovering it. Idaho boomed, increasing by more than a third to nearly a million people in the 1970s. The immigrants were primarily white, upper-middle-class urban refugees seeking cheap land ($200 an acre) and the kind of old-fashioned rural simplicity Idaho represented: a place where cohabitation was still technically against the law but tooling down the road with an open beer was not, where kids could drive at age fourteen, and where there were plenty of forty-pound chinooks to go around. Most, an estimated 43,000 of those who immigrated to Idaho between 1975 and 1980, were from California, a trend some natives grumpily called "Californication." While residents welcomed Californians' fat wallets as tourists, they were less hospitable to their permanent presence. Natives blamed them for snatching up the few good jobs and driving up real estate prices by paying outrageous sums for property.

"In California it was rush, rush, rush, always a deadline, never a day off," a big-city developer told *U.S. News & World Report* when asked why he had recently taken a 50 percent pay cut to move to Coeur d'Alene. "Here the pace is much slower. My ulcer hasn't bothered me once."

Coeur d'Alene's appeal rapidly reached beyond Californians. *U.S. News & World Report* in 1982 touted it in a national story headlined "If You're Looking For a Great Place to Live—An Outdoor Paradise." Three-bedroom, two-bath homes were selling for between $50,000–$60,000, hospital costs were 30 percent below the nationwide average, and there had not been a murder since 1979, the story boasted.[17] Despite a recession hitting the timber and mining industries, Coeur d'Alene benefited from a surge in tourism, with record numbers of conventions and summer tourists topping one million by the early 1980s. The local high school prided itself on turning out National Merit Scholars, the city's two-year college boomed, and a local musical theater group boasted it was "The place to go before going pro."[18]

The story also could have mentioned that the nearby Church of Jesus Christ Christian-Aryan Nations compound was "the place to go after going to the pen," but there was no mention of the new white supremacist headquarters, the ex-cons it was attracting, and the ulcers it was beginning to cause law enforcement, minorities, and community leaders. This compound was still under the national media's radar, and with Wassmuth's hands full with Schuckardt, largely under his own, too.

But Aryan Nations leader Butler, who himself had moved to Idaho from southern California in the early 1970s, was busy touting North Idaho's assets as well. It was a safe haven from the pesky police surveillance that had become a part of life in Orange County, there were few minorities or Jews, and it was beautiful. But unlike the Coeur d'Alene City Council, with its aboveboard campaign to attract clean industries, Butler was recruiting newcomers to his "white homeland," many of whom had criminal records and a propensity toward violence. While the city council was taking out ads in mainstream magazines, the Aryan Nations was sending literature to state prisons.

Like a sinister wind, Butler and his gaggle of followers began spreading hate through the panhandle's hills and valleys, attempting to capitalize on the growing disenfranchisement among blue-collar rural residents going through hard times in the natural resource industries. By the early 1980s, mills and mines were closing. Farms were going under.[19] Workers were being laid off. Anger toward the government and outside interests was rising, and the Aryan Nations was quietly offering sympathy, conspiratorial explanations, and misguided solutions.

At first, it seemed unfathomable to Wassmuth that such crazy ideas would gain favor among rural residents and hard-core extremists alike. North Idaho was home—quiet and neighborly—not a place that could become one of the nation's hotspots for racist and antigovernment activity.

But, he was a little naive then. The region had a history of extremism long before the Aryan Nations. For years Coeur d'Alene's racist "sundown laws" had prohibited Indians from appearing publicly after dusk. The Ku Klux Klan had recruited throughout the Northwest in the 1920s, especially Oregon, until the group's rabid anti-Catholicism dwindled its support. After the Klan came the Silver Shirts, a pro-Hitler support group that took hold in the 1930s and drew much of its support in Washington State. Pearl Harbor ended the Silver Shirts' popularity, but, in turn, triggered racist conspiracy theories and mistreatment of the region's Japanese Americans, many of whom were forced into internment camps. The anticommunist and anti-Semitic John Birch Society also found broad support throughout the Northwest, especially in Idaho.[20]

For decades before Butler, extremist groups had attempted to recruit the Pacific Northwest's rural blue-collar workers during times of economic hardship: blaming Jews or Japanese, Catholics or Communists, Indians, international bankers, or the Internal Revenue Service— whoever was perceived as responsible at the moment. When Butler began building his compound, the seeds of bigotry had already been sown. He carefully tended this dormant discontent, which some believe might have withered on the vine had he not created such an efficient incubator for hate inside his compound. With the advent of Butler's World Aryan Congress meetings, his bucolic twenty-acre spread became the nation's foremost extremist convention site. The first was in 1979, when Butler sponsored the Pacific States National Kingdom Identity Conference, which drew a host of Christian Identity leaders. The keynote speaker was a Church of Israel leader from Missouri.[21]

The prison ministry Butler had initiated that same year soon began paying off. It was in the Arizona State Prison that violent career criminal and white supremacist Gary Yarbrough first heard about the Aryan Nations. After serving time on drug and burglary charges, he moved to northern Idaho in 1980 and began working as a printer at the Aryan Nations in June.[22] (Yarbrough would emerge, four years later, as a key figure in the terrorist group The Order, after FBI agents found in his North Idaho home found the .45-caliber submachine gun used in Denver to murder Jewish radio host Alan Berg.[23]) But Yarbrough started with a more mundane job, pumping out racist literature on the Aryan Nations press, making flyers such as Butler's "Runnin' Nigger Shoot," which had been showing up on the front porches and cars of some of Wassmuth's parishioners, who then brought the disturbing propaganda to church for their priest to see.

Wassmuth's concerns grew as the Aryan Nations' presence did. He was among the ecumenical group of ministers who signed an interfaith petition speaking out against the group in 1980. He passed the disturbing literature along to members of the newly formed Kootenai County Human Rights Task Force. This group, which met in Wassmuth's church, was a mix of local residents—a Protestant minister, a professor, a lawyer, a teacher, a real-estate agent, and a law enforcement officer. All had a common concern: how to respond to a rash of recent racist activity in town, specifically threats against black families and interracial couples, and nasty graffiti that had turned up on an establishment owned by a local Jewish restaurateur. Swastikas were showing up on local businesses and a Baptist church, too. The small group of concerned residents began meeting to offer emotional support to targets of harassment but soon widened its scope to include pursuing legal remedies for the ongoing problem. They drafted proposed amendments to Idaho law that would make bias harassment crimes a felony and give victims the right to sue. The group also attempted to spread awareness about Butler's growing presence, warnings that fell primarily on deaf ears in the beginning. Several prominent business leaders complained they were simply drawing attention to a harmless bunch of weirdos and hurting business in the process.

Butler held his next conference in Kansas and expanded the invitation list to include Klan, neo-Nazi, and Posse Comitatus leaders. The same year the Kootenai County Human Rights Task Force officially formed, 1981, the ex-Grand Dragon of the Texas Ku Klux Klan, Louis Beam, moved to the Aryan Nations compound. Impressed by Beam's dedication to the movement, Butler had offered him temporary residence. (Beam had recently been ordered to stop violent actions against Vietnamese shrimp fishermen in his home region of Texas.) Beam began building a then state-of-the-art computer network that established a national computerized bulletin board for extremists long before "chat rooms" became popular with the mainstream.[24]

By the time of Butler's 1982 Aryan World Congress, held on the rimrock above Hayden Lake, the racist right was beginning to gel under his leadership. A long list of prominent white supremacists attended, confirming Butler's status as rising star in the movement. The number of high-profile racists gathering in Idaho raised the attention of federal law enforcement, prompting the U.S. Department of Justice to send mediation officials from Seattle to meet with local law enforcement for briefing on the Aryan Nations. A savvy Kootenai County undersheriff named Larry Broadbent was assigned to monitor the Aryan Nations, and with good reason.

Many of Butler's followers were becoming sufficiently riled up by calls for a racial holy war to begin acting out more boldly and violently in support of the cause. Crosses were burned on the lawns of two local families in Coeur d'Alene. Some of Butler's more zealous followers, apparently frustrated that Butler was "all talk and no action," formed smaller, more radical factions. What began as one man yelling threats out his van window would eventually lead to more heinous crimes: robbery, bombings, hijackings, even murder.

In February 1982, a white supremacist named Keith Gilbert pulled his van alongside a Coeur d'Alene High School honor student from a racially mixed family who was walking home from a softball game and yelled, "Your life shall perish. Thou shall not live long."[25]

Gilbert and Butler had both attended Wesley Swift's church together in Hollywood, California, but Gilbert had a rap. He had been heavily involved in a guerrilla organization called the Minutemen and was arrested in 1965 for stealing more than one thousand pounds of TNT, which he later said was part of a plan to bomb a Hollywood stage during a speech by the Reverend Martin Luther King, Jr.[26]

After Gilbert served his five-year prison sentence, he moved to Post Falls, Idaho, at about the same time his acquaintance Richard Butler was establishing the Christian Identity church. Gilbert flaunted his racist leanings, even driving around town wearing a Storm Trooper uniform in a camouflaged Volkswagen van marked with a swastika.[27] Consequently, few were surprised to find out Gilbert was behind some of the continued harassment of the Coeur d'Alene youth. Gilbert's threats had been frightening enough to convince the boy's family to go to court over the incident. Eight months later, a jury would convict Gilbert of misdemeanor assault for the threats. At the time, the law did not differentiate between racially based harassment and other kinds of intimidation. North Idaho human rights activists and local lawmakers had been pushing for legislative changes to make such acts a felony. A malicious harassment bill was introduced in 1983 by Moscow, Idaho, Senator Norma Dobler, and numerous human rights activists testified in favor. Richard Butler and two other Aryan Nations leaders testified against the legislation. Gilbert may have inadvertently helped the bill pass by sending legislators a fraudulent letter signed by a fictitious rabbi representing a nonexistent Jewish organization, in hopes of swaying lawmakers not to vote for the bill. When Gilbert was exposed, several members of the Legislature, angered by Aryan Nations' attempts to manipulate them, voted instead in favor.[28] The bill eventually passed, but only after Kootenai County's prosecuting attorney proposed several amendments aimed at mollifying some of the more conservative lawmakers.

Residents' spirits were buoyed by the legislation's passage and Gilbert's relatively stiff sentence of jail time, a one-two punch that many thought would put a lid on the Aryan Nations' antics.[29]

Wassmuth felt the fight against the Aryan Nations had been in good hands with the Kootenai County Human Rights Task Force, whose successes in helping pass the malicious harassment law and convicting Gilbert had quieted things considerably in the community. The task force went into hibernation after several original members moved away. The box of minutes, flyers, and paperwork was dropped off at Wassmuth's office, as his church had been the group's meeting place. It sat in storage for more than a year.

But the relative calm in the following months was deceiving. As townsfolk breathed a sigh of relief at the return of peaceful times in their small lakeside city, members of the Aryan Nations had gone underground and were stockpiling weaponry, recruiting felons, and planning a violent revolution to take over the five northwest states of Washington, Oregon, Idaho, Montana, and Wyoming as the Aryan white homeland.

Though an Aryan Nations faction had pulled off several small heists throughout 1983 to raise money for their grand plan, neither law enforcement nor the mainstream media had yet connected the dots between the offshoot group and Butler's compound. One of the few people who knew what was brewing in the fall of 1983 was a Los Angeles-based freelance journalist who had infiltrated the Aryan Nations while posing as a tropical fish salesman. The journalist had talked Butler's supporters into letting him film inside the compound in exchange for propaganda films that he promised to make for them. His videotaped footage would later be used as crucial evidence in the government's case against members of the Aryan Nations offshoot group called the Silent Brotherhood, also known as The Order. The freelancer's scoop became one of the most sensational stories of the 1980s, but it came with a price: The journalist's name wound up on an Order hit list, right alongside radio talk-show host Alan Berg.

The Aryan Nations, and in particular The Order faction, knew better than to commit major crimes in the county of their headquarters. The

Order began its string of crimes across the border in Spokane, in April 1983, with a strong-arm robbery of a pornographic bookstore that netted them slightly more than $300. Throughout 1983, they pulled off a series of small-time robberies to amass a stockpile of weapons and to fund bigger plans.

A year and a half later, the gang had doubled from half a dozen to more than twenty, and had honed their tactics enough to rob an armored car in California, obtaining $3.6 million to further the fight for racial purity and a government overthrow. They went on to bomb a Boise synagogue, spread counterfeit money throughout the Northwest, murder Alan Berg, kill a Missouri state trooper, and wound another.

During the summer of 1984, using part of the loot from that multimillion armored car heist, two members of The Order affiliated with a white supremacist group from Arkansas and Missouri, paid a $30,500 cash down payment on 110 acres in the mountainous region north of Priest River in Idaho's panhandle. Another $70,000 would be used to equip and operate a paramilitary training camp on the property, which started up that fall.[30] The sight of paramilitary extremists decked out in camouflage gear in the remote north woods only added to residents' growing fear that the Aryan Nations problem in Idaho was out of control. When the group was eventually broken up, dozens were arrested, one Order member was eventually convicted of four counts of murder for hire, and leader Robert Mathews died during a fiery standoff with the FBI on Whidbey Island. Idaho had been blazing across the national headlines for a year, usually with "Nazi" or "Aryan Nations" attached to it. From the outside, the state seemed to be brimming with neo-Nazi hit squads, synagogue bombers, and half-cocked Aryan warriors. Those who lived in Idaho knew that was not the case, but few could deny that while law enforcement investigations had uncovered a vast plot that spanned the Northwest, the Order's roots had been planted firmly in Coeur d'Alene's backyard.[31]

Nonetheless, many locals felt resentful that the image of their state, which had before been known for its Famous Potatoes and posh Sun Valley ski resort, was quickly developing a bad reputation thanks to a group of unruly ex-cons and hate-filled retirees, most of whom had moved in from somewhere else. A lot of fingers were pointed: It's their fault for bringing their hate-filled rhetoric here in the first place. It's our fault for tacitly approving of their presence and allowing prejudice to go unchecked. It's law enforcement's fault for treating them with kid gloves. It's the media's fault for giving them too much attention. . . .

The Aryan Nations blame game, and the even trickier question of how best to combat the group's presence, would trigger an intense bout of community soul searching that lasted for decades—in public debates, in the pages of the local newspapers, in boardrooms and brew pubs, coffee shops, and classrooms throughout the region. While not always easy, such frank discussions eventually helped transform North Idaho into a place more sensitive to its own biases, more aware of its own glaring lack of diversity.

Yet the original impetus for change arose from economics as much as from altruism. The negative attention brought by The Order trials not only embarrassed Coeur d'Alene but also threatened to ruin the fragile economic recovery that tourism had sustained. The Chamber of Commerce complained of fewer visitors. Investors backed away from making commitments in northern Idaho. Worried Travel Council officials began slapping together a national advertising campaign to dispel the growing perception that the state was packed with right-wing fanatics.[32] With the community desperate to respond, the original Kootenai County Human Rights Task Force members scrambled in early 1984 to reinstate their dormant group, which was without a current leader. Few jumped at the job. The Order had shown willingness to murder for its cause. Many of the Protestant clergy and outspoken community leaders who would have normally considered such a post were married and had families. Their wives worried they would become widowed.

Father Bill Wassmuth, however, had no wife or children. He was charismatic, outspoken, and he had a large, adoring congregation to fall back on for support. He was respected and admired by the community for his civic activism—he had served on the governor's Idaho Citizens Prison Review Committee,[33] helped start the Idaho Hospice

Program, volunteered at the Anchor House for boys, belonged to Kiwanis, and the YMCA.

With Schuckardt defeated and leaving, Wassmuth already had successfully taken on one right-wing extremist group. He was perfect for the job. And fortunately for the task force members who approached him with the idea, he also had a hard time saying no. In part, Wassmuth was chosen because task force members believed he would not be a target.

They also noted that, "You've got no wife and kids for them to harass, and your house is made of brick so it won't burn," not knowing that Wassmuth actually lived in the modest wooden house kitty-corner to the church.[34]

Wassmuth's drive, gentle persuasion, and unwavering popularity was exactly what the task force needed. He agreed to take the position and, with the remaining task force members, set out to reinvigorate the organization, restructuring it to include an executive council and several standing committees focused on community response, education, law enforcement, victim support, legislation, and a speaker's bureau. He and the newly reorganized Kootenai County Task Force on Human Relations coined a working motto: "Saying yes to justice is the best way to say no to racism," which set a standard for the group's nonviolent, proactive approach over the next two decades. The group incorporated as a nonprofit entity; asked support from the local Native American government, the Coeur d'Alene Tribal Council; and in a politically astute move, drew the mostly Republican members of the Chamber of Commerce into its fold, simultaneously ensuring a nonpartisan atmosphere and gaining the support of Coeur d'Alene's powerful business community. Wassmuth was known around town as a left-wing priest at a time when Idaho was overwhelmingly Republican. (Republican victories in Idaho in 1980 and 1984 were more substantial than in any other state except Utah.)[35] But the desire to combat the Aryan Nations crossed party lines in Coeur d'Alene, which in 1985 elected Republican combat veteran Ray Stone as mayor. Stone had helped liberate a Nazi death camp while serving as a U.S. Army private in World War II, and what he saw in 1945 forever committed him to support the kind of human rights crusades his community was taking on.[36] Another Republican, Kootenai County Prosecutor Glen Walker, was instrumental in the passage of human rights legislation and prosecution of hate crimes in the county. The task force courted support on both sides of the party aisle, steadily increasing its visibility through booths, floats, and outreach activities at county fairs and small-town parades.

The community, desperate to show its distaste for the Aryan Nations' violent shenanigans, supported the task force through donations and by attending public meetings, which Aryan Nations members often disrupted. Wassmuth, busier than ever, spoke at event after event.

In September 1985, the task force co-sponsored a prejudice symposium titled "Racism: Prejudice and Progress," under the direction of one of the city's most active, behind-the-scenes human rights strategists, Tony Stewart, who was also a popular North Idaho College political science professor. The weeklong event featured an impressive list of speakers, including former Georgia Senator Julian Bond and Native American leader Ada Deer. North Idaho College, under Stewart's leadership, produced seven weekly television programs taped at the symposium, which were broadcast through the Pacific Northwest on public television stations.[37] With increased media exposure and growing regional support, aided by a sensational, high-profile racketeering trial against The Order that fall in Seattle, the task force was beginning to feel the wind behind its sails.

In October of 1985, the Chamber of Commerce named Wassmuth Citizen of the Year for his work with hospice, human rights, substance abuse, cult awareness, and the Ecumenical Council of Churches.

His priestly duties, meanwhile, were growing at a pace equal to his community duties. Under his short five-year tenure the parish had doubled from four hundred to eight hundred families, stretching the physical capacity of the church. Before Mass, the parish council would set up folding chairs for overflow into the cafeteria and gymnasium. During services, Wassmuth asked parishioners to join hands as they said the Lord's Prayer, a participation ritual that in the early 1980s was not common in the Catholic Church. He loved humor, music, and drama, and hosted church variety shows that drew hundreds. He showed up at themed church dances in various get-ups: in a leather jacket on a motorcycle, as a pirate, or a cowboy. He wore an afro, jewelry, and jeans. Yet come Sunday morning Mass, or at family baptisms to burials, there was no doubt among the congregation of his deep devotion to God and the gospel. He was a very popular, if unconventional, priest.

As a result of his parish's rapid growth, Wassmuth was given the green light to build a new sanctuary and had been overseeing every aspect of church construction, consulting with parish planning committees and architects and builders, even raising money.

His evenings were also hectic. He ministered to the dying, giving last rites to whomever asked for them, Catholic or not. He ministered to "street rats," troubled teens who showed up drunk at church dances or the Cult Awareness Center. He made house calls, and they were never short, as residents inevitably invited him to stay for a drink, dinner, or a few rounds of bunco, a dice game that usually ended with fifty bucks in the kitty. Like many priests, Wassmuth smoke and drank. But unlike many priests, he did not hide it. When children asked how Father Bill could drink and smoke even though he was a priest, their parents gently explained that Father Bill was not just a priest, he was also a man.[38]

Privately, it was precisely that fact that tormented him. He came home late at night to a dark, silent house where he would watch the late-night news with that day's newspaper spread out before him and a glass of Scotch whiskey from a bottle given to him from a parishioner grateful for this wedding or that baptism. He longed for close companionship, even just someone to talk to at the end of the day, but this job he loved required him to be single, celibate, and alone. When his father had passed away, Wassmuth's mother had been there. The morning Henry Wassmuth died, as he sat by his bedside and comforted his mother, Wassmuth realized he did not want to die alone. That fear kept him up some nights, and alcohol was gradually turning into the most reliable tool for chasing those thoughts out of his mind.

His drinking habit had begun years earlier as one or two martinis to take the edge off during the flights between Washington, D.C., and Boise. In Coeur d'Alene, it was increasing at the same rate as his workload: almost faster than he could handle. The exhaustion from his hectic schedule and heavy habit was taking its toll. His eyes were bloodshot, his face puffy, and the buttons of his favorite tweed jacket strained against the weight he had gained. Though few parishioners knew, as he was never late nor missed Mass, he had delivered his share of sermons over the years with a pounding headache from a wicked hangover.

Ironically, among those Wassmuth allowed to use his church was the local Substance Abuse Council, which offered a step program similar to Alcoholics Anonymous. During the months they had been meeting in his church, Wassmuth had struck up a friendship with the lead counselor, a tough-talking recovered alcoholic who downed cups of black coffee like she smoked cigarettes: one after another. Wassmuth had been helping out with her sessions, stepping in to do the fifth step—acknowledgement of failure and asking for forgiveness—a process Catholic priests knew well. But the more he counseled, the harder it became to ignore his own problem: He was drinking more and always wishing he was drinking less. He never bought liquor. But, confounded as how to best thank a priest, nearly everybody gave it to him as a gift. At Christmas time, or as thanks for services rendered, it was always "Poor Father, he works so hard, he doesn't have a family, at least let's give him a good bottle of whiskey." Around Thanksgiving, one parishioner gave him a half gallon of particularly fine Scotch. By Christmas it was gone. But nobody knew. He lived alone, a bachelor. And if anybody noticed his health was suffering, as a few parishioners did, nobody felt justified criticizing him. He was a priest.

That Christmas, after having helped perform another step session, he began a personal conversation with his counselor friend that ended with an unusual role reversal: Wassmuth confessed. He was becoming an alcoholic, he confided, and pledged to stop drinking come the new year. He gave away most of his liquor at the parish holiday party; just three bottles of leftover Scotch went home with him at three in the morning. He held them unsteadily over the kitchen sink but could not bring himself to pour them down the drain. He was too weak, the Scotch was too good. Instead he gave them to a friend of his, another celibate middle-aged priest with a cupboard full of gift-wrapped whiskey. Wassmuth stopped drinking cold turkey that January and continued his human rights advocacy without missing a step. Only those closest to him noticed the change.

In January, the task force began coordinating plans to mark the first national holiday commemorating the birthday of Martin Luther King Jr. Though the state of Idaho did not officially recognize the holiday (in 1990, Wassmuth's lobbying would help change that), the task force pushed forward with plans for a local celebration. The school district responded positively and began teaching about racism. District officials recognized January 20 as an official holiday, suspended classes, and encouraged its student body and staff to attend human rights programs being sponsored by the task force. North Idaho College joined the momentum, freeing its students from classes to take part in the midday celebration downtown. Wassmuth delivered the keynote speech to a crowd of more than a thousand people. All three national networks sent local television crews to cover the event, as did local radio stations and newspapers.

Not to be outdone, in the spring Butler announced plans to host his annual Aryan World Congress at the compound during three days in July. He touted the imminent arrival of several hundred sympathizers from across the nation, which residents feared would cause trouble and inevitably draw a barrage of national media. The task force began planning a counterevent and devised a plan to contact all Northwest cities with populations over five hundred and all counties in the five Northwestern states asking them to submit statements in support of human rights. The letter, dated May 23, 1986, went like this:

Dear County Commissioners,
We are writing you regarding a situation which will command your immediate attention. As you know, Coeur d'Alene, Hayden Lake and Kootenai County in North Idaho have been targeted by the media as the

center of the Aryan Nations' Neo-Nazi activity in the Northwest. Recently, however, it has become evident that this activity is a problem not only to us here in Kootenai County, but for all of the Northwest. The Neo-Nazis and the Ku Klux Klan have stated that the Northwest, specifically the states of Washington, Oregon, Wyoming, Montana and Idaho, is an area that will welcome them, or at least not actively oppose their activities. We believe they are relying on local government neutrality and plausibility to accomplish this.

Robert Miles, head of the Mountain Church of Jesus Christ the Savior, a leading exponent of the Identity Church Movement, and a convicted felon, jailed for six years for blowing up ten school buses in Michigan, claims that the Northwest is the place to create a separate nation made up exclusively of whites. He is moving to the Northwest and, allegedly, encouraging his congregation and 1,500 prison inmates to move to the Northwest as well. A separate white nation to be created out of the Northwest is also a stated goal of the Aryan Nations.

In the past, local governments in the Northwest have largely ignored the organized racists growing in our midst. Please remember, however, the violent manifestations of these Neo-Nazi and Ku Klux Klan beliefs that have occurred in just two short years.

Members of The Order were responsible for two armed car robberies in North Seattle in the spring of 1984.

Walter West, a white supremacist, was beaten and killed in Idaho by a member of The Order in May of 1984.

Alan Berg, a talk-show host, was murdered in Denver, Colorado, by a machine gun wielding member of The Order in June of 1984.

Robert J. Mathews, a member of The Order, died on Whidbey Island Washington during a shoot-out with SWAT teams and FBI agents in December, 1984.

Eugene Kinerk, an Aryan Nations member, committed suicide in a Boise, Idaho prison on Feb. 22, 1986. Earlier he had robbed a bank in Grey's Harbor County, Washington.

David Tate, a member of The Order and former Aryan Nations member, shot and killed a Missouri State Trooper and seriously wounded another trooper in April, 1986.

David Louis Wright, associated with the Duck Club, an ultraconservative tax protest organization, has been charged with murdering four members of the Charles Goldmark family of Seattle, Washington, in December of 1985, allegedly believing that he was killing Communists and Jews—the Goldmarks were neither.

(Information concerning the crimes enumerated above came from a Seattle Times copyrighted story dated April 20, 1986.)

Other activities by the Neo-Nazis and the Ku Klux Klan and other hate groups continue in the Northwest despite the reduction in the ranks of The Order.

We are writing to cities and counties throughout the Northwest because we are presented with a unique opportunity. The Aryan Nations is holding its annual convention on the 12th and 13th of July in Kootenai County, Idaho.

We believe if each of you enact a resolution similar to the one attached, the Northwest will be sending a message of absolute clarity to the Aryan Nations, the Ku Klux Klan, Neo-Nazis, and other hate groups that their racist, supremacist and prejudicial beliefs are contrary to those embraced by the Northwest and their local governments.

We need your resolution prior to July 4, stating your support for the federal and state constitutions as these documents apply to racial equality and religious freedom. Let's join together in this opportunity to publicly express our support of the rights and equality of all the citizens of the Northwest.

The letter was signed by Norman Gissel, who had included his phone number for questions. Gissel, a respected and well-spoken Coeur d'Alene attorney and task force leader, signed the letter alongside the mayor and the chairman of the Kootenai County Commissioners.

In response, a dozen letters came in, then fifty, then a hundred. In the end, nearly two hundred cities and counties sent back statements that their communities supported human rights.

North Idaho and Spokane-based human rights task forces began planning the July human rights celebration, calling it "Good Neighbor Day." It was aptly named, as residents throughout the region donated time and labor to prepare the July event, timed to coincide with the Aryan Nations World Congress.

The day before, volunteers set up tables and typewriters for the press.

A local rock band contributed sound equipment and agreed to stay for the day to operate it. A Coeur d'Alene sign painter provided free publicity, and a local florist put together an arrangement for the podium, which was loaned by the school district.

When Wassmuth arrived at the city park the next morning, the press was already buzzing around the bandstand, plugging in cables and wires, setting up microphones and minicassette recorders. Wassmuth made the rounds, from *Good Morning America* to the *Today Show*. FBI agents were also there, in plainclothes, watching for men who had made threats against Wassmuth. There was a certain unease with so many extremists gathered just a few miles away and a big crowd arriving at the downtown park to protest by celebrating human rights. There were always those, especially college students and more radical protesters from Seattle, Portland, Missoula, and other Northwest university towns, who wanted to confront the Aryan Nations directly at its compound—a tactic that had resonance among some members of the human rights supporters as well. But Wassmuth, and most members of the task force, worried that such action risked a violent confrontation that would take away from their proactive message.

In the end it was not necessary to go to the compound for direct confrontation with the Aryan Nations because several members came to the park dressed in fatigues to hear Wassmuth's speech.

"These people here are proclaiming their commitment to justice and equality," Wassmuth said, his voice booming out over the crowd of more than a thousand. "Saying 'yes' to human rights is saying 'no' to racism. Today is the time to stand up and be counted. No one after today can assume any part of Coeur d'Alene, North Idaho, or the Northwest is a haven for racism. The people of the Northwest will actively resist the spread of such."

The crowd rose to its feet in a standing ovation.[39]

Idaho Governor John Evans spoke, and state and local government officials were recognized as proclamations were read from four Northwest governors, and many cities and counties.[40] Altogether, the resolutions covered a population of nearly 4 million. Only Wyoming did not participate.

The crowd size was double what task force members and law enforcement officers had expected. A horde of media had shown up, a public relations coup for the task force. Although most reporters would not have come if not for the "other" rally, Butler's World Aryan Congress, which had kicked off the night before with a press conference at Butler's compound. Veteran national news reporters noted that the scene at the compound looked like a presidential press briefing, with Butler and Robert Miles, pastor of the Mountain Church in Cohoctah, Michigan, fielding questions while more than seventy reporters and photographers jockeyed for positions behind the bank of microphones.[41]

Television crews from throughout the Pacific Northwest were doing the predictable live reports from the compound, and other reporters had flown in from Chicago, New York, Denver, Detroit, Sacramento, and Salt Lake City.[42]

Despite their grumbling that the Aryan Nations was bad for business, Coeur d'Alene Resort officials took advantage of the media contingent by handing out letters at the press conference welcoming the press to "beautiful North Idaho" and inviting them for free dinner and drinks at their new sixty-million-dollar resort. The letter also reminded them of the next day's human rights counterdemonstration. Maybe it was the free drinks, but the pitch seemed to work. Nearly all the media organizations in town for the Aryan Congress, including the major television networks, the *New York Times,* and the *Guardian* from the United Kingdom, attended the human rights rally. Though reporters scattered in the afternoon to cover Butler's press conference at the compound, many returned later to file their stories and take in the entertainment, everything from Idaho folksinger Rosalie Sorrels, to Tribal storytellers, and Israeli folk songs.

It was a strange day. While Coeur d'Alene residents gave Wassmuth a standing ovation for urging support for human rights, Aryan Nations followers gave a standing ovation for the late Robert Mathews, founder of The Order.

The human rights crowd cheered when the president of the Great Falls, Montana, Hebrew Association said "We're all here because we're

Americans; the ideas those people in Hayden Lake espouse are as un-American as the goose step." At the compound, white supremacists were giving the "Heil Hitler" Nazi salute.

"It is only 15 miles from this picture book town in the Idaho Pan-handle to the Church of Jesus Christ Christian, Aryan Nations, near Hayden Lake," wrote *Seattle Times* reporter Don Duncan in the story he filed for the next day's paper."It might as well be 15 light years. The people are that different."[43]

That is exactly the point Wassmuth and the task force were trying to make. Judging by the next day's press reports, the event had success-fully drawn attention away from Butler and onto community support for human rights. It also had triggered important discussions among human rights supporters from Idaho, Washington, Montana, Oregon, and Wyoming, who were now talking about a five-state umbrella or-ganization that could lead smaller task forces being modeled after Kootenai County's.

Butler and other Aryan Nations leaders were reportedly incensed at the community's ability to steal their thunder. The harassment started a few weeks later. Members of the Kootenai County Task Force began getting hostile telephone calls threatening them and their families. The FBI urged extra personal precautions, especially for Wassmuth, who as Catholic priest and chair of the task force, was a vulnerable public target.[44]

Wassmuth changed few of his habits, instead logging a few more miles onto his nightly jog to ease his anxiety. Things were disquietingly calm but only for about a month. After members of The Order were convicted in Seattle during August, a series of new incidents began.

A black man was assaulted with racial epithets while shopping in a Coeur d'Alene K-Mart store by a white man who told officers he had come to Idaho to join the Aryan Nations.[45] A pipe bomb was mailed to a North Dakota judge who had been trying a case against the Posse Comitatus, and on August 7, a similar bomb exploded at an auto body shop in Coeur d'Alene. Butler held a press conference to denounce the bombings and deny that he had anything to do with either incident.

On August 18, the body of a Baltimore, Maryland, man named Kenneth Shray turned up near Bonner County's Clark Fork River. The FBI knew Shray had moved to the region to join the Aryan Nations. They did not yet know that he had been killed because members of a new Aryan Nations faction calling itself the Bruder Schweigen Strike Force II thought he was a police informer.[46] The FBI did believe, however, that the small criminal cell (which also became commonly known as The Order II) had some of the original Order group's stolen money, and warned Wassmuth and other local high-profile members of the task force that they could be at risk.[47]

In early September, law enforcement began closing in on the Order II's counterfeiting operation when one of the members, Ed Hawley, attempted to buy cotton candy at the Spokane Interstate Fair with a bogus $20 bill. The concession stand vendor called law enforcement to report that a man wearing camouflage pants and army boots had attempted to pass fake money. A county sheriff's deputy arrested Hawley, and found fifty-nine counterfeit $20 bills in a diaper bag that he and his wife had been carrying. That night, worried that Hawley had blown their cover, two other members of the small group flushed their green printer's ink down the toilet and took counterfeit paper and a paper cutter from Hawley's home.[48]

Money so poorly manufactured that it could not pass muster at a cotton candy booth was not the only thing getting in the way of the group's plans. Hawley, whose sloppiness had attracted law enforcement to the counterfeit bills, would be the point man on the group's next action. It would make the cotton candy caper look like child's play.

Bill Wassmuth was sitting in his living room chair talking on the phone to a friend in Seattle when Hawley snuck up to Wassmuth's rectory and placed a bomb in a garbage can by the back door. He lit the fuse, ran to a waiting car, and sped off with another man. It detonated at ten minutes to midnight, September 15, 1986, just a few feet away from where Wassmuth sat, winding down after his nightly jog.

The explosion threw him violently against the wall and sent shards of glass flying as the windows and doors blew out of the house. Shrapnel and splinters of wood shredded the kitchen walls and perforated the ceiling like Swiss cheese.

Wassmuth thought his furnace had blown. He looked outside and saw the corner of his house hanging in shards. Lumber and tarpaper littered his lawn.

Shaken and confused, but unhurt, Wassmuth dropped to his hands and knees and crawled across his floor to call 911. The few minutes it took for their response seemed to tick on endlessly. Neighbors came scurrying out of their homes, startled by the blast, which rattled doors five houses away. Pieces of Wassmuth's house landed on the neighbor's roof across the street. An off-duty policeman called in to report he had heard the explosion thirty blocks away. Police, firefighters, and inspectors from the Bureau of Alcohol Tobacco and Firearms began arriving to investigate, setting up a high-power spotlight under which to work. His cozy church rectory was now a rubble-filled crime scene.

Before that night, Wassmuth had been confident the Aryan Nations would never make such a bold and stupid move as to attack a local resident. He had always lived with what he called "purposeful naiveté," but now it had failed him, and he was afraid. No one had ever even raised a fist at him, but it was now clear there were those who hated him enough to do much worse.

Wassmuth felt that if he was still visibly scared when the press arrived on his doorstep the next day, his role as community leader would be drastically diminished. He knew two surefire ways to relieve stress: laugh and talk with God.

He recovered his characteristic sense of humor within hours of the bombing with a phone call to Marshall Mend, a local realtor and outspoken Jewish member of the task force who loved to jest, especially with Wassmuth. He had joked before that Wassmuth should lead the task force because he had no family to harass and a house that would not burn. Once he had humorously lamented to Wassmuth about how difficult it was being a minority in Idaho. "Being a Jew's not easy," he had said. "Just ask Jesus."[49] The night of the bombing, Wassmuth finally had a comeback for him. First he told Mend to turn on all the lights and call the sheriff because his house had been bombed, and Mend could be next. Then he asked Mend if he remembered Richard Butler being quoted shortly before the bombing, calling Wassmuth a "closet Jew" who was impersonating a priest. Mend said yes, to which Wassmuth quipped: "Well, I've only been a Jew for a couple days, and I already don't like it."[50]

The two men shared a laugh. For a brief moment, the mood lightened. Mend asked if he should come over; Wassmuth said no, he was better off staying home with his family, watching over his own place.

After the call, Wassmuth went to his chapel and wore out the carpet in front of the altar pacing back and forth, praying. The anger arrived after he had returned home and had to clear debris from his bedroom to lie down for a rest. All this wasted energy, he thought, tossing glass from his bed.

By the time news-crew cameras rolled in the morning, he had transformed his anger, fear, and frustration into passion—a talent Wassmuth would later become noted for—and was urging others to do the same. He railed against the attack as a "real slap in the face of the whole community" and pledged not to "put steel bars around myself."

"If someone wants to get me, I won't live in fear. We believe in the correctness of what we are doing, and we are not going to let the actions or decisions of a few people affect it."[51]

He even poked fun at his aggressors' apparent incompetence.

"Whoever was after me could have done a better job,"[52] he said, unaware that seconds before the explosion, the original plans to kill him had been modified to just scare him. Law enforcement later discovered that the placement of the bomb at the back of the house was the result of one man's decision to thwart the more deadly arrangement originally agreed to. The last-minute change of plans, and the young man's decision to later turn himself into law enforcement, likely saved Wassmuth's life.

That afternoon, ministers of a dozen different religious denominations prayed together for nearly an hour in Wassmuth's meditation chapel in a show of spiritual solidarity. Idaho Bishop Sylvester Treinen urged the region's Catholics not to "buckle under the face of this kind of inane terrorism."[53] Parishioners showed up at Wassmuth's home with garbage bags and toolboxes to help clean up and repair the bombed-out rectory.

But despite Wassmuth's public pleas for nonviolence, the community was hopping mad, barely able to keep a lid on its fury. The editorials that followed in the local newspapers—notably the *Coeur d'Alene Press*, the *Spokesman-Review*, and the *Lewiston Morning Tribune* —reflected the barely contained anger pulsing through the region in the wake of the bombing:

"This community and this newspaper stand fully behind Bill Wassmuth and what he believes in," said editorial writers in the *Coeur d'Alene Press*. "Whoever is responsible for the attempt to murder him has threatened all of us and we will not be frightened. No, we are not safe from the acts of terrorists here. But neither are the terrorists safe from us."[54]

"The bombing of a Coeur d'Alene Catholic priest's home by person or persons unknown has unleashed forces louder and more powerful than whatever shook the Rev. Bill Wassmuth's neighborhood Monday night," wrote a *Spokesman-Review* columnist. "It's true that those suspected of committing crimes in this country are innocent until proven guilty. But in this instance, our sense of protocol concerning the dispensing of justice has been justifiably tossed off the belfry. Call it righteous pragmatism, if you will, but we've had enough. Richard Butler and his colony of mental lepers have earned all the suspicion and contempt we can dish out. Jurisprudence be damned."[55]

The week was filled with the strident comments of task force members, editorials, letters to the editor, all echoing the same chorus: "We've had enough."

Midweek, Jewish Defense League leader Mordechai Levy contacted Wassmuth from New York to alert him that members of the organization were coming to Coeur d'Alene to violently avenge the bombing. Wassmuth pleaded with the militant group to stay home, noting the task force's insistence on nonviolence. They agreed, but offered their protection if he needed it.[56]

At Saturday's Mass, Wassmuth broke from his customary ritual to thank his parishioners for their cards, calls, and offers of shelter.

"I say from the bottom of my heart, there's nowhere else I'd rather be right now," Wassmuth said, encouraging his parishioners to turn anger into positive action by attending a rally the following week at North Idaho College, and to support minority families who may have been frightened by the week's events.

"If we can move one step further in our fight, then God will once again have used evil to accomplish good. It doesn't mean I'm not afraid. It doesn't mean I'm a hero or a martyr. I think fear is a prison, and I refuse to be in a prison."[57]

Yet, his life changed after the bombing. He stopped jogging alone and began locking his house. He was offered police protection, and he took it, wherever he spoke. When a cousin came to visit, he sent her home rather than leave her alone in his house for two days while he was attending a priests' support session out of town. But his courage and commitment to nonviolent principles helped funnel the community's rage into a productive passion for human rights whose momentum was growing daily.

The governor of Idaho, John Evans, asked to be on the program for the Gathering for Solidarity, the rally planned for the following week. Local human rights activists urged the community to attend, as a way to relieve frustration and anger. Norm Gissel, the attorney who had written the letter to counties and cities for the human rights rally, drafted another letter for publication in the region's newspapers. It ran the night before the rally, September 24, in the *Spokesman-Review*:

> The bombing of Father Bill Wassmuth's home Sept. 15 was a brutal and vicious attempt by racial terrorists to take Father Bill's life.
>
> But it was more than that, more even than an assault on the Kootenai County Task Force on Human Relations to quell its voice and blunt its spirit. This bombing was an attack on our city, our county, our community and our way of life.
>
> The racial terrorists who planned the bombing, made the bomb, drove to Father Bill's home, set the bomb next to his home, detonated the bomb, and stole away in the night, had more motive than the death of one parish priest. The terrorists want all of us to feel the fear of that explosion, to carry with us that fear in our daily lives, and because of that fear, to cease our commitment as a community to equality of all races and tolerance of all religions.

Our community is placed at a crossroad by this bombing. How we respond as a community will be watched closely by the terrorists and by the rest of our country.

Will we bow silently to the terrorists' bomb or will we stand fast, confident in our beliefs and our way of life?

We have an opportunity to demonstrate our community resolve to the crisis thrust into our lives by this bombing, an opportunity not to express our outrage, anger and hostility toward any one group or any one terrorist or act of violence, but instead an opportunity to channel those feelings into a deeper understanding of the dignity of all people and to come closer together as a community now victimized by its first terrorist attack.

The Task Force is holding a "Gathering For Solidarity" at the Bonner Room of the North Idaho College Student Union Building from 7 to 8 p.m. on Thursday, September 25. We should all be there.

More than seven hundred turned up at the emotion-filled meeting. Some drove from Portland and Spokane. The governor was there. So was Richard Butler, with at least two supporters. Afterward, Butler complained to a reporter for the Coeur d'Alene paper that there was no similar outcry when the Aryan Nations church was bombed, his dogs mutilated, or his car vandalized.[58]

For days Butler had been contending in the press that his group had nothing to do with the bombing and were victims of a setup by those wanting to pin the blame on white supremacists. He even tried to arrange a joint press conference with Wassmuth to announce a $1,000 reward to apprehend the bomber. Appalled and convinced Aryan Nations followers were somehow connected, Wassmuth declined. His hunches were right. Law enforcement officers later discovered that the same night of the rally, several of Butler's followers began hatching plans for a series of bombings in the already embattled city, with the downtown Coeur d'Alene Federal Building as their primary target.

On Sunday, three days after the solidarity rally and nearly two weeks after the bombing at Wassmuth's rectory, members of the Jewish community, the predominantly black Calvary Baptist Church in Spokane, and the American Indian community held a rally at Spokane's Westminster Congregation Church to show their unity. "Finding nonviolent solutions to our problems is the best response to the bombing of my house two weeks ago," said Wassmuth, whose remarks drew a standing ovation.

As he was leaving the podium, the quick-witted priest glanced around the periphery of the stage, then added "You know I don't like to stand next to garbage cans these days."[59]

At that moment, the men who had detonated the bomb at his back door were busy building four more, carefully packing gunpowder into one-pound canisters, fitting them with blasting caps, connecting them to batteries and travel-alarm clocks wired into the bombs' detonator circuits.

When the bombs were finished that Sunday night, the three men drove to Coeur d'Alene and left them at four different blast sites, with the first set to go off at 8:30 a.m., the others following every ten minutes.[60] The next morning, they drove to Coeur d'Alene around dawn to await the explosions, which were to create confusion and divert police while the group robbed two area banks, and then stole weapons and explosives from a nearby National Guard armory. Like their Order predecessors, the men planned to use the money to further finance their white revolution, which had been experiencing cash-flow problems since law enforcement closed in on their counterfeiting.

But the plan did not go as expected. Their cheap travel-alarm clocks did not keep accurate time, delaying the blasts until after 9 a.m. The first bomb ripped open a downtown retail building, Gibb's Mercantile. The second went off in a basement window well of the Federal Building, shattering windows for three blocks, the third in the parking lot of Jax Family Dining, a downtown cafe. Unexploded bombs were later found atop a finance company building and at the armed forces recruiting offices, kitty-corner to the Federal Building.

Police and fire officials responded efficiently, making the target banks harder to rob than expected. In the end, the trio returned home having created only a dangerous diversion, which amazingly injured no one. But the twenty-three minutes of chaos—multiple bombs in the heart of the city's downtown business district—panicked residents.

Surrounding towns and counties sent extra law enforcement, sirens blazing, into town. Area schools announced a lockdown. One radio station barricaded its parking lot with employees' pickup trucks in case there was an attempt to take over local media. Public offices were evacuated while bomb squads conducted roof-to-roof searches. The stunned city's fear reverberated through the region. Less than two hours after the first bomb went off in Coeur d'Alene, someone called the U.S. district court clerk's office in nearby Spokane and said, "You're next," prompting the courthouse to immediately go on alert. Security was then stepped up at federal buildings in Seattle and Tacoma as well.

The following day, the *Coeur d'Alene Press* carried a front-page story quoting Butler, who claimed the bombings were "orchestrated well enough by whomever doesn't like white people or like the Christian message to point the finger at us."[61]

Wassmuth seethed when he read it, but resisted calling the reporter to tell him the story was off base. Arrests made two days later would prove it after a troubled twenty-two year old man named Robert Elliot Pires from Baltimore, Maryland, turned himself in to the FBI. In exchange for security in a witness protection program, Pires told investigators that he had organized the bombings with two other men, Ed Hawley, and an ex-sheriff's deputy from California named David Dorr, and their wives. The five had formed a white supremacist criminal cell modeled after The Order, that called themselves the Bruder Schweigen Strike Force II. Though all had loose ties to the Aryan Nations, the group claimed to be operating independently. Attorneys for the federal government, however, argued that the bomb at the Coeur d'Alene Federal Building was to avenge the FBI's investigation of The Order.[62] Pires originally told law enforcement that they had bombed Wassmuth's house to discourage opposition to supremacist activity in the region.[63] But he would later admit that the group had considered killing Wassmuth rather than just scaring him into silence. In an interview from the Latah County Jail where Pires was being held in the nearby college town of Moscow, Pires would tell a *Spokesman-Review* reporter that Hawley had wanted to leave the bomb at Wassmuth's front door and ring the doorbell, but Pires persuaded him not to. Instead, Hawley placed it in the garbage can near the back of Wassmuth's house, which, perversely, was just down the street from Hawley's mother's house. Pires also said he sat in on a discussion after the Coeur d'Alene bombings at which Hawley had told Dorr he wanted to go to Wassmuth's home and "blow him away."[64] A special agent for the FBI later testified that Hawley and Pires had discussed a desire to "throw a pipebomb in [Wassmuth's] front window and follow with a burst of machine-gun fire."[65] It was after that discussion that Pires surrendered to the FBI, saying he feared for his (and others') safety. The next day, agents raiding Dorr's home found stacks of counterfeit bills, uncut sheets worth nearly $30,000, as well as the paper cutter taken earlier from Hawley's house. According to court documents, investigators also found a sheet of steel that matched scraps found at Wassmuth's bombed house.[66]

When Dorr, Hawley, and Hawley's wife were ushered into their initial court appearance on October 3 at the federal courthouse in Moscow, Idaho, they were met by angry protesters holding signs that read "Hate Group Leave Idaho." One bystander even jeered: "Hang them and burn them, hang them and burn them and throw away the key!"[67]

Community anger brewed during the fall as sensational press and law enforcement accounts revealed the group's violent plans. FBI agents testified they had uncovered a hit list that included members of the Kootenai County Task Force on Human Relations, federal judges, prosecutors, FBI agents, and the popular Republican Undersheriff, Larry Broadbent.[68]

If Wassmuth knew the extent of the group's malice toward him in the days and weeks immediately after the bombing of his house and the downtown buildings, he did not let it show. He engaged his signature optimism to focus on the positive, which was easier with renewed support flowing in from around the region. Galvanized by the North Idaho bombings, opposition to the white supremacists' presence had begun to mount in a big way.

Talk of a possible five-state consortium on human rights began solidifying into a real organization. Cities throughout the Northwest were passing resolutions urging racial harmony, and human rights activists in Washington and Idaho had begun lobbying their lawmakers to enact laws that would limit paramilitary training. Even *LIFE* magazine got in on the buzz, dedicating a story in its November issue to the town's battle with the Aryan Nations.[69]

Meanwhile, Butler was losing support. He held a cross burning in late October at the Flaming Cross Ranch, the farm of a neo-Nazi in the small southern Idaho town of Jerome, but it was a bust, with press and protesters far outnumbering those attending the official start of Butler's new five-state white Christian nation.[70]

The following month Butler received a cold reception in neighboring Utah, where the Republican governor, the Mormon Church, and the legislature all publicly denounced the Aryan Nations after Butler showed up to kick off a planned "Aryan Nations Hour" radio show and announced he might open a Utah office. The Southern Poverty Law Center, meanwhile, urged Wassmuth to consider a civil suit against the Aryan Nations. But he and task force members thought litigation should be a "last resort," something that comes only after concerted efforts to raise public awareness. The task force focused instead on out-of-court tactics, such as, monitoring racial harassment; providing support for victims; offering community education through seminars, conferences, television programs, and public events; and recommending new laws. This strategy would later become a model for similar groups nationwide, as Coeur d'Alene's battle with the hate group began drawing national attention.[71]

The task force also was not sure there was enough evidence to convincingly tie Butler's church directly to the attacks, though in hindsight, there likely would have been. Wassmuth would later say he regretted not suing after the bombing of his house, as the battle between the community and the Aryan Nations would continue for another decade and a half before the kind of civil remedies he had considered pursuing would finally break the supremacist organization's back.

In January 1987, the Coeur d'Alene community received the first Raoul Wallenberg Civic Award "for standing up to the forces of evil."[72] Wassmuth, Mayor Stone, and Undersheriff Broadbent traveled to New York to accept the award.

"Coeur means heart, doesn't it?" asked Swedish diplomat Hans Anderson at a dinner honoring the Kootenai County men. "It's very appropriate for your city."[73]

The city used the $5,000 cash prize to purchase more than three hundred human rights books for its public library.

Over the course of that spring of 1987, Pires eventually pled guilty and was sentenced to twenty years in prison on charges of attempted bank robbery, malicious destruction of federal property, possession of an unregistered firearm, and counterfeit money: part of a plea bargain agreement in return for his testimony against the others involved. The husband and wife couple involved, Ed and Olive Hawley, pled guilty, while Dorr was tried and convicted later that spring of conspiracy, firearms, and counterfeiting charges. Dorr received a forty-year sentence for his string of crimes. Pires was also later sentenced to life in prison for his role in Kenneth Shray's murder,[74] and served as the chief witness against Dorr in the case.

Butler himself was never proved guilty of any charge, despite government attempts to convict him and a band of national white supremacist leaders on sedition charges in April 1987. A federal grand jury in Arkansas indicted Butler and eleven other extremists on charges of participating in "a seditious conspiracy between July 1983 and March 1985 to overthrow the government." Specific crimes included the firebombing of a Jewish community center, purchasing explosives, and stealing more than $4 million from banks and armored cars in Washington State. Butler would later be acquitted of all charges by an all-white Arkansas jury.[75]

Wassmuth, the task force, and other human rights activists across Idaho, meanwhile, were on a roll, and had moved ahead with forming a five-state board to fight hate, with help from the U.S. Justice Department's Community Relations Service. In April, representatives from Washington, Oregon, Montana, Idaho, and Wyoming officially launched the Northwest Coalition Against Malicious Harassment, marking the first time in U.S. history that a private, nonprofit organization with links to governors regionwide had banded together.[76] The coalition's members included a mix of public officials, private businesses, government agencies, human rights activists, civic groups, and churches. The group agreed to start a fundraising drive and take a high-profile regional role, focusing on five goals: to determine the scope of prejudice and monitor hate groups; to provide education; to help communities develop strategies for combating prejudice; to encourage uniform hate crime reporting; and to support legislative initiatives to combat hate groups. Officers included human rights activists from Portland, Seattle, and Montana. Wassmuth, representing Idaho, was the last to sign their mission statement, and received a standing ovation when he did.

At the coalition's first conference later that fall, members of the Northwest gay and lesbian community asked that the coalition also pledge to combat bigotry based on sexual orientation. The coalition would eventually agree, but only after a cantankerous meeting that threatened to destroy the fragile nonpartisan organization. Although Republicans and Democrats could come together easily to combat the Aryan Nations, the sexual orientation issue proved much more divisive within the human rights community. Early on, Wassmuth had been opposed to including sexual orientation under the human rights umbrella, but changed his mind after hearing a poignant speech in Spokane by a man who had been targeted because he was gay. Over the years, Wassmuth would become an outspoken proponent of extending hate crimes protection to gays and lesbians. Few Northwest states—only Washington and Oregon—offer such protections, a significant oversight given the rise in violence directed toward members of this group.[77]

The formation of the Northwest Coalition Against Malicious Harassment triggered a series of efforts to improve human rights legislation on the books. Idaho was one of the first states to push hard for change, but it did not happen without a fight. Back in 1983, the state legislature had already passed new legislation making malicious harassment a felony punishable by five years in prison and a $5,000 fine, and passed the Civil Remedies Act, giving victims the right to sue for damages and attorney fees.

Five years later in 1988, human rights activists were emboldened by favorable momentum in the wake of the bombings and the recent election of influential Democratic Governor Cecil Andrus, who had served as Secretary of the Interior in the Carter administration. During spring legislative deliberations in Boise, human rights activists lobbied for legislation known collectively as Idaho's Terrorist Training Act, which would outlaw paramilitary training for violent purposes.

Cosponsored by Andrus and then Republican Attorney General Jim Jones, the first version of the legislation called for forfeiture of property or assets used in illegal firearms activity or paramilitary training. The National Rifle Association (NRA) opposed it, arguing that the bill would interfere with Idahoans' right to keep and bear arms, an argument that effectively stopped the bill in its tracks.

Andrus, an avid hunter who had bagged more game in his lifetime than most NRA lobbyists combined, was livid. He publicly attacked the NRA for its stance, saying the gun lobby organization had "run amok" and was alienating regular sportsmen like him with its increasingly radical positions.

A different version of the legislation eventually passed, without the forfeiture provision and with the NRA's support, despite Andrus's objections that the new version was "watered down."[78]

Even so, it was arguably one of the toughest antiterrorism bills of its kind in the country. The bill allowed sentencing up to ten years in prison and up to $50,000 in fines for two or more individuals engaged in paramilitary training with intent to attack a group or individuals or to subvert the government.

The legislature eventually passed the Uniform Hate Crimes Reporting Act requiring law enforcement agencies to report all crimes apparently committed on the basis of race, color, national origin, religion, or creed; the Idaho Explosive Devices Act prohibiting possession of explosive devices with intent to commit a crime; the Common-Law Courts Act prohibiting impersonation of a public official or acting as a public official with intent to intimidate private citizens or lawfully appointed officials; and the False Lien Act prohibiting filing a false lien with intent to intimidate or harass a private citizen or public official.

These five key pieces of legislation made Idaho one of the most progressive states in the country on human rights law.[79] It was an achievement that Wassmuth hardly had time to relish. As his human rights activism intensified, so did work as a priest. His parish had grown to a record nine hundred families and he was conducting seventy to eighty marriages, fifty to sixty funerals, and more than one hundred baptisms each year, along with five liturgies a week, at an average of one or two a day. This he did all for a salary of about $15,000 a year, including benefits. Yet despite success in both his human rights endeavors and parish responsibilities, Wassmuth was still struggling personally. The newfound sense of mental clarity he had developed since he quit drinking brought the real dilemma he faced sharply into focus: He was being required to live a life of a celibate priest when he no longer wanted to be alone. He had friendships with members of the opposite sex, but their development was always stunted by guilt, avoidance, and fear that such friendships could lead to trouble. It was increasingly difficult to maintain the distance and artificial barriers required when it came to relationships with women, especially one of whom he was particularly fond.

Over the course of a year, it had become clear to him that leaving the priesthood was inevitable. It was time. He talked first with a support group of priests, who backed his decision. His closest friends encouraged him to do what he felt was in his best interest. That summer, in what he would later call one of the hardest moments of his life, he told the Idaho bishop of his disagreement with church doctrine on celibacy, his fear of aging alone, his plans to leave the vocation. Saddened, the bishop resigned himself to the rising trend within the Catholic religious ranks: priests and nuns rushing for the exit because of personal unhappiness with the requirements of celibacy and other rigid demands of religious life. Defections were greater than ever across the nation, and fewer young men were choosing priesthood, with ordinations virtually half what they were in the mid-1960s.[80] In a time when the number of priestless parishes was on the rise, Wassmuth's shoes would be that much harder to fill.

The bishop grudgingly agreed to Wassmuth's yearlong timeline that would allow him to plan his exit, and give the bishop time to plan how to fill the void left by his departure.

That summer, in July 1987, the Aryan World Congress was much smaller than in years past. Numerous arrests had weakened the organization. No one burned a cross or displayed rifles. Butler was there, but weakened from recent open-heart surgery for a quadruple heart bypass. This time, media were banned from attending the two-day meeting and instead were invited to pay a fifty-dollar fee to attend a press conference for the event. Most refused.[81]

The corresponding human rights rally also had fewer attendees and suffered some negative publicity after Wassmuth rescinded an invitation to a self-described witch who wanted to sing British folk songs at the rally. The woman had joined a support group for those being harassed because of race or religion, but to have a pagan witch singing at the rally seemed unreasonable to a man of the cloth. The unsavory, controversial situation tested the limits of Wassmuth's tolerance and momentarily threw into serious conflict his dual public roles as a priest and a human rights activist. But at the rally, Wassmuth apologized publicly to the half-dozen witches (Wiccans) who had come from Spokane to support the woman, admitting he should have been more inclusive.

Aside from that flap, Coeur d'Alene's accomplishments on behalf of human rights in the Northwest that year spoke for themselves.

"Nineteen-eighty-seven has been the most successful year for human rights in Idaho," said Tony Stewart, then president of the newly formed Northwest Coalition, in a front-page story in the Boise-based *Idaho Statesman* newspaper, "and Bill Wassmuth has been right in the middle of all of it." That New Year's Day story announced the *Idaho Statesman*'s decision to name Father Bill Idaho's "1987 Citizen of the Year."

When asked what inspired him to dedicate so much time to human rights, Wassmuth pointed to the profession he planned to soon leave.

"Being a follower of the Gospel is building a just world," he said. "Working as a priest was a way to do something good for society and the world. It was a way to make a difference."[82]

Two weeks later, he would shock his congregation with the news he was leaving that life behind.

Wassmuth always made announcements at the end of services. So-

and-so's birthday, a fiftieth wedding anniversary, a church dance slated for next Saturday night, and then the usual recessional hymns. But this time, hardly anyone sang after the announcements. The parishioners at St. Pius X sat upright in their pews, too surprised to engage their vocal chords: Father Bill was leaving.

"This last announcement doesn't come out good anyway that I do it," he said. "I need time to deal with personal issues in my life; it doesn't have anything to do with you. I've had good years here."[83]

The bishop had known since the previous summer, Wassmuth said, and the process of selecting a new priest would commence in the next month. Wassmuth declined to discuss the details of his decision, or future plans, saying only that he would be leaving the area. He was purposely vague. Any more detail might have revealed an important underlying factor: Since he had made the decision to leave, the object of his growing affection happened to be a former member of the St. Pius X congregation, an aspiring artist named Mary Frances. He had met her when he first arrived in Coeur d'Alene, and they had developed a close friendship over the years. After he made the decision to leave the priesthood, and after she had left Coeur d'Alene in the mid-1980s to pursue her art career in Seattle, Wassmuth allowed his feelings for her to develop. He visited her in the city, and their relationship flourished in the comfortable anonymity of an urban atmosphere. Still they kept a low profile. When he made the announcement to the congregation in January 1988, Wassmuth worried his parishioners might react negatively to the news of his interest in a female companion. He could not have been more wrong. When he revealed the truth six months later, they rallied behind him.

"I am choosing not to spend the rest of my life as a single person," Wassmuth told the four hundred people gathered at Mass that May. "That means that I cannot continue in priestly ministry, as I cannot function as a priest and pursue marriage according to current church discipline."

Wassmuth apologized for the mystery, for not explaining himself earlier, saying he had been advised not to when he announced his plans in January.

"I know I created a lot of rumors," Wassmuth said, adding that his favorite was that he was an undercover government agent assigned to monitor North Idaho's white supremacist movement. "Whoever said that doesn't know that no one would go through twelve years of seminary for a government job," he joked.[84]

Wassmuth announced he would move to Seattle, where he would focus on fundraising for the newly formed Northwest Coalition Against Malicious Harassment. He also said he planned to marry but did not name his bride. After Mass, several parishioners expressed frustration that the church doctrine on celibacy was chasing men like Wassmuth out of the ministry.

"I can't think of a reason why a priest can't be married," one parishioner told a local reporter covering Wassmuth's announcement. "Everyone needs somebody."[85]

Wassmuth's revelation triggered a flurry of regional debate over the impact of the celibacy rule, which Wassmuth had been protesting unsuccessfully for years within the church hierarchy. The Apostolic Delegate's internal church file on Wassmuth was filled with letters he had written urging the church to drop the celibacy rule and allow priests to marry.

To further prove his point, Wassmuth had played a key role in helping one married man become a priest through a loophole that makes exceptions for those who have been ministers in other denominations, if they have special papal permission. Wassmuth helped secure such rare permission for an Episcopal priest who went on to be ordained as a Roman Catholic priest in Wassmuth's church in 1985. Until the death of the converted priest's wife a year later, he was one of only a handful of married priests nationwide.

The church's reluctance to adopt the optional celibacy rules that had been under consideration was one reason behind a large exodus of clergy in the 1970s and 1980s. Of the twenty men in Wassmuth's seminary class at St. Thomas, approximately half eventually abandoned the priesthood. Wassmuth's decision to speak out publicly against the celibacy rule drew criticism. A leader in the nearby traditionalist Catholic SSPX church in Post Falls wrote a letter to the editor of the local newspaper saying he would "pray for [Father Wassmuth] and hundreds like him who desire to tarnish the crown of priesthood by removing from it the jewel of celibacy."[86]

But such voices were in the minority. Wassmuth's parish, human rights friends, and the greater Coeur d'Alene community sent him off with a hail of festivities. Wassmuth knew it would not be an easy transition into the role of a regular man. His life had revolved around becoming or being a priest for more than thirty years. In 1967, Wassmuth had gone from being just Bill, to Father Bill. Now, twenty-one years later, he was going back to being just Bill.

He could hardly remember what that was like.

DIVERSITY
ACTIVITIES
"The only thing necess
is for good men to do n

8 The Role of Community

Human Rights the Grassroots Way

PERHAPS BECAUSE he was from a small town himself, Wassmuth understood early on that rallying support for human rights was more effective if it welled from the ground up inside a community, rather than being pushed upon it from the outside. Using Kootenai County as a model, Wassmuth traveled the West creating a broad-based coalition of people representing a cross section of the community who could all agree on the importance of human rights. Wassmuth explained:

> Our vision with the coalition was to have a task force in every community, no matter how big or small. The task force model approaches the problem from all sides—from education, public awareness, faith groups, government, etc. In that way, it helps create both institutional and attitudinal change because it represents a cross section of the community and therefore has a good chance of having a real impact on the community. If there's a better model, I'm all for it. But this one works.

To what degree society's most acute problems should be addressed by church, government, or volunteer organizations has long been a matter of debate. While Roman Catholic Church higher-ups argued with feudal landlords in medieval Europe over who should care for the poor and ailing, small committed religious orders tended to their needs. As the industrial revolution modernized early America, basic services one might expect the government to provide—roads, schools, prisons, hospitals—were being built by small groups of citizens banding together to improve their communities in a speedier, more efficient way.

European observers of early American culture, most notably French philosopher Alexis de Tocqueville,[1] noted that one of the most distinguishing characteristics of American democracy was the citizens' tendency to join together and form volunteer groups or associations to address the needs of communities, separate from the sometimes cumbersome workings of government.

Such willingness to engage in civic volunteerism is an important cog in the engine driving America. In urban areas, neighborhoods decline or improve depending on the grassroots activism of its inhabitants. In outlying areas, wilderness is often paved or saved depending on citizen participation in hearings and protests. When disasters hit in the United States, nearly a third of the relief is handled by nonprofit agencies that mobilize the resources and volunteer efforts of concerned citizens.[2] In the West, where the barn-raising ethic of the frontier still inspires spontaneous cooperation among residents, mutual aid is a part of everyday rural life. Citizens' grassroots efforts have started, prevented and stopped wars, and shaped modern democracy by bringing about changes in voting and labor laws, civil and women's rights, as well as environmental and consumer protections.

How a community solves a problem at hand depends not only on its available financial and administrative resources, but also on its political vision, which can help members of the community better understand the events unfolding in the present while imagining the possibilities of change in the future. In the Northwest, this political vision began as the Kootenai County Task Force on Human Relations, then as the Northwest Coalition Against Malicious Harassment, and still later, as hundreds of other small-town task forces that sprang up in these groups' wake.

Grassroots civic groups often have a distinct life cycle. It begins when an idea is conceived, the mission is determined, start-up money is scraped together, volunteers recruited, and the effort takes off. Over time, an organization's programs are tweaked and modified to better address the problem. Then in the end stage, such organizations usually either become well established, are absorbed into larger entities, or they shrivel up and die. Experts' general rule of thumb is that if a non-profit agency can make it for five years, the organization has a good chance at permanently surviving.[3]

The citizens' grassroots human rights campaign there both out-maneuvered and outlasted supremacists' efforts to turn the region into a white homeland. The racists had a lot more money, much of it stolen, at their disposal for their campaign. But as Wassmuth demonstrated, money is not everything when it comes to successful grassroots activism. Human rights activists won the first round of the battle fueled by determination, genuine concern for the quality of life, health of the region, and vital leadership of civic activists like Wassmuth, his fellow task force members, and the dedicated community that supported them. Wassmuth stated:

> There was the general premise that a great deal had been accomplished in the civil rights movement in terms of national legislation, but the next step that needed to happen, especially here in the Northwest, was the changing of minds and hearts and that couldn't happen by federal legislation or the passing of more laws. That had to happen community-by-community, and person-by-person. That's why we felt community organizing was the most important thing we could do. When the national leadership is focused elsewhere, it is even more necessary to focus attention on the local level.

Wassmuth saw early on that while national organizations such as the Southern Poverty Law Center, Anti-Defamation League, and the National Council of Churches lobbied for changes on the national scale, much of the day-to-day work in the small rural communities of America where hate groups hide would have to be done by small and midsize nonprofit organizations like those Wassmuth helped get off the ground in the Northwest.

Civic action at the local level is the bedrock of democracy. When grassroots movements create momentum, smart politicians will jump on board, as Idaho lawmakers did in support of human rights legislation in 1987. Public officials often wait for others to organize such efforts, while holding their fingers in the air to gauge the fickle winds of public opinion. In Idaho's case, Kootenai County human rights activists organized such a successful campaign that politicians from around the Northwest asked to be on the agenda for rallies held to counter Aryan Nations events.

What the Kootenai County Task Force on Human Relations did, which was later mirrored by other task forces that cropped up across the West, was textbook grassroots organizing: set clear goals, gain the support of public opinion, welcome volunteers, gain respect of government officials, devise creative responses to opponents, and persevere to accomplish tangible results.[4]

Ideally, groups also have an appealing leader with a sense of humor, an understanding of how to resolve conflict, a gift for public speaking, and good time management: someone like Bill Wassmuth.

When it came to lobbying and persuasive writing skills, Wassmuth had cut his teeth on one of the bigger fish: the Roman Catholic Church. When it came to communicating with supporters, Wassmuth relied on what he learned as a priest—that church bulletins are an effective means of communicating with his congregation. When the task force began planning a large rally in the spring of 1986, volunteers realized they needed the equivalent of a church bulletin. They recruited a community professional to oversee a volunteer newsletter to help them stay abreast of upcoming events. With the donations the newsletter brought in, they increased media spending and printed up a brochure detailing the group's work. In conjunction with the five-state Northwest Coalition, the task force bought ads in a 30,000-circulation 80-page tourist magazine distributed throughout the Northwest and Canada to reassure minorities that they were welcome in Idaho and the region. This happened in spite of having almost no budget and no paid staff. What Kootenai County had, however, and what any successful grassroots campaign needs, was an army of volunteers willing to roll up their sleeves and work. These were the ordinary folks who mobilized others like themselves to do extraordinary things, while the group's figurehead absorbed the credit and criticism that came along with constantly being in the public spotlight.

Researchers believe that for civic education to be successful in a community, three phases are crucial: information development, formation of public policy, and the development of coalitions.[5]

The task force model founded in Kootenai County managed all three of these elements. But first it had to convince the community of what was at stake: their livelihoods, their safety, and their quality of life.

When human rights activists first attempted to sound warnings about the Aryan Nations, some members of the business community blamed the messengers, accusing the media and human rights activists of blowing a "handful of whackos" out of proportion. Wassmuth noted:

> Our savior on that issue was Larry Broadbent. Larry was undersheriff. He was Republican. He was conservative. And when they would bring this up and he was in the group he would say, "Let me tell you from a law enforcement perspective where I think this community would be right now in relation to the Aryan Nations if it wasn't for the public nature of the task force." He would give them a picture of what he thought would have happened and they backed right down. He was an effective voice for that, but it was and still is an ongoing battle and not everyone is convinced. Some people still think we gave them too much credibility. I think they are wrong and I would still argue with them.

Critics were right to complain that national news coverage was, in general, overly sensational and chronically incomplete. Reports rarely mentioned the large counterdemonstrations and persistent home-grown efforts to drown out the Aryan Nations message with an even louder one of inclusion and commitment to human rights. That story never was as sexy as skinheads and swastikas. Local news was measurably more balanced, however, with vigorous investigative and beat reporting by regional Washington and Idaho newspapers, most notably veteran investigative reporter Bill Morlin of the *Spokesman-Review*.

Each year the Aryans marched uninterrupted, the din of negative media coverage intensified and fears that the region's identification with hate groups would hurt tourism and other businesses began to materialize. Large regional corporations like Micron and Hewlett Packard found it increasingly difficult to recruit and retain a diverse work-force. The Coeur d'Alene resort feared it was losing corporate confer-ence business because "the city by the lake," also happened to be the "city by the compound." The University of Idaho and Boise State Uni-versity reported that the state's tarnished image was complicating ef-forts to attract and keep faculty and students. Other universities and businesses throughout the Northwest expressed similar concerns.

In Coeur d'Alene, what eventually moved some of the established businesses and community members toward a more aggressive ap-proach with the Aryans was the very real prospect that unless some-thing more was done, the state, the region, and especially the beautiful lakeside city itself would suffer serious economic damage. Wassmuth believed:

> But that's okay. You move a community in whatever way you can. Some-times you dangle the economic development carrot, or you speak through the faith community or the educational system. There's a whole bunch of ways of motivating folks to take a look at what they are doing. Use them. We used them. It's not like major change is going to be able to occur based only on the pure theoretical, rational civil rights argument.

In the West, one of the foremost challenges of grassroots organizing is literally bringing people together, when vast distances make it geo-graphically difficult to go door-to-door or to convince people to come to town for meetings. Yet rural civic campaigns do have a few advan-tages: many small-town residents already have established traditions of mutual aid and cooperation, and when there are events, there are few other activities competing for the populace's attention. Cam-paigns in metropolitan areas bring their message to a concentration of people via billboards or door-to-door pamphleting. Rural campaigns, in contrast, must reach not only townfolk, but also the hundreds of residents living in the isolated country that surrounds any given hub. In the West, there are two places where most of those people are gath-ered at one time: county fairs and local parades.

As American as baseball and apple pie, it seems like if you have seen one quirky small-town parade you have seen them all: the big-haired rodeo queens and waving junior misses, the high-school marching bands competing with circling Shriners' motorcycles, antique cars, city fire engines, political candidates, and clowns tossing candy. Almost every rural community has an annual parade. They are one of the few events that draw crowds onto Main Street anymore, one of the few remaining collective expressions of a small-town's identity.

Likewise, annual county fairs express a community's regional character through the local produce, goods, and artisan crafts displayed in the livestock barns and exhibition halls.

While it may seem trite and folksy to some, human rights activists in Kootenai County found participating in the communal atmosphere of parades and county fairs an effective means for reaching rural residents who could not always partake in city events but who proved to be among some of the strongest supporters of human rights.[6]

In parades, the task force gathered community members from diverse backgrounds—blacks, whites, Native Americans, Hispanics, Jews, and Asians—to walk side by side behind banners that read "Good Neighbors Come in Many Colors," and "North Idaho Is for Everyone."[7] Given the tense backdrop of North Idaho and its nest of white supremacists in the mid-1980s, the normally innocuous act of simply walking down Main Street in a parade took considerable courage, especially for the minority members. But that brief fifteen-minute walk demonstrated several key concepts: respect for difference, unity within the community, and a lack of fear (though task force members later admitted they were anxious about exposing themselves by marching publicly).[8] The occasional slurs shouted from the sidelines were almost always drowned out by applause and encouraging shouts of "keep up the good work," and "we're with you."[9] Marching in the local parades was a low-cost way to gain broad community exposure and to give the local community the chance to feel, by clapping and supporting as the float or marchers go by, that they were a part of the grassroots effort. The community pride that later inspired residents to rally more vigorously behind task force members targeted with intimidating acts of violence began germinating then, in the Main Street parades, county fair booths, and other basic human interactions with the community at large.

Ironically, the small-town parade also would be used as a tool by the Aryan Nations, whose angry marches through downtown Coeur d'Alene in the mid and late-1990s attracted goose-stepping skinheads, angry counterprotesters, and a barrage of national media.

These Aryan Nations parades and the debates swirling around them each year they happened were the city's worst nightmare come to pass. The city spent thousands of taxpayer dollars on additional security precautions, overtime pay for police officers, frivolous legal attempts to stop the parade, and not so frivolous legal claims that required the city to defend its sometimes overzealous handling of counterprotesters—all of which became a point of contentious public debate.

The community divided sharply over whether to face down the Aryan Nations on the street, turn their backs and hold a counterprotest somewhere else, or ignore them altogether so as not to give them any attention.

In hindsight, task force members insist their two-decade-long, nonviolent, and proactive tactic was the right approach. It was not easy. Those who spoke out did so at significant personal risk and sometimes lived for years with character assassination, intimidation, and outright threats.

There were threatening anonymous calls at home, graffiti at their workplaces. Aryan Nations members often showed up at task force meetings, sometimes filming participants with handheld video cameras. Richard Butler himself confronted human rights activists at various meetings and events, notably the 1986 county fair. That year task force members had rented a space, slapped together a booth out of stray lumber, handed out pamphlets, and invited visitors to sign a statement of support for human rights. Butler and his supporters came to the booth asking for a list of human rights supporters' signatures and then began haranguing a volunteer to hand out his literature. The public, and eventually someone from another nearby fair booth, intervened to support the woman.[10] In other cases, such as the bombing of Wassmuth's house, the threats were serious attempts to intimidate, harm, and even kill activists.

Veterans of grassroots campaign organizing maintain that the best weapon in such cases is a nonviolent means to a nonviolent end—an internal personal grit that helps one rise to large challenges, an agenda that is clear and straightforward, and a good sense of humor.[11] Wassmuth had all those things. Power in numbers does not hurt, either. A large group not only spreads the workload and fosters creativity but also reduces feelings of personal fear or vulnerability that can come with standing up against threatening elements in the community. Task force members note, however, that many of their meetings and rallies would never have happened had there not been the reassuring presence and firm support from local law enforcement. When the task force held events, it had cooperation not only from city police but also from the sheriff's department and the FBI.[12]

A good working relationship between a local human rights coalition and the police is crucial, and not only for security concerns. The first and most important step in healing racism in a community is recognizing what is a hate crime. Wassmuth explained:

> When police investigate an assault between people of different races, they need to do their investigation keeping in mind what the criteria of a hate crime is, because if they are met, it can be prosecuted as a hate crime. If the police do not appropriately investigate the incident and get the evidence they need, it's lost right away. The problem is that hate crime law demands you look beyond the action, at the intent, and that's more complicated. For example, if police come across a fistfight in a bar between a black and a white man, all they used to have to do is say, "Who threw the first punch and who came out bloodier?" But if you are going to investigate the possibility of a hate crime, you have to find out why the fight broke out, what kinds of words were said, at what stage of the fight they were said, and what the backgrounds of both people are. It's a more complicated investigation and a more complicated report that isn't always a priority for police officers, some of whom carry into their job the same level of bigotry and prejudices that everyone throughout society has.

Criminal acts that are motivated by a bias on the part of the offender against a particular group to which the victim belongs are classified as hate crimes. These include violent crimes against people because of their race, ethnicity, gender, religious beliefs, or sexual orientation. But hate crimes, usually triggered by rage, also manifest themselves in slurs, vandalism, arson, intimidation, and assault.

The term "hate crime" was added to the American lexicon after the Hate Crime Statistics Act was signed into law in 1990. The act requires the federal government to collect data on bias crimes, which the FBI currently does. But whether local law enforcement agencies recognize and report hate crimes is still largely subject to local sensitivities. When law enforcement does investigate a hate crime, are public prosecutors trained to handle it as such? Human rights task forces, as part of their educational role, can help fund or encourage training for local public officials in recognizing and responding to hate crimes. Once local law enforcement officials determine a hate crime has occurred, it is helpful if they are able to notify a local coalition to support the victim. In return, coalitions can act as an early warning alert system for law enforcement authorities, as they did in Kootenai County, where the undersheriff was a member.

Effective civic campaigns bridge social and economic classes by bringing together a diverse coalition of community members, old and young, rich and poor, Democrat and Republican. Human rights organizing is no different. A community's human rights task force should be a coalition of people from across the spectrum of the community—churches, schools, clubs, media, business, law enforcement, municipal government, and other civic groups. Wassmuth believed that ecumenical associations and church groups are particularly good allies because they already have networks of volunteerism built into their structures and a commitment to basic Christian principles of fairness and tolerance at their spiritual core.

Additionally, business groups, clubs, and unions often value community service and can contribute the labor of their members, not to mention key political support. For example, five days after a mixed-race couple's house was spray painted with nasty graffiti in Billings, Montana, in the mid-1990s, more than two dozen volunteers from the local painter's union painted over the defaced house in less than an hour. Veteran of war groups have been effective voices of reason when it comes to combating neo-Nazi movements in the Northwest.

A local chamber of commerce may put business first, but business is often affected by other factors crucial to a community's well-being, such as tourism or tolerance of diversity. For example, the Greater Seattle Chamber of Commerce sponsored banquets aimed at encouraging business professionals to share personal experiences across race lines. After the annual banquet, the chamber coordinated hundreds of integrated dinner parties in private homes.[13]

In the Northwest, a few private sector corporations proved powerful partners in the fight against hate, albeit because they feared the negative economic impact of prejudice. When Hewlett Packard's laser-jet printer unit in Idaho tried to recruit workers in the late 1980s and early 1990s, potential hires balked, inquiring warily about the Aryan Nations. During many of these years, the company's attrition rates in Idaho for people of color were double the national average, a factor that company officials blamed not just on Idaho's image but also on prejudices within the community and the plant's workforce.[14] In 1998, convinced it could no longer afford to lose quality minority employees, HP-Idaho began a large-scale campaign to show its public commitment to tolerance. The company bused its employees to human rights rallies at the statehouse, produced nationally televised commercials urging support for diversity, and sponsored symposiums on race, among other things.

When a community forms a coalition that includes members of the business, education, law enforcement, and religious sectors, the diversity of interests represented and breadth of the group's influence significantly increases its effectiveness. Yet, as Wassmuth later found out, casting the net too widely can limit a coalition's successes.

Researchers who have studied the rise and fall of grassroots organizations believe that small locally based community groups have a better chance at survival than larger umbrella organizations. There are three basic reasons. First, the directors and staffs of smaller organizations are usually more willing to take risks in order to be flexible and

stay ahead of changes that could impact their effectiveness. Second, financial limitations require them to operate cost-efficiently, therefore
smaller organizations are usually able to bounce back from short-term
fiscal crises such as shortfalls, unexpected fundraising needs, or personnel layoffs. Perhaps most important, small organizations are able
to operate on a more personal level with the community itself. No
matter how caring or humanitarian a large organization may bill itself,
it inevitably gets caught up to some degree with conventional bureau-
cratic lethargy.[15] Criticism of the Red Cross in the wake of its response
to September 11 is one such instance. The Northwest Coalition Against
Malicious Harassment nearly went under after Wassmuth left in 1999
and it merged with the Portland-based Coalition for Human Dignity.
Financial problems, in-fighting, and a series of leadership missteps
plagued the once innovative and widely supported five-state organization. Its long-term survival is still not certain. The Kootenai County
Task Force on Human Relations, meanwhile, is humming along successfully, planning to help raise the roof on a new multi-million-dollar
human rights center in Coeur d'Alene. Human rights organizers in
Boise recently completed the nation's only Anne Frank Human Rights
Memorial and are developing an education resource center that would
provide teachers and researchers with easy access to human rights
materials. Other local task forces that Wassmuth helped form in Montana, Oregon, Wyoming, and Washington continue to operate successfully as small, locally based grassroots organizations.

This task force model works well in small-to-medium-sized towns,
Wassmuth noted, but is considerably less effective for urban organizing:

> We went to Portland to set up a task force and it backfired on us. There
> were too many special interest groups involved there, and when you
> brought them all together they tried pulling the group in their direction
> instead of working together on the issue. There was a history of battling
> it out in some cases. They were incapable of working cooperatively as
> groups in smaller communities were able to do. It just did not work in
> big cities. Then you had the additional problem of the very radicalized
> progressive elements that exist in big cities. In Portland you had radical

progressives—primarily young white men—who very quickly sent politicians, law enforcement, and people of color scrambling for the hills because the group became too liberal for the business community and law enforcement, too radicalized for the politicians, and too white for the people of color.

In the spectrum of political attitudes, Wassmuth was able to capture the middle by appealing to basic Christian values.

Everybody could come together to fight the Aryan Nations or racist skinheads because it wasn't a conservative–liberal issue, they are as much an enemy of Democrats as they are of Republicans.

But the task force had to make exceptionally clear that its agenda did not include providing political advantages for any particular group or party. Key to nailing down broad public support is nonpartisanship, a form of political moderation that demands self-discipline for those accustomed to having strong political opinions. Though Wassmuth never made public his political affiliations, he was known as a left-wing priest. His occasional political remarks chafed his Republican colleagues on the task force, who once even gently chided him for mixing politics with human rights advocacy. While Wassmuth made a concerted effort to keep out of the political fray, he was committed enough to rooting out racism that he was not afraid to publicly upbraid popular politicians for remarks he felt were inappropriate, regardless of potential political risk. Wassmuth:

It's tricky because you have to be non-partisan but yet be willing to identify bigotry when it shows up. For example, we needed to be clear that former [Idaho] Congresswoman Helen Chenoweth said some things we felt were racist, but not because she was Republican, but rather because of what she had said. Sometimes the line between Christian patriots and some ultra-right Republicans got pretty shady. But you have to constantly identify the issue, not the party. It is a core enough issue that if bigotry is a part of a person's life they are not going to make decisions that are good for the community at large and should not hold a public position. We should not elect them.

Wassmuth constantly faced the pitfall of "crying wolf" and losing credibility. Claims that a particular group was a hate group, or that its leader advocated hate, had to be carefully substantiated and accurately researched, so as not to paint groups that may simply have conservative viewpoints with the same brush as right-wing extremists.

> There is the constant risk of exaggerating for the sake of grabbing attention, grabbing a headline. There are those who accused us of that. But I made it a personal goal to be sure we did not abuse that, because we would lose credibility with the media. Reporters are smart enough that if you abuse their trust once they won't come back. You can mislead a media person once, but not twice. The fact that they kept coming back to us meant that we were keeping things in perspective, that they believed they could count on an honest statement by us.

Often, a grassroots campaign's biggest obstacles are self-made, a result of the kind of fraternal infighting that occurs when small factions of groups become too protective about particular issues. This is particularly the case in human rights organizing, where the needs of diverse groups of minorities have to be balanced sensitively, so as to avoid allowing a "wedge issue" to divide supporters. Wassmuth:

> When we started taking on antigay bigotry it became much tougher to hold our coalitions together. When we started a coalition in Boise, some more radical members of the gay community felt the coalition did not push hard enough on antigay bigotry, while some of the established members of the black community thought the issue had been pushed too hard. We just tried to hang onto the middle as much as we could. Human rights task forces today, however, must incorporate antigay hatred into their missions. If gays and lesbians are left out, it gives bigots tacit permission to attack them because it is an obvious absence.

Members of a task force may have differing opinions on homosexuality, for example, and that is okay, according to Wassmuth. More important is for them to agree that violence against gays and lesbians because of their sexual orientation is not acceptable. Task forces have to focus on working within the limitations of their common ground, which can stretch activists' self-discipline when they feel ethically bound to stick up for their particular issue. A move too far in one direction risks allowing human rights opponents the chance to use these sorts of wedge issues to pry apart coalitions.

In Oregon, Colorado, and Idaho, for example, outside groups attempting to pass antigay initiatives tried to use the gay issue as a wedge to divide the social justice movement. The Oregon Citizens Alliance's (OCA) messages in 1992 and 1994 played on class, race, and gender differences in order to divide members of diverse constituencies, such as church groups, ethnic groups, and business associations, who had before been united against bigotry. In one particularly crass example, a man affiliated with the Oregon Citizens Alliance published "The Pink Swastika: Homosexuality in the Nazi Party." The piece was intended to deflect charges by the group's opponents that Oregon Citizens Alliance members were bigots or Nazis and at the same time drive a political wedge between the gay rights organizations and Oregon's Jewish community. The work linked Adolf Hitler's regime to homosexuality by expanding on a few known facts (some of Hitler's top officers were homosexual) and ignoring other crucial ones (those leaders were later killed in a murderous purge of the Nazi party, and antigay laws led to the eventual rounding up of homosexuals, who were sent to concentration camps with an identifying pink triangle on their clothes). After the article's release, the Oregon Citizens Alliance formed a group called Jews and Friends of Holocaust Victims for Measure 13, an antigay measure. But most of Oregon's Jewish community distanced itself from the OCA and criticized the group for using Holocaust revisionism to further its political aims.[16]

In Idaho, human rights task forces helped defeat an antigay initiative in 1994 by arguing that if the initiative passed, other groups—such as Idaho's Mormons—could be targeted next. Wassmuth pointed out:

> Once you allow a premise that says we in society have a right to determine there is a group amongst us that shouldn't have full rights because of . . . whatever . . . then all you have to do is change the blank. It can be because you are a woman, or a lesbian, or because you are black, because

you are a communist, or a conservative, or a Muslim or a Mormon, whatever. Once you set up that premise, it can apply to anyone.

When Idaho faced an antigay initiative in 1994, Wassmuth met with church leaders and argued that point—if gays and lesbians could be targeted with such an initiative, so could Mormons, and judging by some of the group's anti-Mormon literature, just may well be. Indeed, the antigay initiative failed in the normally conservative Mormon southeast. Interestingly, hate group experts have found that Christian Identity adherents, along with their racism and anti-Semitism, are also often anti-Catholic and anti-Mormon.[17] Though not covered equally by the press, acts of vandalism and prejudice toward Mormons and Catholics were common during the wave of extremist right-wing violence that washed over the Northwest in the mid-1980s. Around the time of the bombing of a Boise synagogue, Mormon centers were vandalized in Idaho Falls and Meridian, and Catholics leaving Mass in Idaho and Oregon found their cars leafleted with anti-Catholic propaganda. While working in the Idaho diocese, Wassmuth contacted Mormon officials for solidarity in the fight against hate. But he also clashed with LDS officials in some parts of southeast Idaho, where non-Mormons were in such a minority they themselves felt discriminated against. Wassmuth related:

> When I was in the [religious] education office I once went to the superintendent of public instruction and said, "You know, you've got a case down in one of these little towns in the southeastern part of the state where I've got a Catholic person who is qualified to teach, who wants to teach in the public school system, and they won't give her a job because she's not a Mormon. Why don't you do something about that?" He looked me right in the eye and said, "I like my position and it is an elected position and I'm not going to do anything about it."
>
> There are places where Mormons have created a theocratic society, in the same way that Greencreek was Catholic and theocratic. If you can get it moving in the right direction it can be a positive force, but it can also be divisive.

Though Wassmuth helped prevent it from happening in Idaho in 1994, ideological differences over sexual orientation are often used as a wedge to successfully divide human rights supporters. In Washington State, a tenacious critic of the local human rights task force managed to get himself appointed to the Kitsap County's human rights council. The citizen, Jim Craswell, had criticized the task force for its defense of gays. By creating a schism in the group over the issue, one faction was eventually forced to break off and form a separate human rights group in late 1998.[18] In this case, opponents hijacked the organization, creating the irony of a human rights organization that criticizes human rights more than it defends it. Craswell then used his human rights post to send "Religious Freedom Alerts" to county pastors alleging that human rights organizations were "anti-faith" because of their criticism of some Christian evangelical groups for attacks against gays, civil rights, and religious minorities, including Jews and Muslims. Wassmuth responded to Craswell by reiterating that the coalition points out bigotry in all cases, including those where prejudice is taught in the name of religion. Because he had been a priest and knew the Bible, Wassmuth felt it was important to expose Christian groups whose religion crossed the line into hate. One such example was in 1998 when some members of a Kansas church congregation demonstrated near the funeral for slain gay student Matthew Shepard in Wyoming with signs that read "God Hates Fags," noted longtime Idaho columnist Jim Fisher in a *Lewiston Morning Tribune* editorial he wrote defending Wassmuth against Craswell's criticism. "Christianity is hardly a synonym for bigotry, but calling yourself a Christian doesn't inoculate you from being identified as a bigot, either."[19]

Homosexuality may be one of the most common wedge issues, but it is not the only one. In the early 1990s, the Aryan Nations used environmental concerns to draw working-class residents into its fold by sending recruiters to meetings of out-of-work loggers who were upset by the federal regulations and environmental restrictions that had slowed timber harvest in the Northwest.[20] Former Aryan Nations recruiter Floyd Cochran once bragged that he raised $8,000 on one swing through Oregon denouncing the federal government's efforts to protect the spotted owl. "Nobody cared about the spotted owl or the logger," he told the Spokane *Spokesman-Review* about the Aryan Nations. "If someone is pissed about something you can send them in many directions."[21]

Bridge issues, such as resentment of government regulations or unfair taxation, are common wedges used for recruitment into racist groups. Similarly, white supremacists have used free speech to divide academics and human rights groups attempting to counter their hateful messages. This has been especially evident in cases where Holocaust revisionists come to speak at public university campuses, sponsored by small student associations, sometimes no more than a few skinheads who have banded together in order to give bigots a technical foothold. In 1998, human rights groups and city officials in North Idaho and Eastern Washington organized a counterevent on the evening a controversial British revisionist was scheduled to appear at Washington State University. As 150 people watched a Holocaust survivor weep through her wartime stories, David Irving stood at a podium across town discouraging another crowd from believing such eyewitness accounts. Irving's appearance had been sponsored by a WSU student who maintained a controversial Holocaust revisionist site on the WSU Internet server. The college student newspaper's decision to print a lengthy letter from the student promoting Irving's claims drew criticism from fellow students and professors.

"The First Amendment protects [the student's] right to say what he wants, but where is it written that one has the right to a media spotlight?" asked one professor attending the counterevent.[22]

Wassmuth agreed completely:

For those who say you should allow these guys to speak in the name of academic free speech issues on college campuses, who say we are stifling free speech, I don't agree with that at all. They have a right to say what they want to say, but they don't have a right to demand a bullhorn. That's not a part of free speech. If [Aryan Nations leader Richard] Butler wants to say Jewish people are the children of the devil, he's got a right to say that, but we have a responsibility to counter that and say "that is an absolutely stupid, unjust, un-Christian point of view." Free speech does not mean someone tolerating what is being said as being acceptable. If you say something unjust, I have a responsibility and a right to call that wrong.

Without a task force in place to organize a counter event, Irving's claims might have gone unchallenged.

The task force Wassmuth remained proudest of was the one he helped set up while he was head of the fledgling Seattle-based Northwest Coalition Against Malicious Harassment. As director, he helped form the Bonner County Human Rights Task Force in the small Idaho town of Sandpoint, an hour north of Coeur d'Alene.

Sixty miles from the mountainous U.S.–Canadian border, Sandpoint sits at the edge of Idaho's deepest and largest lake, Lake Pend Oreille, covering 94,600 acres. Formerly a gritty Scandinavian lumberjack's town, outdoor recreation activities like skiing and sport fishing have diversified and supplanted the old timber-based economy.

Today, more SUVs with ski racks and out-of-state license plates cruise along Main Street than logging trucks. Like many small communities in the rural West, Sandpoint is undergoing a transformation from "old West" to "new West" as wealthy newcomers and out-of-state retirees move to town to take advantage of ample outdoor recreation and the beautiful lakeside setting. All kinds of eccentrics have made the remote folds of North Idaho their home in the last four decades—survivalists living off-the-grid, hippies from the back-to-the-land movement, religious oddballs, artistic loners, and paranoid veterans. They come and go, along with Bigfoot rumors, lake monster sightings, and recycled conspiracy theories about secret military weapons testing installations in the region. These unconventional characters are not distinguished by any one political or cultural affiliation but rather are bound by the isolation that separates them and their collective appreciation of privacy and general distaste for government intrusion. On some backcountry roads, residents still draw their mail up to their homes on a pulley.

Some of those attracted to remote Idaho by hate and antigovernment conspiracy theories embraced one radical right fringe group after another—the John Birch Society, Posse Comitatus, Minutemen, and later the Aryan Nations. In the 1970s, extremists such as Robert Mathews began writing hate-filled letters to the local newspapers in North Idaho and Northeast Washington.[23] They were early warnings of what would become a violent legacy of racial hatred with shocking ties to Sandpoint and the greater Bonner County a few years later. The 1985 Order trials would expose North Idaho as part, if not the hub, of a nationwide criminal hate vortex that resulted in the arrest of forty-two people in seventeen states. In 1989 America's Promise Ministries, a church with white supremacist ties, moved from Arizona to Sandpoint.

Less than a decade later, Sandpoint was hoisted into the national spotlight when the standoff began at Randy Weaver's mountain cabin on Ruby Ridge, just twenty-five miles north of town. The botched siege by federal agents resulted in the death of Weaver's wife and young son, as well as one U.S. Marshal. Weaver later received a $3 million wrongful death settlement from the government. This tragic showdown between federal SWAT teams and the Weaver family fueled widespread anger against the federal government for its overreaction to what most saw as trumped-up charges accusing Weaver of selling a sawed-off shotgun to an undercover agent. White supremacy groups eagerly capitalized on that anger by courting sympathy for Weaver and his white supremacy beliefs.[24] Ruby Ridge, combined with the ever problematic Aryan Nations compound just to the south, only added to North Idaho's, and particularly Sandpoint's, unwelcome reputation as a haven for bigots, religious zealots, and conspiracy-theory crusaders.

But even before the Ruby Ridge debacle and the media frenzy accompanying it, Sandpoint residents had determined it was time to take back their town. Wassmuth came to town in 1991 to help them form a human rights task force modeled after Kootenai County's. More than three hundred residents, many of them from local church groups, packed into the high-school cafeteria to hear Wassmuth speak. As the citizens rose to their feet to give a standing ovation in support of Wassmuth's inspiring speech, a small knot of people (some wearing swastika armbands) remained seated. It was Richard Butler and a cadre of

Aryan Nations followers. Butler attempted to speak but was booed down by the crowd. Afterward, the community decided to heed Wassmuth's call and form its own task force. A series of organizational meetings were held over the following year, and the task force incorporated in 1992.

Over the next decade, the Bonner County Human Rights group held rallies and counterrallies, sponsored diverse speakers and cultural events, even held workshops on how to raise tolerant kids. When the antigay initiative was put to Idahoans in 1994, only three of North Idaho's ten counties rejected the discriminatory initiative. Bonner was one of them, after the task force canvassed the county door to door with information about the initiative. In 1995, residents sent Christmas cards designed by local children to their friends and family carrying messages of tolerance and racial harmony. When residents heard that former Ku Klux Klan grand dragon Louis Beam was planning to move to town, the task force planned a rally to raise awareness and expose Beam's racist ties. The bolder the task force became in countering hate groups' public moves, the more local support grew.

In 1995, former Los Angeles Police Department officer Mark Fuhrman moved to town after being convicted of perjury for denying he had used racial slurs (tapes later revealed he had) during the OJ Simpson trial. That he chose to make his home in Sandpoint only worsened perceptions of the town as a haven for racists. A human rights rally drew five hundred people to hear Wassmuth speak again, and again Richard Butler and a dozen skinheads showed up outside to scowl at those going into the meeting. Recognizing that Sandpoint's human rights activists were fighting a losing battle in the court of public opinion, Governor Phil Batt, whose bill created Idaho's Human Rights Commission, pledged that the state would look into ways to offset the negative press being generated by "a small population of fringe groups in Idaho." Many shared his frustration. Sandpoint could not shake its negative image.

Rarely did national and international news stories about the region's white supremacy ties include mention of the ongoing grassroots battle to counter their messages of hate. In 1996, the German-language Swiss newspaper *Weltwoche* ran a multipage spread about Sandpoint under the headline "America's Nightmare." While the reporters claimed to have been in the area for weeks, no one ever contacted the Bonner County Task Force, and no community efforts to combat hate were mentioned in the story. *Gentlemen's Quarterly* (GQ) magazine menacingly described Sandpoint as the "heart of whiteness," in a story that marketed the small resort town on the cover as "Fascistville, Idaho."

Despite the task force's persistent efforts, things worsened in the late 1990s when two retired California businessmen began pouring cash into what had been, up until that point, a fairly low-budget white supremacist movement. Vincent Bertollini and Carl Story both had grown wealthy in California's Silicon Valley computer industry boom and then moved to Sandpoint in 1995. They were not exactly inconspicuous. They bought fancy homes in the nicest neighborhoods, drove Lincoln Towncars, and developed reputations for flashy clothes and flamboyant gestures, such as leaving $100 tips to waitresses they liked. A reporter at the *Spokesman-Review* later revealed that Story had been convicted in 1979 of shipping nearly $300,000 worth of computer-chip-handling equipment to the Soviet Union—equipment authorities believe may have been used to develop Soviet missile-guidance systems during the Cold War. Story managed to avoid federal prison through a plea bargain but was placed on probation and forced to pay a $25,000 fine.[25]

Under the guise of the white supremacist 11th Hour Remnant Messenger organization they had founded earlier in California, the two men spent millions to bring antigovernment speakers to town and to mass mail racist and anti-Semitic propaganda to thousands of Idaho addresses. Included in the mailings were a forty-five-minute videotape of an interview with Aryan Nations leader Richard Butler and a chilling six foot by three foot full-color Christian Identity poster, "The Adamic Race, Adam's Pure Blood Seedline," which purported to trace the history of the world's races according to the Christian Identity interpretation of the Bible. Like other Identity believers, Story and Bertollini believed whites were among the Lost Tribes of Israel, who they believe are the chosen people described in the Bible.

The huge "Adamic Race" Identity poster, which Bertollini claimed cost $9.45 per copy to print, fold, and mail in the fall of 1998, was noted by watchdog groups as "one of the most professional pieces of white supremacist propaganda in recent years."[26]

Though the Bonner County Human Rights Task Force did not have the resources Bertollini did, it countered his every racist thrust with an equally clever human rights parry. In one local business Bertollini used to frequent, the poster he had mailed out was laid on the floor for those behind the counter to walk on. The business owner hung up a sign that read "We are proud to live in a community that supports human rights." Fed up with the hate mail being sent out by Bertollini, the owner eventually refused his business.[27] When Bertollini began sending out racist mailings, the task force established a human rights scholarship fund as a means for community members to react. For every donation that came in, the task force mailed Bertollini a postcard notifying him that a donation in support of human rights had been made in response to his racist mailing. That generated several thousand dollars in human rights scholarships.

The task force also teamed up with the school district, forming human rights clubs in the high schools and promoting projects such as the Art for Tolerance contest, which drew entries and support from high-school students throughout the region.

The committee put together an Emergency Hate Response Kit, complete with tolerance bumper stickers, window posters on human rights, and tips on how to respond. The community held a contest for creative alternative uses for unwanted mailings. One resident sent in a recipe for hate compost: Mix manure liberally with white supremacist literature. Cover the garden and watch something positive grow. Another person made a candleholder out of a videotaped interview with Richard Butler and submitted it wrapped in paper with "Let There Be Light," written in English, Japanese, Russian, Arabic, Greek, and Hebrew.

The suggestions eventually became part of a humorous document entitled: "Sandpoint Residents Stand Up to Bigotry: The Ten Best Ways to Recycle Hate Literature."

The frequent hate mailings so angered Sandpoint residents that they packed a meeting of the Bonner County Human Rights Task Force that was called to develop a unified community response and to give antira-cist speakers a forum. Bertollini showed up at the meeting with Rich-ard Butler and a skinhead video crew to tape local human rights lead-ers and attendees. Though the move was intended to intimidate human rights supporters, it had the opposite effect. In front of more than three hundred people, the steely director of the Bonner County Human Rights Task Force at the time looked Butler in the eye and said, "No one should have to live in fear or shame."[28] The mayor of Sand-point warned that the mailings were more than just an occasional abrasive act, they were acts that would call into question the quality of the atmosphere of the town as a whole, adding "I don't like having people in our Community Hall dressed like Nazi soldiers."[29]

One of the former Aryan Nations recruiters who attended the filled-to-capacity meeting later said he did not go back to Sandpoint to re-cruit because there had been such a large turnout.[30]

But Bertollini and Story did not let up. In November of 2000, they mailed out a pamphlet titled "Idaho, the Hue Man Rights Jew con-trolled Marxist Communist State" in an attempt to mock the new "Idaho, the Human Rights State," credo of the Kootenai County Task Force on Human Relations. The pamphlet featured a map of Idaho marked with the locations of the state's human rights organizations and the names of human rights leaders, a move that many activists (some of whose names appeared on the mailing) felt targeted them. In response, twelve hundred Sandpoint residents publicly declared their support for human rights with ads in the local newspaper and by ramping up their own grassroots activism. The task force marched in a community parade behind a "Building Better Community" banner (and to applause from those standing on the sidelines). When the Aryan Nations planned a march through town in the summer of 2001, the task force and community quickly mobilized, planning a separate human rights event that drew hundreds to the county fairgrounds.

Both the Sandpoint City Council and the Bonner County Commissioners adopted human dignity resolutions pledging government support for programs that enhance a civic environment of tolerance. The local police department kept a close watch on Bertollini. (He was charged three times with drunk driving and once for resisting arrest after a scuffle broke out between him and several officers who said he had been disorderly.)

Eventually, the intense scrutiny from across the community spectrum—law enforcement, schools, government, media, private residents—had the desired impact. Bertollini vanished (but only after buying a new home for aging Aryan Nations leader Richard Butler, who remained in Idaho but whose assets were liquidated to pay off a civil suit judgment against him). On his way out of town, Bertollini, apparently a federal fugitive and the focus of an undisclosed grand jury investigation, railed against the Sandpoint community for being so supportive of human rights and unsympathetic toward his racist views.[31] His partner, Story, also disappeared from the public sphere.[32]

Since then, North Idaho has continued to experience a welcome exodus of bigoted individuals and organizations. Bertollini and Story skipped town, and at about the same time, a separate white supremacy publishing and Internet operation called 14 Word Press that had been based out of St. Maries, another nearby small North Idaho town, packed up and moved.[33] Bankrupted by a civil suit, the crumbling Aryan Nations moved its headquarters to Pennsylvania and began sniping among themselves about who would pick up the sad pieces of the crippled organization.

Although these local successes have gone largely unnoticed and underappreciated by the national media, the region's grassroots campaign is beginning to attract attention in national and international human rights circles. In October 2001, a group of human rights leaders for the central Asian republic of Uzbekistan visited Sandpoint to talk with community leaders after choosing the town as a model for grassroots human rights activism. Coeur d'Alene, meanwhile, is building a multimillion dollar human rights education center.

The region's recent successes gave Wassmuth hope that these small-town grassroots efforts to challenge hate with support for human rights will continue to be a model for communities throughout the West. Wassmuth:

> When I heard about Bertollini and Story [leaving Idaho] I felt thankfulness for the strength of the Sandpoint community, which was responsible for encouraging these two people to find their domiciles elsewhere, and excitement about the continually changing image of what Idaho is about. It is not just a place that attracts these folks, it is also a place that mounts a huge campaign that ultimately results in some of these folks leaving town.

9 | Seattle

1988-1999

IT ONLY TOOK a few hours to pack. As a priest he had been married only to voluntary poverty. Everything he owned fit in the hatchback of his car except his king-sized waterbed and beloved overstuffed plaid pillow. Driving away from Coeur d'Alene with a whole new life ahead of him reminded him of the morning he left St. Thomas Seminary in Seattle and headed home to North Idaho for ordination. Except this car did not have that new car smell, the shine had definitely worn off his vocation, and this time he was headed in the other direction—back to Seattle.

He backed out past the budding pear tree in his yard, glancing one last time at the corner of his house where white supremacists had detonated a bomb. It had not even been two years, but so much had changed, and so many adjustments still lay ahead. For six months he had been meeting with a counselor and former priest, who had himself resigned to marry, to aid in the transition from priest to layman. Most told him the same thing: This, turning in his cup and book, will be traumatic. Prepare to feel aimless, alone, and confused. Many priests who sought laicization during the post-Vatican II decades were advised by church officials to testify that either they suffered from psychiatric problems that prevented them from carrying out their duties or that they had not really wanted to be priests in the first place. Honorable exits from clerical life were not easily granted—and marriage was certainly not one of them. This fact made such a decision (to resign in order to marry) difficult also for the women the priests intended to marry. When their existence was recognized (and that was rare), women were often viewed as wily accessories who tricked and tantalized the priests into a relationship. Wassmuth and his bride-to-be were not immune from this criticism. Wassmuth dutifully prepared for his "scandalous" choice to have a punitive, traumatic effect on his spiritual and personal life.

Leaving Coeur d'Alene that June morning was bittersweet. He drove across eastern Washington's pocked scablands toward Seattle feeling heavyhearted about leaving behind the congregation he had served, the human rights activists he had befriended and worked alongside, and the security of what he had done for twenty-one years, almost to the day, as an ordained Roman Catholic priest. Once he crossed over the Cascades and caught a glimpse of Seattle's shining city skyline, an unexpected surge of relief and excitement washed over him. That he had only a meager $500 severance check after twenty-one years with the firm did not matter. That he had been denied the vested interest in his church retirement plan did not matter. That he had nothing except what was in the trunk of his car did not matter. He had freedom, in a way he had never had before.

He rented a small first-floor apartment on Alki Beach in West Seattle, just two blocks down from the woman who would be his wife. There he settled in to wait for the trauma his counselors had predicted would arrive. He waited four months for an emotional breakdown that never materialized. He had left publicly, with the support of his parish (who had passed the hat to come up with a several-thousand-dollar send-off), which effectively blunted the loss he thought he might feel the first few Sundays he did not don his collar and step up to the pulpit.

But Wassmuth did miss his friends and colleagues who were still serving the church—particularly the clergymen he had confided in for years about the struggles of priesthood. They, along with church leaders, largely ignored him. If he had not been excommunicated (and he had not), why did it feel as though he had fallen off the face of the Earth? It had been his choice to resign, but he felt somehow defrocked of an entire segment of his life. Some colleagues avoided him as if he had done something shameful, inadmissible, and essentially dishonorable. In their eyes he had been reduced to a loner "lay state." When a priest friend died of a heart attack, Wassmuth heard about it from a non-Catholic acquaintance. When he contacted members of his former spiritual community, they were polite but distant. Wassmuth felt distinctly that they were ignoring him to avoid talking about some of the controversial questions they all faced, but he was working through—the church's celibacy requirements and the poor treatment of priests who stepped out of service, for starters. It took Wassmuth twelve years, and the diagnosis of a terminal illness, before he would receive retirement benefits from the Roman Catholic Church.

But despite the church's cold shoulder, Wassmuth felt confident that God himself understood, and the deep faith that extended beyond institutional boundaries propelled him forward on lonely days, as it had for years. He considered working in hospice or as an alcohol counselor—both human service jobs he had done on the side in Coeur d'Alene. But in January 1989, the board of the Northwest Coalition Against Malicious Harassment, then led by Wassmuth's good friend and Coeur d'Alene human rights activist Tony Stewart, proposed the hiring of a new executive director to lead the five-state effort. Wassmuth went to the board meeting, said he was looking for a job and would take it if they would hire him. The board said they had no money. Wassmuth said he would raise it. The board asked when he could start.

Wassmuth would have to raise his own salary, but he would have a new job heading the coalition he helped found. He moved to a bigger apartment overlooking Elliott Bay and set up shop in the spare bedroom. After a few months, he had raised enough money to move into a small, handsomely restored downtown office with a view of the Sound. He began hiring staff and put them to work on direct mail solicitations for donations.

These were inspired days and not only because of the challenging new work opportunities. After years of voluntary celibacy, he was finally free to pursue a relationship with a smart, attractive woman he had admired and been friends with for years. Seattle artist Mary Frances had met Wassmuth while attending St. Pius X in Coeur d'Alene as a member of his congregation. In 1986, she moved to western Washington to paint and pursue her art career, putting several hundred miles between them. Now, with the burdens and limitations of his vocation behind him, they finally could be together. Considerably younger than he, she carried her tiny, lithe frame with an energetic lightness that lifted his spirits every time she entered the room. She was lovely, her dimpled smile and delicate features framed by jet-black hair. But equally, he respected her quiet intelligence and how she loved to laugh, and the way her unbridled creative streak colored their days with imagination and art. She had been a loyal, understanding, and patient friend and would prove to be an even more dedicated wife, loving him unconditionally for thirteen years, in the best and worst times.

They married July 1, 1989, in a small ceremony in Seattle, with a honeymoon afterward in Newport, Oregon, just a few hundred feet from the beach. Those first precious evenings of their marriage they sat for hours outside their beach house, hunkered down in two white plastic lawn chairs. She painted a watercolor portrait of those chairs, the seats sunken from Bill and Mary Frances' long evening talks. It still hangs in their living room. Bill spent days on the beach building sandcastles, a hobby he loved, and he used his temporary sand creations to strike up spiritual conversations with passersby who would stop to admire them. Over the years, he had even developed what he called "sandcastle theology," which he had preached occasionally to his parish, about how one's spiritual development was not unlike building a sandcastle. In both cases it is the process that is important, he would say, not the end result, because the end result is going to go away with the changing tide. It is what happens to you and others while you are building that is more important.

His wife began working the sand alongside him, adding her own flair, transforming his hulking square fortresses into whimsical chateaus with a decidedly more artistic touch. They complemented each other in many ways. He made her laugh. She taught him to love. He was happier than he had ever been.

With Mary Frances at his side, he was more motivated than ever to work, and she encouraged him to continue reaching out into this rural West where they both had made their homes. The summer they married, they camped their way through most of Montana, from small town to small town, helping to build the state's human rights network by day, sitting around the campfire under the wide Montana sky at night. Except for that first trip, she did not often travel with him, and when she did, she rarely made public appearances. Wassmuth was extremely cautious about her public exposure because he worried for her safety. Because he had been a target, he worried that those who did not like him might see harming or threatening her as one way to rattle him. He rarely spoke about her in interviews, articles, or speeches. Some even wondered if he really had a wife. When white supremacists suggested he was gay, he let the assumption go unaddressed. Though they had an ebullient love, they kept their relationship very private and low profile, divulging their tenderness only before close friends and family.

He traveled to Wyoming, Colorado, Oregon and of course back to Idaho, sometimes with her but more often with one of the U.S. Justice Department's mediators on race relations, Bob Hughes, who was with the department's Community Relations Service. Hughes had been on the front lines of the civil rights movement in the South, helping to build community coalitions in the 1950s and '60s in Alabama. He helped the Kootenai County Task Force get started in Coeur d'Alene and facilitated the formation of the five-state coalition. With his access to federal law enforcement resources and extensive experience in race relations, he was a quiet, persistent, and underappreciated government presence throughout the Northwest's struggles against white supremacist extremist groups. He was also a former Methodist minister. That made him and Wassmuth an almost unbeatable team on the speaking circuit. They would drive into town, hold a meeting, and in their wake, almost inevitably, a task force sprang up.

Concerned about the Northwest Coalition getting swallowed up in the urban politics of Seattle, Wassmuth spent most of his time on the road, trying desperately to cover all half-million square miles in the five-state region his coalition represented. Eventually, Colorado would join the effort, bringing the number of states represented to six. By the end of 1992, Wassmuth was averaging more than 35,000 miles a year on his red Subaru and had built up the coalition's annual budget from zero to $100,000. The only such regional coalition in the nation established to fight hate, Wassmuth's organization had earned the support of six governors (Washington, Oregon, Idaho, Montana, Wyoming, and Colorado), plus the backing of human rights organizations, businesses, and multiple local, regional, and state officials. He conducted workshops and seminars and drove to hundreds of tiny towns in the vast rural West to provide concerned residents with the tools they needed to make their communities safer.

It was a good year both professionally and personally: He was awarded the prestigious Gleitsman Foundation award, for which he was flown to Washington, D.C., to meet with consumer advocate Ralph Nader and the U.S. Assistant Attorney General for Civil Rights. The honor came with a $50,000 cash award that he used for a down payment on a small bungalow-style house in a modest neighborhood of West Seattle called the Junction, the first home he had ever owned. Ironically, the home he bought was right across the street from a Catholic Church, next to the Catholic school, and had a backyard that looked out across the Catholic Church playground. He surrounded himself with the life he was trying to let go.

Over the next several years, Wassmuth showed up in nearly every community in the region that was fighting a white supremacist presence. He drove to rural Wyoming to galvanize a small community group that was trying to speak out against a white supremacist who was spouting bigotry from his remote ranch. He urged Montanans to show their solidarity when a Jewish woman from Billings was targeted because of a menorah in her window, and when an African American man was taunted and beaten with an ax handle in a Butte mall parking lot.

He warned Idahoans that passing an antigay initiative could result in more hate crimes against homosexuals, exposed hate crimes when they happened, and publicly called for a more vigorous official response when minorities felt their cases were not being properly investigated by police.[1] When a twenty-seven-pound rock covered with racial epithets was thrown through the bedroom window of the Boise National Association of Colored Persons president, Wassmuth flew down to help Ada County residents establish a task force.

He had friends on both sides of the political aisle and appeared often with Idaho Republican Governor Phil Batt, sticking up for him publicly when Batt came under fire for "betraying white Americans" with an initiative to improve the lives of Hispanics in the state.

In Washington State, Wassmuth jumped to the defense of black Gonzaga law students who were being harassed and threatened, prompting fifteen hundred students to rally behind them. And despite significant criticism, he publicly exposed a large survivalist expo being held in Spokane as a thinly veiled cover for a gathering of white supremacists and antigovernment extremists.

Throughout the 1990s, Wassmuth (acting in part on warnings he had been given by the FBI) sounded the alarm about new recruitment of younger skinheads into the Aryan Nations movement. The FBI had busted a 1990 plot by three Aryan Nations members to bomb a gay bar in Seattle after the men were arrested in the Seattle area with bomb parts and weapons. In fall 1991, the FBI began monitoring another small group of skinheads that had been meeting in rural North Idaho. According to an FBI informant, three skinheads and two teenage girls at one meeting had discussed assassinating Wassmuth and Marshall Mend, another well-known human rights activist, as well as firebombing a Spokane synagogue. The participants were later identified as a thirty-five-year-old New York native, a nineteen-year-old California skinhead, and his girlfriend, a fifteen-year-old Portland girl, along with two skinheads from Canada and Italy.[2] No one was ever charged in the terrorist plan, as it fell apart when the government began deportation proceedings against the Canadian and the Italian. The group broke up, and the FBI notified Wassmuth that the threat against him had ceased.[3]

A year later, Wassmuth's hunch about the dangerous young skinheads was confirmed when two other men, aged twenty-two and nineteen, were arrested in connection with the murder of another skinhead who had been an employee at the Aryan Nations compound and whose body was found by woodcutters on the side of the road near Sandpoint.[4]

As the Aryan Nations recruitment tactics changed, so did their message. They mainstreamed it to include antigovernment, anti-immigration, antigay, and anti-environmentalist themes. As in the previous decade, there were those who justified racially motivated violence with the Aryan Nations' pseudo-Christian, hate-filled rhetoric. In the fall of 1993, a Texan named Alan Lindholm shot an interracial couple at Spokane's bus station. Lindholm, who had met with skinheads in Hayden Lake, later said in court that God had told him the white woman and black man should die. They survived multiple gunshot wounds. Lindholm received a twenty-four-year prison sentence.

Racist flyers surfacing throughout the Northwest were increasingly aimed at exploiting tensions between white and minority communities. Rural towns with a booming Hispanic migrant worker population—places like Sunnyside, Washington—became white supremacists' new breeding ground for hate. Wassmuth, who had experience working with Hispanic populations as a priest, traveled frequently to those communities to combat the Aryan Nations' efforts and to urge tolerance. When antigay initiatives were introduced to voters in Oregon and Idaho in 1992 and 1994, Wassmuth worked alongside human rights activists, lawmakers, and others to defeat them both.

He carried his message with him everywhere, from the big urban centers to the smallest rural hamlets, regularly urging public audiences not to make the mistake of assuming someone does not support civil rights "just because they're Catholic, Mormon, or male."

He even held a daylong workshop and public meeting near his hometown in the Grangeville High School cafeteria after survivalist Bo Gritz announced he was building his Almost Heaven covenant community nearby.

He urged community members to keep tabs on the antigovernment, militia, and Christian Identity movements that blossomed in the wake of the botched 1992 Ruby Ridge standoff at Randy Weaver's cabin, the fiery end of the Branch Davidian compound in Waco in 1993, the passage of the gun control Brady Bill, and the standoff with the Montana Freemen in 1995.

Wassmuth feared that white supremacist groups were tapping into a broader anger that was being fueled by tax protests, land feuds, gun control measures, and mounting resentment of the federal government. He could talk about these issues with rural residents; being from Idaho he understood them well. But he feared white supremacists were taking advantage of the brewing antigovernment sentiment. He began publicly warning across the West that the rhetoric could soon escalate to violence.

In January 1995, Wassmuth called an emergency two-day meeting of researchers and human rights activists who were monitoring the militia movement. The meeting's attendees agreed that the group's paranoid, violent rhetoric and arsenal of weapons was a ticking time bomb. Despite the Northwest Coalition Against Malicious Harassment's attempt to bring the issue to the fore, the government and media had not yet grasped the seriousness of the militia movement.

A few months later, as Wassmuth had predicted, the simmering hate exploded when Timothy McVeigh detonated the 4,800-pound bomb outside the Alfred P. Murrah federal building in Oklahoma City that slaughtered 168 people. At that point, the FBI formed a domestic terrorism task force to monitor antigovernment groups in Eastern Washington, North Idaho, and Montana. McVeigh had ties to the Northwest (he was allegedly spotted in a Spokane motel shortly before the bombing, where witnesses said he was visiting Chevie Kehoe, another criminal character who spent time at Butler's compound).[5]

After the Oklahoma City bombing, which repulsed many sympathizers, militia activity nationwide dropped significantly. But a small core of white supremacist extremists continued to operate and plan acts of domestic terror in the Northwest and elsewhere, refocusing their efforts away from the antigovernment concerns of militias to their original focus on racial superiority, anti-immigration, and anti-Semitism.

In 1996, a group with links to a white supremacist "church" in Sandpoint bombed a *Spokesman-Review* office and a Planned Parenthood Clinic, and robbed a U.S. Bank branch. That same year, two white su-

premacists with ties to the Aryan Nations, Danny Lee and Chevie Kehoe, murdered an Arkansas family of three and helped bomb the Spokane City Hall, crimes they were convicted of five years later. Lee was
sentenced to death; Kehoe was sentenced to life in prison.

It was expensive to keep tabs on the extremist violence unfolding in
the Northwest. Something new and terrible seemed to happen every
few months, and Wassmuth's nonprofit Northwest Coalition Against
Malicious Harassment suffered from chronic poverty. He was constantly fundraising and seeking grants to keep it afloat. He insisted,
however, even in tight fiscal times, on the importance of physically
traveling to these small communities—all the while living on the cheap
and staying in the spare bedrooms of community leaders—rather than
just speaking out from Seattle. It was more effective, he argued, and
was the best way for his group to monitor the pulse of hate in the West.
His knowledge of what was really going on in the rural West's most
isolated outposts—places like Rawlins, Wyoming; Noxon, Montana,
and Kamiah, Idaho—soon made him a reliable source for reporters
covering hate groups in the Northwest. Wassmuth was surprisingly
media savvy for an ex-priest, able to deliver sound bites, sources, and
compelling interviews from which television broadcasters could easily
pull a ten-second quote. When the media had a story on the Aryan Nations, neo-Nazi skinheads, or the dissemination of racist literature,
Bill Wassmuth became the reliable voice of reason countering out-
breaks of bigotry.

He was not only reactive, however. He testified in Boise, urging
Idaho state legislators to recognize Martin Luther King Jr. Day as an official state holiday, despite the grumbling of some Republican lawmakers that it was too expensive and that King was a "communist sympa-
thizer." Wassmuth shamed them into changing their minds.

In Colorado, he testified in support of a bill that would have en-
hanced the state's anti-intimidation law to include sexual orientation.
The legislation was defeated, but Wassmuth kept pushing to broaden
hate crime protections.

For those communities Wassmuth did not reach in person, he relied
on the coalition's mass media project, Let's Fight the Fear Together,

which used print, radio, and broadcast mediums for educational out-reach throughout the region. He also connected small communities with larger organizations that could help, most frequently the South-ern Poverty Law Center, Anti-Defamation League, and Center for Democratic Renewal.

But perhaps most important, he taught communities how to re-spond on their own through the formation of community human rights task forces. Wassmuth's rousing, heartfelt speeches that urged small-town residents to speak out were the impetus behind many hu-man rights task forces throughout the West. Long after he stopped preaching, he still had his touch, an uncanny knack to gently inspire regular folks into action. For him, it was not much of a transition from serving people in a pastoral role to serving in a social justice role to help them enrich their lives. Long after leaving the priesthood, he re-mained a preacher at heart, referring to human rights and social jus-tice as his "continued spiritual ministry."

In 1998 Wassmuth and the Northwest Coalition received a flurry of awards, including being hailed as a Promising Practice by the White House. For every accolade in Washington, D.C., however, there was another fire to put out back in the Northwest.

The region was plagued through the end of the decade by a deep community divide over how best to respond to Richard Butler's plans to hold Aryan Nations parades in downtown Coeur d'Alene.[6]

Some argued it would be letting the Aryan Nations "win" to allow them to march down Main Street without demonstrating to let them know they were unwelcome. Irv Rubin, former leader of the Jewish De-fense League who died in 2002 after an alleged jailhouse suicide at-tempt, called the Coeur d'Alene mayor from Los Angeles to promise a massive counterdemonstration to Butler's planned 1998 march. "The only thing bullies understand is the fist," said Rubin, bragging about blood he had recently shed at an encounter with the Ku Klux Klan.[7]

Others, including Wassmuth, argued such a plan would raise the likelihood of violence and give them more attention, exactly what But-ler wanted. Better, he argued, was to hold an even bigger counterevent elsewhere and turn the focus toward human rights. In the end, both tactics were used, though the result was a rift that developed between human rights activists who wanted to face the Aryans down and those who wanted to rally for human rights elsewhere so as not to give them unwarranted attention.

More than one thousand counterdemonstrators showed up at the sidelines of the Aryans' parade, while local human rights groups, business, and political leaders planned a larger counterdemonstration at Gonzaga University across the border in Spokane, Washington, at the same time as the parade. Wassmuth and the Kootenai County Task Force on Human Relations also organized a clever countercampaign called "Making Lemonade out of Lemons." Nearly fifteen hundred people pledged to donate various amounts of money to human rights organizations for each minute the Aryans marched. Once the national media caught wind of the campaign, pledges rolled in from around the country. The local media took an interest in playing a more active role in the debate. The *Spokesman-Review,* the region's largest newspaper and known for its civic journalism, published a lengthy series about race called "In It Together," which, alongside traditional reporting, featured pro-human rights essays written by prominent community members and local high-school students. Many of the essays resulted from forums that the newspaper itself had organized for students, businesspeople, and political leaders. The paper also printed and inserted a pro-human rights placard into that day's paper for the region's residents to display publicly in their homes and offices.

"They have a right to a parade. That right is guaranteed under the First Amendment. But those who disagree with their message have a right and a responsibility to offer a different message," wrote then Managing Editor Chris Peck about the series. "The *Spokesman-Review* believes it has a responsibility to report on these constructive responses as well as report on the Saturday march. This reporting effort is intended to provide the context readers need to cope with what has become a defining issue for our region."[8]

Several downtown businesses shut down during the march and posted signs reading "Closed to Hate." Theaters, skating rinks, bowling alley, and a water park, meanwhile, offered discounts in hopes of drawing young people away from the event.

In the end, the parade lasted twenty-eight minutes and raised $35,000 in pledges for diversity and human rights programs in schools, equal to $1,250 for every minute marched.

Though the community managed to make lemonade out of lemons, the summer had nonetheless been somewhat soured. Taxpayers ended up footing a $100,000-plus bill to train police and staff security for the march, which drew more than one thousand protesters and sparked more than a dozen arrests as police attempted to keep peace on the sidelines. Those arrests in turn brought lawsuits that further cost the city.

Despite the mounting costs, the city of Coeur d'Alene had spent thousands on legal experts in an attempt to deny the parade permit. It had hired a Seattle constitutional law expert for a $40,000 fee, half of which was paid by the owner of the city's large resort, Duane Hagadone, who feared the parades would hurt the tourism business. In fact it did. Groups canceled conferences and argued over whether to give Idaho their patronage. In one such case, Idaho Governor Phil Batt flew to Sun Valley to assure members of the all-black National Brotherhood of Skiers that they were welcome after some members of the group refused to come to the state's premier ski resort town because of Idaho's reputation.

On the expert's advice, city officials tried to force the parade to take an out-of-the-way route near one of the former city garbage dumps. In response, the Aryan Nations sued (with the help of the American Civil Liberties Union), and a U.S. district judge agreed that denying them the traditional parade route had violated the Aryan Nations' First Amendment free speech rights.

Some residents, frustrated with the debate, attempted to solve the problems themselves. One Coeur d'Alene man applied for the right to hold his own one-man parade on the two days corresponding with the Aryan World Congress. He hoped to lock up the parade dates by using his own free speech rights to play "Twinkle Twinkle Little Star" and "Mary Had a Little Lamb" on an accordion as he marched.[9]

Much of the rest of the community was torn between two diverging response tactics, the proactive response Wassmuth favored or the more up front reactive response favored by activists like Berkeley lawyer Larry Hildes, the Jewish Defense League's Irv Rubin, and a coalition of local and regional groups. Seattle activists sent a letter out that June urging protesters to caravan across the Northwest and Canada to attend. They reproached local human rights activists who, in their opinion, "in previous years led civil rights advocates out-of-state for a rally while the Aryans took over one of their streets." Stung by the criticism, the task force held its counterdemonstration in Coeur d'Alene in 1999. The group's then president Doug Cresswell responded in a guest newspaper column:

> Some human rights activists wonder why the Kootenai County Task Force on Human Relations doesn't appear with counterdemonstrators at Aryan Nations marches. Some believe we're afraid or in denial. We, along with thousands of people in the Inland Northwest, have stood against hate for more than eighteen years, and we will continue to do so.[10]
> The Nazis know that a march draws a crowd. They want a crowd. What type of crowd is of little importance as long as the crowd is there. A march is theater; it requires actors and spectators, if either is missing, there is no theater.

The Aryans, all seventeen of them, eventually drew the crowd they had hoped for and held their march, though they were detoured by protesters who locked arms and staged a sit-in at the parade's midway point. While Butler and his skinhead parade marched along carrying Confederate and Nazi flags, approximately four hundred others were reciting the national anthem about a mile away at North Idaho College, where then Idaho Governor Dirk Kempthorne addressed human rights supporters.

Though the Coeur d'Alene Aryan parades garnered headlines and required Wassmuth's attention to help organize counteractivities, other equally important battles were underway elsewhere in the West. In the wake of national repulsion over the 1998 killing of gay college student Matthew Shepard in Wyoming, Wassmuth joined efforts to push legislators in the Rockies to expand hate crime laws to include sexual orientation. Wassmuth testified before several legislatures on the issue, to no avail, despite new FBI figures showing that sexual orientation had been the motivation for 14 percent of the reported hate crimes in 1997. Northwest legislators still did not act. In fact, lawmakers in Colorado, Idaho, Montana, and Utah defeated bills in 1999 that would have added sexual orientation to categories of people protected by existing hate crime laws.

That year—1999—marked the ten-year personal benchmark that Wassmuth had set for staying with and building up the Northwest Coalition. After nearly a decade of traveling, teaching, and testifying, it was time to step down. The organization, if it were to survive without him, would have to transition to new leadership. The coalition was at peak strength—the budget was approaching a half million per year, there were six people on staff, and more than 150 task forces throughout the Northwest that he had personally helped form. Some six hundred individuals, agencies, and organizations had joined the coalition, and Wassmuth had just nailed down a $600,000 grant to fund joint efforts among Northwest-based human rights groups. Wassmuth had even recently begun discussions with Gonzaga University in Spokane about forming an academic institute against hate. Convinced the best time to leave was when the coalition was doing well, he delivered a firm deadline to the board of directors for finding his replacement. But when no clear successor to Wassmuth emerged after a year, a new proposal to merge the Seattle-based organization with the Portland, Oregon-based sister organization, Coalition for Human Dignity, began gaining ground. Wassmuth was lukewarm to the idea.

Although the organizations had collaborated frequently and had similar end goals, the two groups were different in many ways. Wassmuth's Northwest Coalition focused on mobilizing communities, while the Coalition for Human Dignity focused its efforts more on background research and analysis. As the two organizations were often vying for funding from the same donors, many believed they could be more effective if they combined their strengths, budgets, and staff, thereby eliminating duplication.

But merging politics and methods would prove significantly more difficult than expected, partly because the two groups had emerged from very different events and political visions. The Northwest Coalition had been formed in 1987 by community, religious, government, and law enforcement leaders, in reaction to the violence of the Aryan Nations and their followers. The Coalition for Human Dignity grew out of street protests in the wake of the 1988 neo-Nazi skinhead murder of Mulugeta Seraw, an Ethiopian student in Portland. The Portland group had a more confrontational style, while Wassmuth's group was considerably more centrist, relying on coalition building, cooperation, and government involvement. The difference in political vision was not unlike the split that developed in Coeur d'Alene, with one side favoring a more direct, confrontational style of activism and another side partial to coalition building and a proactive response with broader appeal.

But the Coalition for Human Dignity had one thing the Seattle group needed: an effective director, Terre Rybovich, who had turned the organization around during a troubled period and whose administrative expertise made her the best potential candidate to replace Wassmuth. As discussions intensified, however, Wassmuth grew more skeptical of the merger plans. When the merger went through in October of 1999, he asked to transition out earlier than he had originally planned because he was unhappy about some of the proposed changes, yet felt he was in no position to meddle. Rybovich became the director of the merged organizations, which renamed itself the Northwest Coalition for Human Dignity. But Rybovich got off to a rocky start. When she resigned fifteen months later, the merged group was nearly broke and had been forced to lay off almost the entire staff.

With sadness, Wassmuth watched from the sidelines as the coalition he had helped to build nearly crumbled beneath the weight of bitter internal squabbles and a loss of financial support. He believed the coalition would emerge intact after a few tense transition years, but he put more faith in the longevity of the small local coalitions he had helped start in the rural communities.

10 | The Road Ahead

WASSMUTH thought it would be a mistake to assume that the problem has been resolved because a few high-profile groups are leaving Idaho and the Northwest.

The Aryan Nations, despite dwindling membership and the lack of any real headquarters, still threatens to hold its disruptful annual parades. And experts warn that the legal blow dealt the Aryan Nations by the debilitating civil suit against them in 2000 could bolster the leaderless resistance movement, encouraging loners to go underground and act independently to stay out of law enforcement's reach. Already, "lone wolves" are replacing domestic terrorist groups as the preferred method for carrying out hate crimes. Though Buford Furrow had Christian Identity ties, he acted alone when he shot and killed a Filipino postal worker after opening fire at a Jewish community center in Los Angeles.

Timothy McVeigh had connections to hate groups—he contacted a Christian Identity compound near the Oklahoma–Arkansas border just days before blowing up the Murrah Federal Office Building. But officials could not implicate the hate groups in the crime.

As hate groups move away from the compound-in-the-country concept, loners are not the only concern. A decade ago, hate groups shipped their propaganda to mailboxes anonymously, wrapped in brown paper. Today's methods of hate recruiting involve instantaneous communication through the Internet and increasingly popular neo-Nazi white-power music labels.

While the number of hate websites is growing at a more rapid pace than ever before, white supremacists have been using computer-based telecommunications for more than a decade. Texas Ku Klux Klan titan Louis Beam established a computer network in the mid-1980s called the Aryan Nations Liberty Net, which provided users with a variety of services, including a national computer bulletin board that allowed communication via modem. The system also featured a hit list with a point system that allotted credits to participants for killing politicians, civil rights leaders, police officers, and journalists.[1]

Computer services, hardware, and software became cheaper and more readily available in the 1990s, about the same time the militia movement took off. The movement relied on the free flow of instantaneous information over the Internet to spread paranoid conspiracy theories and post instructions for various illegal activity, such as making an ammonium nitrate bomb like the one that went off in Oklahoma City.

Today's hate groups on the Internet are increasingly multimedia and international in scope. Many sites have background music and animation, and some are available in foreign languages. The internationalization of hate on the Internet poses a number of problems, not the least of which is the impression these websites give that they are not fringe elements but rather mainstream groups who are part of a worldwide community movement. On the web, a single person can masquerade as a large organization.

Because most neo-Nazi websites are hosted in the United States, many European countries that ban racist speech complain that the First Amendment has turned the United States into a "safe harbor for racists."[2]

European authorities took the problem into their own hands in March 1995 when they arrested infamous Nebraska neo-Nazi leader Gary Lauck as he was visiting a Nazi collaborator in Denmark. Lauck had been jailed in the 1970s after trying to import twenty thousand Nazi insignia into Germany. This time, he was extradited from Denmark to Germany, where a year later a Hamburg court found him guilty of mailing tons of banned racist propaganda to Germany from the United States, including pamphlets vowing "not to rest until all Jews have been exterminated." German authorities deported him in

1999, after Lauck served four years in prison. The following year, he visited the Aryan Nations compound in North Idaho.

In December 2000, German legal authorities ruled that websites aiming racist propaganda at German audiences could be prosecuted under the strict German law that bans any publications that incite racial hate, deny the Holocaust, or show Nazi insignia and slogans. Germany's laws prohibiting the sale of hate literature is one of the strongest. Authorities there continue to press for more global regulation on hate speech in cyberspace, but in most cases, what is illegal in Germany and other European countries is perfectly legal in the United States.

Still, German officials maintain that private Internet companies, nongovernmental organizations, and Internet users could do more to limit hate-filled websites, which have exploded from just a handful in the mid-1990s to more than two thousand today. Ironically, anti-Semitism expert Ken Stern points out in a recent article in the Gonzaga University-based *Journal of Hate Studies* that the website of a black hate group that dehumanizes whites and a white hate group that dehumanizes blacks are frequently just a few mouse clicks away from each other, bound by rabid anti-Semitism and Holocaust denial.[3]

Some private Internet service providers, such as America Online, have attempted to limit hate groups' reach, but with mixed results. After being notified of the site's existence, America Online closed down the Charlemagne Hammer Skins homepage, a skinhead site that opened to the sound of machine-gun fire and showed a masked and armed man standing in front of a swastika. When visitors clicked on the "access for subhumans" icon, a picture of a concentration camp photo popped up along with the warning "You can be sure that we have a lot of one-way tickets to Auschwitz left." But days after America Online shut down the site, it popped up on the web again, this time through a Canadian server.[4]

But watchdog groups also note that the availability and accessibility of hate material on the Internet—the very information some would like banned—has given researchers, activists, and journalists a valuable new tool for keeping tabs on the groups. Updates on changes in leadership and locations of headquarters are regularly posted on most hate-group sites. Two decades ago the Aryan Nations had to hold "Congress" meetings at a physical location to bring together bigots with similar views. Today, such gatherings happen regularly in cyberspace, where racists openly discuss their hate ideologies and calls to action in chat rooms. Anyone with a modem can access this virtual compound—a welcome development for those monitoring hate groups.

Computer technology also makes hate crimes easier, as became obvious in the first hate e-mail case in the country, tried in California. The case, which resulted in the eventual conviction of Richard Macado, stemmed from a series of bigoted, threatening e-mail messages sent out to approximately sixty students with Asian-sounding names at the University of California, Irvine, in 1996. The e-mail, which made reference to the author's intent to kill "each and every one of you personally," was ruled a hate crime.[5] Critics of the ruling claimed Macado's free speech rights were violated, but those who defend it maintain the key difference lies in that his threat was "action" not just "opinion," and therefore was no more protected than a phone or regular mail used to threaten and harass someone.

Debate over how much hate speech and hate sites should be protected under the First Amendment ignited over university hate speech codes being developed in response to an increase of racial tension on American college campuses. Courts have struck down hate speech regulations both at the University of Wisconsin and the University of Michigan.

The dilemma is essentially this: Is it possible to punish racially motivated violence when the right to free expression of ideas, no matter how distasteful, is a fundamental constitutional right? In his book *Punishing Hate*, Boston University law professor Frederick M. Lawrence argues it is. There are basic differences between bias crimes (crimes motivated by race or difference) and racist speech (the articulation of hateful views), which, no matter how unpleasant, is protected, he argues. The line is not always clear. Burning a flag is conduct, an action, for example, yet it is protected under the First Amendment.

Assuming racist speech is constitutionally protected (although even that is debated), Lawrence argues that the difference between racist speech and bias crimes depends on the motivation behind the hate speech in question. Free expression protects the right to believe offensive views but not the right to behave criminally. This argument views speech *intended* to frighten someone as verbal assault that should be punished and behavior that merely vents a person's bigotry, perhaps upsetting someone in the process, as racist speech protected by the First Amendment. The basic distinction is in the underlying motivation of the actor.[6]

Whether such speech is deemed a hate crime or just racist, Wassmuth believed it always should be challenged. In his words:

> Free speech does not mean somehow tolerating what is being said as being acceptable, especially if it promotes violence. You've got every right to say something stupid, but I've got a responsibility to call that wrong. As for those who say racists should be allowed to speak on college campuses, I saw they have a right to say what they want, but they don't have the right to demand a bullhorn. The right of free speech does not include a platform. The right of free speech does not include the right to urge violence against others.

Some of today's most violent, vitriolic hate speech is being fomented through "White Noise" music marketed by right-wing record labels and white-pride concert promoters who target youth with aggressive marketing and slick, sophisticated publications. Through sales of CDs, concert tickets, and concert videos, white-power record labels are also generating a significant new aboveboard source of income for a movement that used to rely primarily on illegal activities such as counterfeiting and armed robbery.

This recruiting trend expanded significantly after the summer of 1999, when the now deceased leader of one of the most influential neo-Nazi organizations in the United States, National Alliance leader William Pierce, purchased a controlling stake in Resistance Records. It is the biggest white-power music label based in the Midwest, where a dozen labels and even more white-power bands are located. Nationwide, there are at least fifty record labels and distributors of white-power music,[7] which has succeeded in infiltrating various youth sub-cultures and creating a cultural niche for bigotry within those scenes. The music has also united skinheads internationally through sister re-lationships with European white-power labels. The website of Port-land, Oregon-based Imperium Records, for example, boasts "afford-able white power music for Aryans" and allows visitors to translate its site into twenty-three foreign languages with one easy mouse click. The foreign languages available are limited to those spoken by Aryan races, which includes "euro-Spanish." Through use of technology and inter-nationalization, white-power music is creating a following big enough to propel the music's violent, racist messages into the mainstream through concerts and public performances.[8]

In 1998, one of the most radical white power music "zines," *Fenris Wolf*, printed the following commentary on white-power music by Da-vid Lane, an imprisoned member of The Order, who has continued to recruit and propagandize from prison.

"I am overjoyed at the success we are seeing with the White Power bands. I must confess that I don't understand the phenomenon, since my preference runs to Wagner and Tchaikovsky, but the musical enjoy-ment of us dinosaurs is of no importance. White Rock seems to reach and unify our young folk, and that is the first good news in decades."[9]

Lane's former wife, a woman named Katja Lane, operated a mail-or-der hate business called 14 Word Press from 1995–2001 out of her cha-let-style home in remote North Idaho until she announced she was turning it over to a New Jersey man who operates a mail-order neo-Nazi skinhead music company called Micetrap Distribution (though the press now has an address in North Carolina). Hate group analysts say Micetrap Records is among the top ten distributors of white-power hate music. This new medium for spreading hate is particularly worri-some because much of the music embraces outright calls to violence in a contemporary, multimedia way that appeals to younger generations.

The use of mainstream multimedia tools such as the Internet and music labels is part of a larger strategy of bringing about political changes through cultural means. Hate watchdog groups warn that the camouflage paramilitary posturing, survivalist shows, and militia meetings organized around government conspiracies is giving way to suit-and-tie soap boxing on core racial issues: attacks on immigration, multiculturalism, hate crimes legislation, and affirmative action, for example. Wassmuth and others called this latest approach "White Nationalism," and warned that it is insidious because its posturing is packaged in false patriotism and advocated within the system as opposed to outside of it.

Wassmuth cautioned:

White Nationalism can be much more acceptable in mainstream society because it is easy to disguise. You've got things like the Conservative Citizens Council in the South, which is really just the segregationists rejuvenated, and people like Senator Trent Lott have addressed their group. Aryan Nations is going to appeal to a very limited number of people. Christian patriotism appealed to more, and white nationalism is going to appeal to a lot more. They are cousins if not brothers.

It's a more acceptable, sugar-coated way of mainstreaming white dominance.

. . . And it's we, being white folks, who are the ones that need to be working on human rights issues. It's not the job of African Americans, Muslims, Hispanics, and Native Americans to change social justice issues, it's our jobs because we're the ones that need to change our prejudices, our stereotypes.

White nationalists have been particularly quick to seize onto the color clock: census data is predicting a major change in the American social dynamic as a whole, with forecasters suggesting that sometime this century white people will no longer be a numerical majority. The Census Bureau reported that between 1990 and 2000 the percentage of the population who identified themselves as white decreased from 76 percent to 69 percent. By 2050, analysts predict, half of the nation's population will be classified as something other than white. Already in California, no single ethnic or racial group makes up a majority. Instead of considering this a positive development, proof that different ethnic groups with varied cultures and backgrounds can exist peacefully in a community, the demographic data has instead provided ideological ammunition for those attempting to stir up white anxiety and capitalize on resentment. By blaming nonwhite immigration for these population shifts, anti-immigrant issues and attacks on diversity have been propelled to the forefront of white nationalist agendas.[10]

An especially significant transformation is underway in the rural West, an area made up of 299 counties in 12 states east of the Cascade and Sierra Mountains and west of the Great Plains.[11] Approximately three-quarters of this vast expanse of land still qualifies as "frontier" according to the original Census Bureau definition of land that hosts less than six people per square mile.[12] But the region has experienced an explosion of growth in the last fifty years, and is growing considerably more diverse as it booms. According to the 2000 Census, the West expanded 19 percent in the 1990s, faster than any other region. In Oregon, Idaho, Washington, and Utah, the population bulged more than 20 percent, with a majority of that growth a result of rapidly expanding Hispanic populations, which more than doubled. This shifting demographic has exposed an undercurrent of racial tension that is sharpened in debates over bilingual education and other cultural changes.

Boise, Idaho, for example, mushroomed 46 percent in the last decade, primarily due to well-paid professionals moving from large urban areas. With them come immigrants who provide cheap labor for construction and service sector jobs created by the boom.[13]

The expansion of the West's urban centers and mid-sized towns (places like Boise, Idaho; Portland, Oregon; and Bozeman, Montana) is changing the region's social dynamic. The newcomers sometimes present a strong contrast to the old lifestyles of the region, where most people worked the land or supported those who did. The resulting tension between the old and new West presents unique challenges to small towns, not the least of which is tolerance toward newcomers of all different races, religions, and creeds as the face of the West changes.

The tiny populations of the rural West are still predominantly supported by ranching, mining, agriculture, and timber, but since the 1980s, the economies of rural communities have been shifting away from extractive industries and toward tourism, service sector, high-tech start ups, and creative entrepreneurs.

All over the rural West, one-industry towns have been revamping to adapt to the New West economy. The Silver Valley towns of Kellogg and Wallace in North Idaho now make more income from tourists who come to snowmobile, bike, and ski than they do from the mines that once turned precious metals into millions. The same goes for Park City and Moab, Utah, once mining towns that are now ski and mountain-biking meccas. Similar trends are visible in small towns throughout Oregon, Washington, Idaho, Montana, and Wyoming.

Some communities that have long depended on tourism complain it has gone too far. Residents in Jackson Hole, Wyoming, for example, have watched their social core give way to an increasingly stark gap between the ultrawealthy who have moved there, and everybody else, especially the Hispanic laborers who work for them. A high cost of living and a lack of affordable housing have forced many middle-income residents, such as teachers, carpenters, and law enforcement officers, to commute across a mountain pass from Idaho where the land is cheaper.

Shifts in existing regional populations has fueled growth in New West counties. As agribusiness, timber, and mining have become increasingly mechanized, requiring less labor, workers in those industries are looking toward other economic opportunities emerging in New West counties.[14] Some analysts have stretched this trend a step further by characterizing rural West counties into two distinct groups: the booming New West "cappuccino counties" and the declining Old West "cowboy counties."[15] In cowboy counties, census data shows the population is still predominantly working class, and the economy still relies on natural-resource based extraction industries like agriculture, ranching, mining, and logging.

In the so-called cappuccino counties, demographic data shows the population is increasingly college educated, retired or working in professional and service occupations, and the economy is increasingly based on tourism and recreation. While the general population of the rural interior West grew by 103 percent between 1950 and 2000, cappuccino counties grew 241 percent compared to cowboy counties at 87 percent.

Two small Oregon towns, Bend and Burns, are prime examples of these two contrasting snapshots of the New and Old West, respectively. Bend used to be a typical timber town. But nearly a decade after the last mill shut down, the vestiges of its gritty past are being crowded out by New West phenomena, such as a Ben & Jerry's ice cream parlor and even a Porsche dealership. The town grew by 154 percent in the last decade.[16]

Burns, however, has been battling a depression ever since its timber mill shut down. Population growth stagnated, unemployment spiked, and city officials have struggled to diversify an economy now largely dependent on ranching. Communities like Burns, however, are not vexed by snarled traffic and ugly sprawl, the growing pains that threaten to ruin the very qualities of the New West towns that made them attractive in the first place.

As the economy's fundamental restructuring increasingly makes the old ways of life obsolete, rural America faces potentially dangerous feelings of loss, resentment, and fear of change: sentiments that can lead regular folks down the path of hatred. Racism is often rooted in fear and alienation. It manifests itself when one group feels its core cultural or economic security is threatened.[17]

Perhaps recognizing such disenfranchisement as fertile ground for recruitment, racist fringe groups have tried to capitalize on the economic and cultural anxieties felt by those losing their old ways of life. In a letter published in the Chehalis, Washington, *Log Trucker Magazine*, Aryan Nations leader Carl Franklin wrote, "The coming warfare will be literally a war for survival not of the logging industry or a way of life, but the very survival of the white race."[18] The letter exemplifies how racist movements have tried to capitalize on the changing nature of the rural West's economy. Wassmuth believed that as rural areas struggle to adapt to new economic realities that are largely out of their control, both old-timers and newcomers to the West could practice more tolerance. Those moving into the region could certainly be more accepting about some of the rural West's basic old ways: There is slow farming and logging equipment on the roads. There is dust during harvest. People hunt to fill their freezers for the winter.

Wassmuth believed rural residents were poised to embrace and better manage the inevitable economic and demographic transformation of their communities. Natural resources will not last forever nor will the jobs that depend on them. And newcomers often enrich a community, bringing with them new approaches to old problems, added job opportunities, and welcome services. Broad, nonpartisan human rights task forces often form a crucial bridge of tolerance for communities undergoing major economic and demographic transformation.

Wassmuth:

> We wanted to help task forces form in these small communities but we also wanted to help them broaden their mission, to see that the best way to deal with racism was to build communities where diversity is respected and valued and make sure that would be ongoing whether the bigots were around or not.

Caring for one's neighbor is a commandment in nearly all social philosophies, both religious and lay. Wassmuth was convinced that not only was more tolerance in the face of the changing rural West the right thing to do but a matter of self-preservation in an interconnected, interdependent world economy that recognizes few boundaries—local, national or international. Wassmuth argued that civic groups like human rights task forces can play a proactive role in helping them adapt, by building on and expanding the existing foundation of altruism and neighborliness that courses through rural America's tightknit communities.

Wassmuth:

> It's important that we don't give up on small towns. For human rights groups, and others as well, it's easy to write these small communities off, because the larger populations are more attractive and there's more energy there, but these little communities are the heart and soul of what the West is about. The people that are there are not any less capable of making the moves toward justice than the people in urban and suburban America are. I think too often they are written off as country bumpkins and that is unfortunate. That is a different kind of discrimination, an anti-rural, anti-farmer, anti-get-your-fingernails-dirty sort

of thing. Some of my good friends from long ago and some of the most successful human rights advocates I know are from small, rural communities and they are as open-minded and progressive in their thinking and intelligent in their understanding of these issues as anybody.

Small towns have the advantage that you don't have to change big huge institutional structures to make a difference in a community of a couple of hundred people. The change can happen on a much smaller level, so it's much easier to bring about. We absolutely cannot give up on those rural communities.

Understandably, many in the Northwest felt the region suffered an unfair battering. But deep prejudices do remain in this historically white pocket of the West. Once considered a phenomenon of the South, seven out of eight hate crimes today happen in the North and West, according to the Southern Poverty Law Center.

Despite a rapidly growing Hispanic population, the legislatures in the Northwest states are among the nation's least diverse. Idaho's Legislature is the nation's "whitest." It is also mostly male and nearly all one party. Instead of bending over backward to fight bigotry, given the state's sullied reputation, some legislators have openly expressed derogatory comments about the state's farmworkers and used terms like "Jew 'em down," during committee hearings.[19] Across the Northwest, anti-Indian campaigns and laws limiting tribal sovereignty continue to make legitimate progress at both the legislative and local level.

According to FBI statistics, hate crimes against homosexuals is one of the biggest growth areas in bias crime reporting. A lesbian couple from Montana narrowly escaped death in 2001 after their house was set on fire not long after the two women filed suit asking for health benefits from the University of Montana. Police believe their attempts to assert their rights as a gay couple motivated the arson. Except for Washington and Oregon, the other Northwest states have yet to add protections for gays and lesbians into their hate crime statutes, an omission that Wassmuth and other human rights activists argued makes them even more vulnerable to such attacks.

More recently, since the attacks of September 11, 2001, rural parts of the West are experiencing an increase in hate crimes and discrimination against residents of east Indian or Middle Eastern descent and those who simply look Arab.

Wassmuth:

There's a new kind of paranoia that is creating a real divisiveness in society. It makes me very concerned that we are living with this new level of hype—people who have prejudicial attitudes in their background already are going to be looking for people to blame for all that's happening. There's a huge rise in nationalism going on now—I believe in being patriotic—but this business of good against evil is very concerning to me because it means America, God, and good versus the rest of the world, Islam, and evil. I don't think politicians should be determining what is good and evil.

There are also major violations of civil rights going on with the imprisonment of middle eastern-looking people, many of whom were held without due process. It seems to me we are a long way from being through with this, whether we have more terrorism, more violence, more economic downturns, or we start losing people in war efforts, we are not through this by any means. If there ever was a time to work on human rights, it's now.

Just as the presence of the Aryan Nations hurt North Idaho's economy as some tourists stayed away, prejudice against Muslims also will have an economic impact on the region. Universities have already lost valuable students, faculty, and researchers who contributed to the economy directly with the business their families do in the community and indirectly through research and development that benefits America's public and private sector.

Wassmuth was particularly disturbed by the ways in which home-grown racism is going global, such as with the bumper sticker he spotted in eastern Washington that read "Anybody want to play cowboys and Muslims?" The message is doubly racist. It plays first on our local history of suppressing and killing Indian tribes, and then promotes aggression toward Muslims. It is a reminder of how racism even in the most innocuous forms—a bumper sticker, a child's game—can incubate dangerous prejudices. While those who act out violently—hate groups or lone wolves—may be few, the sentiments that lead them to believe their actions are acceptable stem from everyday bigotry and an unwillingness to confront it.

Wassmuth:

The actual followers of Butler were very few. The people who were not card-carrying members of the Aryan Nations but those who sort of agreed with some of the things he said and are sort of sympathetic and kind of glad he's around because it keeps things the way they like it, well that's a larger number. Then there's a third strata that does things like elect somebody like [former U.S. Congressman] Helen Chenoweth or [Kootenai County Commissioner] Ron Rankin, who pushed for Eng-lish-only laws . . . or for example the whole battle in the [Idaho] Legis-lature over the issue of the name "squaw." That was embarrassing. For a white legislator to stand up and say "I call my wife squaw all the time and I don't see anything wrong with it." That was horrendous. . . . that is arrogant white pride American nationalism and it's unfortunately more widespread.

As citizens start their own campaigns to confront prejudice locally and peacefully, Wassmuth believed they deserved government and in-stitutional support. Even after he had left the Northwest Coalition for Human Dignity, Wassmuth lobbied leaders to support civic engage-ment as a top priority since the Northwest's sense of civic duty had been reawakened by its success against the Aryan Nations. One of Wassmuth's last pleas was for Northwest governors—starting with Idaho—to appoint a Blue Ribbon Task Force on Human Rights that would have helped unite and link the varied efforts throughout the re-gion to make sure groups like the Aryan Nations never again take seed. To declare victory and move on is the biggest mistake the region could possibly make.

Wassmuth:

My biggest concern is that now that we've gotten rid of some of the high profile white supremacists, the white folks will declare the battle over, but they aren't talking to the victims, the people who have been mis-treated for a long time. They may feel that the whole issue of civil justice is taken care of, but that just ignores the fact that those guys were the worst manifestation of what is an ongoing problem. We must continue to address the issues of prejudice and racism that are still present in Idaho and the rest of society. It's the Aryan Nations and their like that give Idaho a bad name, but it is the bigotry manifested at a check-out counter in a grocery store that keeps people from feeling welcome.

Until every person who is different—and that includes minority groups of gender, race, ethnicity, religion, sexual orientation—can honestly and genuinely say I am being treated just as fairly as everybody else in this city or this community—until we can get to that stage, the battle isn't done.

11 | Ellensburg

1999~2002

SEATTLE'S DREARY WEATHER and dull gray skies grew more wearisome for Bill and Mary Frances with each year that passed. She had been offered a job working at a noted art gallery in Ellensburg, Washington, a two-hour drive east, over the Snoqualmie Pass and across the Cascade range and into its arid rainshadow. With Bill's retirement from the struggling coalition and with Mary Frances' promising opportunity, the prospect of a fresh start on the sunnier side of the state appealed to them both.

Though just a few hours apart, the difference between Ellensburg and Seattle is nearly as formidable as the mountain range between them.

Ellensburg is, in many ways, an enigma. Geographically, it is where the expansive sagebrush plains of the Columbia basin give way to a jagged chain of Cascade mountain peaks rising on the western and northern horizons. It is a town in transition economically, too. Bullet's Gun Shop shares a downtown storefront with the Skate & Snow gear store, across from an ethnic import clothier. On one end of town is the John Deere dealership and an agate & gem shop. At the other end of town is Central Washington University, home to U-Tote-Em burgers and a Starbucks. The Rodeo City Barbecue hosts the hundreds who help transform Ellensburg every year into a rough and tumble cowboy town for a few days during Washington State's biggest rodeo, while art aficionados browsing the downtown galleries flock to the Valley Cafe, where Manila clams are delivered fresh from Seattle and a good bottle of Washington wine can easily tack $50 on the bill. At the Tav, the bar-room pool tables are cheap and popular, like in most small western towns, but then, across the street at the Pub, there is that touch of Seattle: the sharks carrying their own pocket chalk and custom pool sticks.

Quirky Ellensburg had both grit and grace, and a cowboy poetry kind of rural–urban sophistication perfect for a small-town Idaho guy who had moved to, and then away from, the big city. Wassmuth fit right in.

After spending the first half of his life saving souls, and the last ten years raising social consciousness, he was looking forward to a quieter existence. Though not exactly retiring, he was nearing sixty years old and hoping to mark a slower pace than he had in years past. He even looked forward to being a househusband, since now it was Mary Frances' turn to work. Upon marrying, they both agreed on a simple life based on the democratic arrangement that Wassmuth would work for ten years as the major breadwinner, then they would trade off and she would work for ten years, and so on. The art gallery job was perfect. She started the summer of 1998. Wassmuth sold their house and wrapped up loose ends in Seattle, where he had agreed to stay until late fall to help the coalition's transition into new leadership. She drove over to Seattle on weekends; he drove over to Ellensburg other days. In October, dismayed with some of the changes underway at the coalition, he said his good-byes and left a month earlier than expected. He moved in with her, into a small house converted from a cabin that they planned to remodel. While cozy, they soon discovered it was too small for both of them and their two dogs—a greyhound-shepherd mix named Pluto and another charity case named Alki, otherwise referred to as "little rat dog from hell." They offered their original purchase price to some interested Bellevue friends and sold it the same week that their offer was accepted on another house across town. The new place was a stately, if slightly neglected, Victorian fixer-upper on a street lined with old maples and well-kept homes near Central Washington University campus. The turn-of-the-century house was a handyman's dream. Bill, with his penchant for fixing things, and Mary Frances, with her artistic eye, looked forward to creating a home together.

It was not clear if the Northwest Coalition would survive, much less thrive without Wassmuth's vital leadership, but the decision to leave had been a good move for him personally. That spring, he traveled to Paris to fulfill his lifelong wish to see Europe. The trip's impressions stayed with him for months. He formed his own nonprofit consulting business called Stand Together Publishers and Consulting, and through it, with his personal friend Tom Alibrandi, published the dramatized account of his fight against the Aryan Nations, *Hate Is My Neighbor*. He also began to consider the manuscripts of human rights activists struggling to find publishers for their work. He was still in strong demand nationally for workshops and presentations on human rights and community activism. He traveled on business to Chicago and Santa Fe and then throughout Washington State on a speaker's circuit contract with the Washington Humanities Commission. He was attending meetings of the regional ecumenical ministers associations throughout the West Coast. Always a consensus builder, Wassmuth felt that because such associations bring together pastors from various denominations they were an ideal context for religious leaders to begin combating hate on a more unified level. He did not view religion as a force of intolerance but rather genuinely believed that faith groups provided the kind of moral compass and social networking needed for combating prejudice. This faith in the role of religion set him apart from some of the more radical urban activists, who sometimes viewed religious groups as inhibitors of social justice.

Between trips to work with state and regional ministerial associations, Wassmuth periodically visited Coeur d'Alene to follow developments in a civil suit against the Aryan Nations and Butler. The suit was being brought to court by a woman and her teenage son who were assaulted on a road near the compound in 1999 by several security agents working for Butler. The mother and son had stopped to pick up something that had fallen from their car, and the 1977 Datsun backfired. The loud noise caught the attention of several skinhead security guards at Butler's compound, who jumped into a pickup and sped after the two. The men started shooting, and when a bullet punctured one of the rear tires, her car careened into a ditch. The two security guards, dressed in fatigues from the Aryan Nations compound, pulled the mother and son from their car and assaulted them with the butts of their rifles, threatening to kill them. Another car passed by, which interrupted the assault. The guards saluted in Nazi fashion, warned the two not to talk about the incident, and left the scene. Butler had avoided prosecution up until this point, but Wassmuth and other human rights activists in the region felt a jury would likely hold him responsible for this action, committed by paid employees under his watch. They urged the mother to take the case to court. She agreed and retained respected Coeur d'Alene attorney and human rights activist Norm Gissel, who worked in conjunction with Morris Dees, the renowned Montgomery, Alabama, civil rights attorney from the Southern Poverty Law Center. Dees had an impressive courtroom record on similar kinds of suits, having bankrupted or severely crippled five other white supremacy groups over the last twenty years, including the Klan. In 1999, Dees helped win a $37-million judgment in South Carolina against a Ku Klux Klan group responsible for an arson attack against a predominantly black church. In fact, he had not ever lost such a case, and this sensational trial in August 2000 would be added to his long list of high-profile successes. Wassmuth was present in the courtroom the day the all-white jury delivered its guilty verdict, along with a $6.3-million judgment that bankrupted Butler and his organization, resulting in the eventual destruction of his compound.

To see Butler finally held responsible for the violent acts of his minions was a poignant moment of sweet justice for Wassmuth, one of the finest before his life changed altogether.

In between trips back to Coeur d'Alene to keep tabs on the trial, Wassmuth had been busy remodeling his two-story home. He had set up scaffolding and hammered and scraped along its old walls. Several afternoons he had noticed a tingling sensation in his left thumb that made it difficult for him to hold the nail straight as he was hammering. He expected it would go away. Just a case of the jitters. But little signs that the problem was worsening troubled him: He began struggling with the toothpaste tube, it became difficult to make a fist, then his bicep began quivering. In September of 2000, he went in for a battery of tests to get to the bottom of the problem. He continued work on the house, despite the strange feelings in his limbs, until October, when he slipped and fell off the roof. Two days later, he received a final diagnosis of amyotrophic lateral sclerosis (ALS), a motor-neuron disease sometimes called Lou Gehrig's disease. It is an often fatal degenerative disease that attacks nerve cells in the brain and spinal cord. Stunned and upset, he and Mary Frances and friends began researching all possible causes and cures, neither of which are known. He learned that motor neurons located at the base of his skull were connectors between his brain and the nerves that reach the muscles. Body parts move by initiating a signal in the brain (upper motor neuron), which relays the signal to another motor nerve cell in the spinal cord (lower motor neuron). It was as if there was an electrical circuit going from the transformer box to the light bulb, but someone took the light switch out, he reasoned. When motor neurons die, the brain can no longer control or make muscles move. He looked at before and after pictures of the motor neurons, witnessing how they wither up and die, and discovered that the disease would impact only the voluntary muscles, not the involuntary ones. His taste buds, for example, were not affected, but his tongue muscle would deteriorate, because speech is a voluntary function. He began to try to predict how the disease would affect him by determining if a muscle was voluntary or involuntary by deciding if it was something he could move by choice. He would keep breathing, since it is involuntary, but he would not be able to control his breathing, for example, to take a deep breath, because that is a voluntary function of the diaphragm. Sight, touch, hearing, taste, smell, sex drive, and his mind would remain unaffected, but the rest of his body would begin to atrophy. It was a maddening realization.

He tried nearly everything over the next year, spending $40,000 on medical bills not covered by insurance, including $17,000 on naturopathic supplements. Together, he and Mary Frances waded through vastly conflicting material on the little-understood disease. They had heard about the famous physicist, Stephen Hawking, who has lived forty years with the disease. That gave them hope. But there were also many ALS patients, like famed New York Yankees pitcher and Hall of

Famer, Jim "Catfish" Hunter, who died just a year after diagnosis. Wassmuth was not sure how long he would have to live. He had all the metal fillings removed from his teeth on the belief that heavy metals were particularly detrimental for those with ALS. He participated in experimental bovine stem cell research, imported from Germany and shipped to Ellensburg in a brown paper bag because it had not yet been legalized for use by the Food and Drug Administration. He was ready to do anything medically available (short of new-age healing or magic, which he did not believe in) to fix the ALS. He did believe, however, in the positive energy that happened when a large group of supportive people were gathered around him. And while he appreciated the thousands of prayers across the Northwest, he never expected they would convince God to fix the motor neurons and make it all better. He did not believe God gave him the disease, nor did he believe God could take it away. He was angry at the disease, not God.

By Christmas 2000, he had lost nearly all use of his left hand, some use of his right, and was having trouble buttoning his shirts. The constant improvements they had planned for the house were a welcome distraction. They painted the dining room a rich chocolate brown and the other rooms equally mouthwatering shades of butter yellow, light blue, peach, and pea soup green. They painted the trim white and polished the old hardwood floors.

By late spring of 2001, his legs had weakened to the point that he needed to carry a cane, though he resisted using it, especially in public appearances. When he was awarded an honorary degree from the University of Idaho, Wassmuth left his cane near the podium and took a small step forward to shake UI President Bob Hoover's hand. Though unsteady, he preferred to stand on his own.

He was still just strong enough to walk, with the help of his cane, arm in arm with human rights activists through the Aryan Nations compound shortly before it was razed. There were stacks of timbers and poles the group had set aside for cross burnings and photos of minorities that had been used for target practice, blackened scraps of Martin Luther King Jr. images left among the ashes in the burned barrel. He watched with pride in his heart and tears in his eyes as a huge construction crane took a destroying bite out of a swastika that had been painted on the corrugated metal roof of the cookshack. The dismantling of that shed sent shivers through his whole body. He would outlast this place.

When friends asked Wassmuth what he wanted for his sixtieth birthday in July, he jokingly told them he would like the gift of motor neurons. One friend, a professional window washer, cleaned all of his windows to increase the amount of sun that streamed in, which he believed to be good for motor neuron regrowth and for the clarity with which Wassmuth, increasingly housebound, could see out. Around the region, his friends and supporters prayed for the disease to stabilize, as some ALS patients can live for many years if the deterioration plateaus, but it rarely does. Bill and Mary Frances could see it was progressing. There was twitching, muscle weakness, and his speech had slowed and was more labored. There were fundraising dinners and events throughout the Northwest to help raise money to pay for Wassmuth's mounting medical bills.

About a month later, during the week that Wassmuth was getting accustomed to using a walker, Mary Frances arrived home from work to find him lying in a daze on the dining room floor, confused. He had apparently fallen while trying to navigate his walker through a doorway. He kept repeating the same questions, was uncertain of his whereabouts, and clearly not himself. Mary Frances knew his injury was potentially life threatening when she asked him who was pitching for the Mariners and he could not remember. She listed off a series of his favorite baseball players. No recollection. She rushed him to the emergency room, where doctors confirmed he had suffered a serious concussion during the fall. After a week, he had recovered fully. The two decided, however, that his walker days were over. It was time to transition to a wheelchair.

The attacks of September 11, 2001, shocked and disturbed Wassmuth deeply, as it did most Americans. But perhaps more than most Americans, Wassmuth was troubled also by the immediate rise in hate crimes on the basis of race, religion, or nationality in the days and weeks following the attacks. Mosques were being vandalized and inno-

cent Americans unjustly attacked because they were foreigners. Wassmuth was especially bothered by the case of Balbir Singh Sodhi, a gas
station owner in Mesa, Arizona, originally from India. Sodhi, who had
actually donated blood for the survivors of the terrorist attacks and
was deeply patriotic, was shot dead the week after September 11 by a
deranged local man who killed him for no other reason than because
he was dark skinned, wore a turban, and had a thick dark beard. He
was the first to die in a nationwide series of attacks against Arab-look-
ing people in the wake of 9-11. Wassmuth kept tabs on all the cases
but especially those unfolding in the Northwest. Islamic Centers,
Muslims, and dark-skinned immigrants were threatened in southern
Idaho, Oregon, Montana, Spokane, and Seattle. Two Seattle-area
mosques and a Tacoma synagogue were defaced. The post-9-11 rise in
hate crimes weighed on Wassmuth's conscious heavily, and he quietly
urged his successors at the Northwest Coalition to take a strong stand
against such incidents. He did not believe it was just for the government to detain thousands of persons on the basis of race and nationality alone. He was also thoroughly convinced that the anthrax attacks
were the work of domestic terrorists, a theory the FBI was also considering.

But the rapid progression of his disease limited his ability to speak
out against the surge in hate crimes that years before would have had
him calling a press conference and rallying Northwest residents to respond. A surprising silence filled the void left by Wassmuth's physical
inability to continue his gentle but persistent calls for justice. America's anger had overwhelmed its capacity for tolerance, and too few
seemed to care, which deeply concerned him.

By early October 2001, Wassmuth was confined to a wheelchair and
had lost nearly all upper body movement, save for some muscle tone in
his shoulder that allowed him to lift his arm enough to navigate his
wheelchair and press the large 9-1-1 buttons on the phone in an emergency. He had two college-age caretakers—Justin and Mary—in the
house almost every day to help him with hygiene, dressing, and other
daily needs while Mary Frances was at the gallery. She called home
from work a lot that fall just to tell him that she loved him.

He considered taking a trip for experimental surgery, but it was determined he had deteriorated too much for the necessary follow-up care in Europe, as the research had not yet been approved for use in the United States.

He traveled to Boise in October for the city's declaration of October 11 as Bill Wassmuth Day and soaked up the love and support from former parishioners and Boise human rights activists, such as his loyal friend Marilyn Schuler who helped raise money for his treatment. There was a celebratory mood—the Aryan Nations compound had been purchased by philanthropist Greg Carr, an Idaho native, who had in turn donated the land to North Idaho College as a peace park. Inspired by the demise of the compound and eager to aid Wassmuth, twenty-one artists held a songwriting workshop in Boise and from it compiled *We Will Always Stand As One*, a CD of mostly original music inspired by Wassmuth's life and work. All proceeds from CD sales helped pay Wassmuth's many medical bills not covered by insurance. Wassmuth was deeply moved by the outpouring of support he received that day, one of the last major public celebrations he attended. They bought an $18,000 modified van for transporting him safely in the wheelchair and paid for it out-of-pocket with help from donations from friends and supporters, including those in Boise.

Over the next three months his respiratory capacity dipped dramatically from 78 percent to 65 percent. His speech grew more slurred each week. He felt constantly hot, so he wore running shorts and a t-shirt and left the doors wide open despite a fall breeze brisk enough to blow the dry golden maple leaves off the trees. He enjoyed sitting in his recliner because sometimes it felt as though there was nothing wrong, and he could forget, until he reached for the remote. He also enjoyed e-mail and chatted occasionally on ALS support-group websites, such as <http://rideforlife.com>.

By Christmas he was giving away his possessions and thinning out his personal belongings. The few books he saved were donated to Ellensburg Public Library and the Gonzaga University Institute For Action Against Hate in Spokane. He threw out boxes of photos, letters, and documents. Nobody cared about pictures of him waterskiing, he argued, and he did not want his wife to have to face piles of his stuff after he was gone. He did not fear dying nearly as much as he feared how Mary Frances might be hurt by his dying. His lack of fear stemmed largely from his unwavering belief in life after death. He thought he would still be himself after he died and that he would encounter others who had passed away—his mother, his father—and that he would recognize them. He was not afraid or scared of what was on "the other side." Actually, he was comfortable with it, even excited about what he thought would be an adventure, something to look forward to. Thinking about himself dying was not hard, it was thinking about Mary Frances living afterward that hurt.

But the dying process is a part of living, Wassmuth believed, and experiencing the death of a loved one is part of that, too. He had watched so many people pass on as a priest, while delivering last rites or tending the ailing during hospice, that he knew the sense of awe that occurs while holding the hand of someone who is dying and helping them let go. He would say "Go, trust in God, it's going to be okay," and each time he witnessed death, it deepened his belief in the sacredness of life. Though he encountered death often as a priest, it did not prepare him for his own.

To make the process as peaceful as possible, they began planning in late 2001 for his eventual death. She bought the silk his body would be wrapped in before cremation. He called a reporter to help him write his obituary so it would be ready at a moment's notice. It was a benefit of this particular disease, Wassmuth thought. Those killed in a car wreck do not have the time, the opportunity to do it this way, to die well.

By the New Year 2002, his trunk muscles had weakened to the point that he was unable to hold himself upright for long while sitting on the edge of the bed, or lean forward over his knees, or sit in his electric armchair. He bought a neck brace to help stabilize his head while riding in the van. He could no longer type, which meant less e-mail correspondence, but he could still hit the speakerphone button on the phone. He decided to stop struggling with "I can't anymore" everyday. Practicing how to do things would not make it easier, because he would lose that ability in a few months anyway. He stopped fighting the changes; he needed to avoid the frustration and exhaustion of trying to adapt. Instead, he tried to stay ahead of the curve: stop before getting frustrated and wait on the help he needed to do something. He focused on the things he could do—like enjoy good food and music—not the things he could not do. This approach helped him emerge from a difficult phase of Lou Gehrig's, the loss of physical independence despite a mind that is still thinking as clearly as ever.

Friends visited often, but Mary Frances was his main pillar of support. Together they came to terms with what lay ahead: this was a fatal disease that was going to kill him. He was likely going to continue to get worse. Today was as good as he would be for the rest of his life. Tomorrow could be the same, or he could be weaker, but he would not be better.

He and Mary Frances and a friend went on a November trip to the ocean, for him to say goodbye. There was so much he could not do anymore—walk on the beach, dip his feet in the water, build a sandcastle— that he felt at peace closing that chapter of his life. They stayed for a week in a beachhouse with large picture windows just yards from the ocean. A huge storm front moved in, with thunder, lightning, and eighty-mile-an-hour winds. No one could be out on the beach, so he did not feel he was missing anything. It was dramatic, overpowering, perfect. For hours he watched the angry surf pound the shore and the sea lions swim by. He had his own little chat with the Pacific about his plans to have his ashes spread over her after his death.

Wassmuth's sense of humor and sharp wit penetrated even the darkest corners of his last months. He was constantly making macabre jokes about his declining health, using laughter to help ease the stunted conversations when friends would call. Visitors would walk in, see him and say "Hi Bill, how are you?" and, with a glimmer in his eye, he would perkily retort, "I'm dying, how are you?"

In February 2002, his new wheelchair arrived. It was a $16,000, state-of-the-art Quickie S-686 with a joystick and Rock Shox that sped along at six miles per hour. It was the Mercedes of wheelchairs, and he showed it off to all his friends, even challenging a few to races.

At a fundraiser held for him in Seattle, Wassmuth and Seattle-area human rights supporters rewatched the videotape taken of the day he walked through the Aryan Nations compound before the buildings were set ablaze as practice for local firefighters. Sitting in his new wheelchair in a Seattle living room, he watched himself on the screen, still able to walk across the compound grounds with the help of a cane. When the camera zoomed in on the construction crane taking a large bite out of the shed's roof and destroying the red swastika painted there, he could not help but smile. Wassmuth knew he might not be around to see it, but the scab where the guardtower once stood would heal over and fill in with soft grass, and the gates of hate that for years opened to "Whites Only" would become the new entrance to a peace park open to everyone, a reward for a community that fought bigotry together, with common courage. As the video's credits rolled, Wassmuth wheeled back around to the clapping crowd who were gathered around the television with him. He could not help but cry.

In spring, he ate meals packed with cholesterol and began drinking moderately again—the loss of the use of his hands prevented him from pouring himself a glass, thereby preventing him from the possible abuse of alcohol. He relished the smoothness of 1970s-vintage Napa Valley cabernet sauvignon wines brought by one of his best friends, a Methodist minister from Seattle, on his every other week visit.

He stopped wearing sunscreen when he sat in the sun. When one friend called to ask how it was going with his new feeding tubes, Wassmuth wisecracked that he thought "that eating thing" was overrated, and that once the mainstream populace tried these tubes out they were really going to catch on.

He arranged to have a backyard art studio built for Mary Frances, and he watched with satisfaction as local construction students put the finishing touches on the building over the summer. In July, Mary Frances and his caregivers considered taking him to Jazz in the Valley, Ellensburg's local music festival, but it was getting emotionally much harder, frustrating and exhausting in fact, to see so many people he knew and not be able to communicate with them. Only Mary Frances, a few close friends, and his two caregivers could still understand his slurred, labored speech.

They took him instead to a place just a few blocks away, where communicating did not necessitate speaking: Ellensburg's Chimpanzee Human Communication Institute, an innovative research center where the primates have been taught to communicate through sign language.

With so little physical ability left, yet his mind still alert, he began taking pleasure in the smallest silly things, like when his female caregiver painted his toenails with neon blue nail polish after giving him his bath. Normally he might have protested, but it was particularly funny now because he could not do anything about it except laugh until she agreed to remove it.

He loved watching baseball. His mother had been an Atlanta Braves fan. After she had a stroke, she requested him to watch so many games that he began to better understand it and became a diehard fan. His last big trip had been in April to see a Mariner's game in Seattle. He tuned his television to all their games that season, including the 5-2 loss to the Minnesota Twins on the August day he died.

After coming down with pneumonia that month, his lungs could no longer pump out fluid, requiring those around him to use a manual pump and medication to ease his breathing. He had decided against any surgery that would leave him dependent on life support or breathing devices, and sensed the pneumonia could be fatal—most with ALS die of respiratory failure. The last day, Mary Frances tended to him lovingly and told him he could let go when he wanted. Four close friends were at his bedside. His sister drove up from Idaho. Everyone held onto a part of him until the moment he closed his eyes.

The disease held his body hostage for the last two of his sixty-one years, but in the end it was Bill, not Lou Gehrig's, who decided when it was time to die. He had spent many months preparing for that moment.

There was warm sunshine and bright blue skies on the day his service commenced a week later at Ellensburg's St. Andrew's Catholic Church. There were readings from the Scriptures (Micah 6:6–8) and the Desiderata. As they entered the church, each of his family members and closest friends carried with them personal items representing his life: the chalice he used as a priest, seashells found at the beach, human rights awards, his cane, cherished photos. The urn was placed in the center. Tears were not only accepted but encouraged. Yet the service was orchestrated with grace and a positive spirit he would have appreciated. There was an abundance of laughter, music, and poignant moments of reflection when the diverse crowd in attendance spoke of how he affected their lives at an open microphone near the altar. Those in attendance were then invited to write notes to him that would be burned, added to his remains, and spread across the ocean.

Other memorial services spontaneously developed out of respect and mourning across the Northwest, especially in Idaho. The University of Idaho in Moscow held a memorial tribute and showed video clips of him bowing his head to receive an honorary doctorate and president's medallion. More than one hundred people gathered in Boise to swap stories about what a cool priest and effective human rights activist he was, how he urged them to serve their communities, how deeply he had touched their lives. Several noted they had a "Bill's room" in their homes for when he had business in their towns and needed a place to stay.

In Coeur d'Alene, a crowd of five hundred gathered in the sanctuary built under his watch at St. Pius X to weep, laugh, and sing the hymns Father Bill loved: "Pan de Vida," "Make Me A Channel of Your Peace." Several priests, including two who were cousins from Greencreek, hailed him as a heroic model of courage who followed in Jesus's footsteps and then gracefully handed over their pulpit to non-Catholic members of the human rights task force. Near the end of the service, a Jewish man stepped up to the altar from where Wassmuth had delivered so many homilies. With candles flickering from the pulpit, the choir looking on, and eight priests and deacons in white robes and holy vestments standing behind him, he urged those sitting in the pews before him to continue fighting bigotry whenever it surfaces and for whatever reason. He paused, then added: that includes sexual orientation.

For a moment, there was awkward silence in the sanctuary. Then, from the back of the hall, one brave person began clapping. Within seconds, the church burst into full applause, for Father Bill—such a good priest—and for Citizen Bill—such a good man. They clapped loud and long, nodding their heads in remembrance of all the honorable values he stood for, continuing their spirited ovation long after the priests had refolded their hands into prayer, applauding like they believed he could hear them.

EPILOGUE

MAYBE IT was the post-Christmas blues, or the foggy winter chill that frosted all the sagebrush in eastern Washington that morning, but the interview I did with Bill on January 7, 2002, took a particularly difficult turn. Our rhythm up until that point had been for me to send sets of questions to him a few days in advance of my arrival, giving him time to think about them and setting the framework for that week's interviews. Some days, though, it felt more natural to just have informal discussions that began, continued, and ended much like a conversation. This was one of those. It was just after the rush of the holidays, and I was not prepared with a set of scripted questions. We always began our interviews with a little small talk, and this interview just unfolded spontaneously after I asked him how he was doing, how he was feeling that day. The interview naturally bumped into what he called "the elephant in the middle of the room," his pending death from Lou Gehrig's disease. We had not ever really discussed it in such a frank way before. That evening after we had finished, I drove four hours home from Ellensburg to the Palouse, squinting to see through thick banks of fog along the Columbia River, my eyes watering all the way to Dusty, the tiny farm town that signaled I was almost home.

After Bill's death in August, 2002, I decided to reprint the excerpts of this January interview, even though some of this material had been covered in the book. His own wisdom about death, dying, and faith are, I think, more poignant as he said them than what I have written. They reveal through his own words, slurred when spoken, but not on paper, what he believed would come after his life on earth was finished, and therefore are a fitting epilogue to his story.

The interview begins here as Bill and I are talking about the manifestations of Lou Gehrig's disease, how it was progressing and how he was feeling that day. We were sitting in his living room, he in his specialized wheelchair, I across the coffee table on his couch. Close enough that I could reach over and hold his hand.

Can you feel when I put my hand on yours like this?
Oh yea, there's nothing wrong with my nerves there. What has died is the connectors. That is right at the base of my neck, at the base of my skull is where they are at. It's the connectors between my brain and the nerves that reach the muscles. They are called motor neurons, and I've seen pictures of them before and after, and they essentially just wither up and die so it's as if you took an electrical circuit from your transformer box to the light bulb and took the light switch out, that's essentially what it is.
But you still have feeling in your limbs.
Yes, see it doesn't have anything to do with the nerves themselves that cause feeling. It's the nerves that carry the electrical impulses from my brain to my muscles. And it's only the voluntary muscles, not the involuntary ones—the voluntary muscles, which are also connected to the brain by motor neurons. For some reason this crazy disease just picks on voluntary ones and wipes them out. My feeling and nerve sensation is all fine. My taste buds are fine, but my tongue muscle is going. That's why my voice sounds strange. That's my tongue for the most part. The movement of it is what affects my speech, it's a voluntary function.

It's sort of like you can tell the difference between the two, voluntary and involuntary, by just stopping and figuring out if you can move it by choice. So, I can stop and say move my tongue; I can move it, so it's voluntary. I can breathe deeper by moving my diaphragm, so my diaphragm is voluntary even though breathing is not. I can stop breathing, but as soon as I relax I am going to keep breathing even if I am unconscious or sleeping. So that's an involuntary.

Do you have control of the diaphragm still? How is the progress through your body? Do you feel different each day?

I am losing it. I can't breathe as deeply on purpose anymore as I could before, and sometimes I can't move my diaphragm at all, so there must be a number of muscles down there and some of them are already gone.

My whole trunk is weakening, for example, so it is harder to hold my head up now. I can hold it up when I am sitting still but if I hit a bump in my wheelchair, for example, I snap around. So I actually today ordered a neck brace that I am going to wear when I am outside of the wheelchair, like when I'm in our van. And I can feel it in my trunk muscles, too. If I am sitting somewhere without a back rest, like when I am sitting on the edge of the bed, I can't hold myself straight for very long, and I can't pull myself frontward when I am sitting. I can't lean over my knees anymore, or even just to lean forward in the chair—I can't get my back away from the backrest anymore.

I can't type anymore, but I can go to the phone, and we've got the phone set up on speakerphone, so I can hit the speakerphone, and we are going to put 911 on the bottom call button so I can hit that. I can't hit the upper buttons anymore. I went to the phone company and this was the most handicapped friendly one they had. It's getting to be a moot question because I'm not home alone anymore for more than a half hour and fairly soon that's not going to be the case either. . . . Plus there's no point in my struggling with that sort of stuff because it wears me out, and it frustrates me, and there's no need for me to fight that because it is only going to get worse, it's not going to get better. I can't make it easier by practicing. It's not like if I practice I will strengthen some muscles or be able to do it in the future. I went through that a couple months ago when I was losing my ability to do a bunch of stuff and I fought it and I fought it and I fought it, and then I kind of had a talk with myself and said, "Now this is stupid." I'm not going to make it any easier and it is only going to make it more and more frustrating, more and more exhausting, so it is much better to stay ahead of the curve and stop doing things before I get so frustrated and get the help that I need to do them. That is what it amounts to, is having the help around to be able to take care of me. I have made it through that stage of not wanting to do that because I was losing independence.

How do you get over that?

Part of it is you have to. I have talks with myself. I have come to some peace with it all. I consider myself very, very lucky to have some really supportive people around me who don't allow me to feel sorry for myself, and Mary Frances is at the top of that list. They help me with a little 2-by-4 to the top of the head every once in awhile. One guy came and visited me and I was moaning and groaning about the things I couldn't do anymore, and he let me whine for a little while and then he said, "Alright, I thought you were working on focusing on what you can do and not on what you can't do," and I said, "Yea, your point being?" And he said, "All you've done since I've got here was talk about what you can't do."

The other thing is just coming to grips with the fact that this is a fatal disease, and it is going to kill me. I am going to continue to get worse. So it's not a matter of if I struggle through this somehow I am going to get better on the other end; that just isn't going to happen. So to accept that fact and to acknowledge that today is as good as I'm going to be for the rest of my life. Tomorrow I could be the same or tomorrow I am going to be a little bit weaker, but I am not going to be better.

Religion played a key role in shaping you as a young man. What role is it playing now, as you face this fatal disease?

I thought we only have a few hours?

(Laughter.)

I know, I said only a few questions today, but they're whoppers.

(Laughter.)

I talk in terms of spiritual journeys, and I think the whole of life is a spiritual journey. For me that journey has gone through a number of very important stages, but also very different stages. That's why it is a long answer, because what my faith says to me now and how it participates in how I deal with things now, is essentially different than it was five years ago, fifteen years ago, much less what it was when I grew up.

On the other hand, everything that was a part of my faith experience on that journey is part of what's gotten me to where I am now. I mean, it's step-by-step, mile-by-mile. It's all been very important. My earlier faith experience was much more fundamental, in the sense of the clear and absolute portions of it. In terms of what I am facing now, there was a very clear notion of heaven and hell, and you would go to one or the other after you had died, and there was a whole set number of things that you did or did not do, or things that were done or not done unto you, and if you did all those right you would go to heaven and if you screwed up on one or two you would go to hell and it was very clear. I like to joke about something that was very true:

When I was in grade school, the school was on one side of the road and the church was on the other side. We were in a Catholic school, and we always went to confession on the first Thursday of the month, and we would go during school hours. So us fourth and fifth graders, we would traipse over to confession and then come back. One of the things the teacher always told us was be very careful crossing the road when you are going over that way. She wasn't concerned about our coming back because if we got killed on the way back we would go to heaven, but assuming that if we got killed on the way over, since we hadn't been to confession yet, and we hadn't had our sins forgiven, we'd go to hell.

Today, it's much less clear, less absolute than that.

Did this lack of clarity develop over time slowly? Was it after you left the priesthood that this perception started to change?

No, it was slower than that. Back in summer school was the major time of transition of opening up a whole different approach to things. I headed in the direction of not being anywhere nearly as scripted. To put it simply, prior to that time the more specificity—oh, there's too many "ss's" in that word for my tongue—and the more exact and detailed and thorough we could be in our definition of who God was, the closer I believed we were to the truth. The more you could picture intellectually and other ways who God was, the closer you were to that God. After that summer school I went exactly the opposite direction. In my mind, if you can picture who God is, you've got it wrong. If you can define who God is, you've got it wrong. Now, I really believe, and I had a card hanging up for a long time, but it's something like, if you can tell me who your God is, I believe you've made up your own God rather than the God that has created us all, or something like that. It's the opposite.

So you are saying you think it's spiritually arrogant to believe one can know precisely what God is?

Exactly.

How in the world can we presume to capture in our frail little brains, as wonderful as they are, how can we hope to capture that ultimate out there, whatever that is. . . . God is obviously much much more than I can ever define God to be. As soon as I try saying this is who God is, I've narrowed God down to where it doesn't make sense to me anymore, so it is expansive rather than restrictive, opening rather than closing, widening rather than narrowing, it's freeing rather than defining.

I think there are some people of faith who, after being diagnosed with ALS, would become very angry with God. Did you go through that?

No, I never did. I have reflected on it because other people have asked me. It's because where I am now in terms of my faith journey as far as God is concerned—God didn't have a tinker stone to do with my ALS. I am angry at the ALS, I'm angry at the disease. God didn't give me the disease, and God isn't going to take it away. I really appreciate all the people who are praying for me; I appreciate that because it's their goodness and some of that is being manifest for that prayer. But I have no expectation that somehow if I have two thousand people praying for me rather than one thousand people that is going to convince God to somehow fix these motor neurons in my back and make it all better.

How does your faith help you during this time?

I am angry at the ALS, and I will do anything I can medically to fix the ALS. I will not go to healing, magical, miracle kinds of things to do it because I just don't believe in that.

I believe in the energy that can happen when a whole group of supportive people are gathered around me and with that energy I could be healed as much as any, and if God's finger is in that, then that's fine by me. It's the energy of the loving people around me, not God sitting up there in heaven saying I gave him this ALS for a purpose, and the purpose has now been accomplished so I'm going to take him now; that ain't my vision of what God is.

Where my faith figures in now is, I very much believe in life after death. I don't believe death is the end of it; I believe there is something beyond. From there on it starts getting pretty unclear, but I do believe there is a personal ongoing presence. I think I will be me after I die, somehow, and I think I will be able to encounter folks who have died and I will know who they are. I will reencounter my mother, I will re-encounter my dad, that sort of thing. I think there is a personal presence somehow, how that all happens I don't know. I see God these days not in terms of a personal Father–Son–Holy Spirit kind of thing, I see God more as the fullness of life, the fullness of energy, the fullness of love, and the fullness of truth, and all that. Somehow I am a part of that already, somehow everybody is, and somehow after I die I am more clearly a part of that. Frankly, I am kind of excited about it. I see it as something of an adventure, something that is worth looking forward to. I am not speeding up the moment that I die, by any means; I've got a lot to live for and intend to stick around for. On the other hand, I'm not scared of dying, I'm not afraid of it. I'm not afraid of what's on the other side. I'm rather comfortable with that.

What about your friends and family, do they feel similarly?

Well, the most important person in my life, Mary Frances, yes. We've talked about that, and we continue to do that. She's to the point of where she teases me about it now, she says, "Yea, easy for you to say, you're going off to this wonderful adventure experience and you are leaving me behind." And in a sense that's very true. The worst thing about dying to me is what it does to her. I'd do anything to not have to put her through that, but I can't do anything about it.

That shows a lot of maturation on her part to accept, and be able to openly discuss the situation at hand.

That has only happened in the last couple of months. She is much more able to talk about what life without me is going to be like and what she is going to do. She can do that now, and we can start making some plans. She's going to get some artist friends together, and they are going to get the box that I am going to be cremated in, and they are going to paint it, ahead of time, so we will have that box sitting around here in the garage or something after they get it painted. She is buying the silk cloth that she is going to wrap my body in. She's got it down to we are hoping that I die here, and she is going to not have my body removed right away and be able to do the washing and the wrapping herself before they have it removed.

While for some people that is unthinkable, even gruesome. But for her, it is her way of being able to start dealing with the grieving process and figure out how she is going to make it through that time and what we need to do to help her make it. We are discussing whom we have around that is energizing to her rather than draining to her so she's got that level of support. She's now doing with her grieving process the same thing I am doing with my disease process. The dying process is part of living, too, and experiencing the death of a loved one is part of that as well, so she wants to go through this process as peacefully, and as well, and as thoroughly as she possibly can. It's like, why do this in anything other than the best way possible? There isn't going to be anything more important or more serious or more vital to what living is about than what we are both going to go through in the next six months or couple of years.

It is one of the benefits we have because of this particular disease. If I was killed in a car wreck, dying would have happened as well, but we wouldn't have the time or the opportunity to do it this way. So we've got the opportunity, let's do it as well as we can.

That's a visionary way of coping with this. . . .

Thank you, thank you.

Do you still consider yourself Catholic?

Yes, by my definition. Maybe not by some other person's definition, but I don't feel the need to fit into all those rules and regulations today. I'm not downplaying them because they were a really important part of my life, and they are important parts of other people's lives so I don't ridicule them in any way. I just know that in my spiritual journey right now they are not an essential part of it.

Did being diagnosed with this disease change your religious perceptions?

Only in a sense of deepening. People in the parish in CDA, which would have been during the '80s, would see me now as being consistent as what I was doing then, even though I would use different words then than I might use now, but they would see me as consistent—in terms of, for a lack of better word, in terms of the spiritual journey. . . . The church is there to be of service to us on our spiritual journey, not the other way around. It is not there as an absolute, it is not there as the only way to God. I don't believe that; I haven't believed that for a long time, and I didn't promote that when I was a priest in Coeur d'Alene.

Did your work as a priest, having seen so much death and grieving up front, help prepare you for this?

Yes, and maybe even more than most priests because I worked with hospice and in that context became sort of the minister to the dying, and the funeral homes and doctors and hospitals. If they had somebody who was dying and didn't have a church they were connected to, but the person wanted somebody to minister to them, I was the one they called because I knew the hospice process, and I knew the dying process, and because they knew I was open enough that I wasn't going to do a Catholic trip on people. Sometimes I would go with my collar on, but often I didn't wear my clerical collar anyway so I would go as I normally dressed, an open-collared shirt like I'm wearing now. . . .

There is a great sense of awe, for lack of better word, that happens to me over and over again as I held the hand of somebody who is dying and helped them let go. I would say, "Let go, trust in God, it's going to be okay." To be holding the hand of somebody as that happens and be with them as they go through that, it is an overpowering experience. And it's very enriching.

Every time you are with somebody who dies, you have to evaluate what it all means, so in that sense, yes, it prepared me. But no matter how often you encounter death, it doesn't prepare you—us—really well for the death of somebody that is close to us. Some of the people I ministered to there were very close to me, but still, when my dad died, when my mother died, that's a whole different ballgame. It's a different ballgame for me as well. In a way I have to do it all over again from a completely different perspective.

Is one of the reasons you are able to believe so strongly in life after death is because you saw so many people pass on?

Yes, I think that is part of it. My basis for life after death is: I respect life so much, and I think the human person is such a wonderful existence that I can't imagine it ending. It's sort of like, as good as this is, is this all there is? No, that doesn't make sense, so there must be more. The human spirit and the human person is capable of so much, and even somebody who lives a long full life, there is so much more that any given person is capable of that it makes no sense to me to have this limited existence, as good as it is, be the whole thing. When you start applying that kind of thinking to somebody who is younger, like a child that dies, or a teenager or a thirty year old or fifty year old, it seems to make even more sense. That human being, capable of so much more of what they had the opportunity to live out. It makes more sense to me if you see the human spirit as being capable of limitlessness.

Did your faith deepen each time?

Yes. It deepened my whole belief in the sacredness and importance of life. I can't imagine that when my dad stopped breathing that time and all that was left was this motionless body. I just can't possibly fathom that that's it, because prior to that there was this wonderful person who had experienced all this life and accumulated all this knowledge. The idea that this person, all of that whole bundle somehow evaporates into thin air, just doesn't make any sense to me. . . . There's something else. I try to remember my most memorable moments of my life and try to take all those, put them all together at the same time and say magnify that by a hundred, and that's what it [the afterlife] is going to be like.

But you could go on to live five more years, right?

Well, it's a potential, but frankly I don't think so. When we were at the ocean I asked Mary Frances, "What does your gut say, how long do I have?" I said, "I've got something in mind but what does yours say?" We both thought exactly the same thing, that I had about a year, and that if I make it to the next Christmas I will consider that a bonus. I am not psychologically shutting down, but I have to be realistic. . . .

We are not going to choose to extend my life as long as we possibly can. The goal is quality of time not length of time, so I am not going to do things and be absolutely miserable the last couple of months of my life. I'm just not going to head that direction.

You mentioned that you and Mary Frances recently made your last trip to the ocean. I wanted to ask you about that connection, since it seems like every time you have made a big decision you have gone to the ocean.

Well, that's been historically the case. Some really really important things have happened to me on the ocean, and I like it there. I find myself peaceful there, looking at things at a different level when I am there. . . .

In December that was sort of my chance to ask some serious questions about things and also say goodbye to the ocean because I really don't expect to get back there. I can't really spend anymore overnight times away from the house and that is too far to go in a day and back. I can't go on the beach anymore, and there is so much stuff that I can't do anymore—like even walk on the beach or put my feet in the water. So that's okay. It was really important to go back, but it is one of those chapters of my life I am ready to close the book on.

How did you say goodbye?

We were in a place for that week where we were almost literally sitting on top of the water. It was a great spot. We had great big picture windows and it was like ten feet in front of the window was the bank and ten feet from that was the high tide, so it was almost like you could spit in it. We had a huge storm; it was that big storm that dumped all that storm here in December. There were eighty-mile-an-hour winds, thunder and lightning. I loved it. It was so dramatic and overpowering. I was inside so it didn't matter because I wasn't being buffeted by the wind; it was warm where we were staying.

So it sounds like you got quite the send off?

Yea, and I didn't miss anything because we couldn't be walking on the beach anyway. Some sea lions went by, so it was fun to watch them. If there was a time to be on the ocean when there was a big storm, that was the time to do it. I sat by that picture window for hours and watched the waves and mentally talked to the ocean in terms of whatever force it has been to me before. It was kind of like "Okay, ocean, I'm not going to be back here with you for awhile but I do expect that soon I will be experiencing you on a whole different level."

No pun intended?

(Laughter.)

Yea, right. No pun intended. Our plans are that after I die I am going to be cremated and John and Mary Frances and anyone else she can find to take along are going to take my ashes to the ocean and spread them across the ocean. Scientifically, life sprang from the ocean so for me to have my ashes returned to there is kind of going back to where I'm from and marking the next phase of the journey.

It was also a time for me to tell the ocean, "Okay ocean, get ready for me because the next time I come here they are going to be sprinkling me on you, and you're not going to be able to get rid of me. Before, you could always throw me out with a big wave or because you got too cold, but now you'll see. Now you'll see. . . ."

NOTES

Preface

1. Letter from Richard Masker, February 1997.

2. The first Jewish governor, Moses Alexander, was elected in Idaho in 1914 and re-elected again in 1916. In 1991, Larry EchoHawk became the first American Indian elected as a state attorney general.

3. CIA abuses against American citizens exposed by the senator's powerful "church committee" included bungled assassination attempts against foreign leaders, as well as domestic abuses such as the unauthorized opening of mail, illegal wire taps, and unwitting medical experiments.

4. A few years later, in 1905, the former governer Frank Steuenenberg was assassinated when he opened the gate to his side door, triggering a bomb blast that killed him. The union activists charged with murder were eventually acquitted of the crime during a sensational trial in Boise.

5. *San Jose Mercury News*, August 3, 1998; *Gentlemen's Quarterly*, March 1996.

1. Greencreek

1. *Atlas of the New West* (Center of the American West: University of Colorado at Boulder, 1997).

2. The community-orientation of Catholics, and the social constraints that accompanied such communalism, was one of the primary objections of the Protestant reformers to the Church because they believed it put community of human relationships between the individual and God. The impact of such communalism on Catholics has been widely debated. Sociologist Max Weber believed Catholic communalism was inhibiting educational achievement of Catholics in early twentieth-century Germany. Others argued Catholic communalism helped maintain an important sense of mutual aid and social ethos. For example, Emily Durkheim argued suicide rates among Catholics were lower due to Catholic social pressures prohibiting self-destruction. For more on the

relationship between contemporary Catholicism and community, see chap. 4, pages 111–136 of Andrew Greeley's, *The Catholic Imagination* (Berkeley: University of California Press, 2001).

3. George M. Klein, Forrest Christensen, and Jean Terra, *The Nuremberg Funnel: Idaho-German Tales* (Legendary Publishing Company, 1996), 123.

4. Jay P. Dolan, *In Search of an American Catholicism: A History of Religion and Culture in Tension* (New York: Oxford University Press, 2002), 181.

2. The Small-Town Challenge

1. David Neiwert, *In God's Country: The Patriot Movement and the Pacific Northwest* (Pullman: Washington State University Press, 1999).

2. Arthur J. Vidich and Joseph Bensman, *Small Town in Mass Society: Class, Power, and Religion in a Rural Community* (Urbana and Chicago: University of Illinois Press, 1958, 1968, 2000), 303.

3. Vidich and Bensman, *Small Town in Mass Society,* 302, 303.

4. Author interviews with human rights activists, Coeur d'Alene 2002.

5. Morris Dees, interview with author, January 22, 2002, Washington State University, Pullman, Wash.

6. Ibid.

7. Vidich and Bensman, *Small Town in Mass Society.*

8. Amitai Etzioni, *The Spirit of Community: The Reinvention of American Society* (New York: Simon and Schuster, 1993), 146.

9. Bill Wassmuth and M.J. Bryant, "Not in Our World: A Perspective of Community Organizing Against Hate," *Journal of Hate Studies* 1, no. 1 (2001–2002): 109.

3. Mount Angel Abbey and St. Thomas Seminary

1. Edward E. Malone, *History of the First Century of Conception Abbey* (Omaha, Nebraska: Interstate Printing Co., 1971).

2. Malone, *History of the First Century of Conception Abbey.*

3. At their peak in 1965, more than 2,413 Catholic secondary schools in the nation were serving 1.1 million students, according to the National Catholic Education Association. By 1994, that number dropped to just 597,425 students.

4. John Maloney, Architect, A.I.A., architect's message, 14 April 1959.

5. Robert T. O'Gorman, *Catholic Identity and Catholic Education in the United States since 1790* (Nashville: Scarritt, 1987).

6. Thomas Oldenski, *Liberation Theology and Critical Pedagogy in Today's Catholic Schools* (New York: Garland Publishing, Inc., 1997), 23.

7. Michael W. Cuneo, *The Smoke of Satan: Conservative and Traditionalist Dis-*

sent in *Contemporary American Catholicism* (New York: Oxford University Press, 1997), 16.

4. The Role of Education

1. Eugene Kennedy, *The Unhealed Wound: The Church, the Priesthood, and the Question of Sexuality* (New York: St. Martins Press, 2001), 55.

2. Colleen McDannell, "Catholic Domesticity, 1860–1960," from the anthology *American Catholic Women: A Historical Exploration* (New York: Macmillan, 1989), 74.

3. Jim Carrier, *Ten Ways to Fight Hate: A Community Response Guide,* ed. Richard Cohen (Alabama: Southern Poverty Law Center, 2001).

4. Adam Stone, "Human Rights Education and Public Policy in the United States: Mapping the Road Ahead," *Human Rights Quarterly* 24, no.2 (Johns Hopkins University Press, May 2002).

5. Ibid.

6. The Southern Poverty Law Center offers a wealth of resources for schools and communities fighting hate. For more information, visit the Teaching Tolerance website at www.splcenter.org or www.tolerance.org.

7. *When Hate Groups Come to Town: A Handbook of Model Community Response* (Atlanta: The Center for Democratic Renewal, 1986).

8. Memo to Bill Wassmuth and Eric Ward, Northwest Coalition Against Malicious Harassment, February 12, 1998.

9. Aryan Nations leaflet left on cars outside Post Falls High School in early 1998.

10. Flyer distributed by Aryan Nations to parents in Sunnyside, Washington, 1992.

11. Author interview, February 2002.

12. Executive Summary of Recommendations of the Center Mission Committee, Amended and Adopted January 10, 2002 by the Human Rights Education Foundation Board of Directors.

13. Monica Andrews, "Educating for Multicultural Perspectives: A Doorway to the Rest of Humanity," *Promising Practices in Teaching Social Responsibility* (Albany: State University of New York Press, 1993), 120.

14. Linda Lovett as quoted by Jeanette White and Heather Lalley, "Schools Vary on Subject of Racism," *Spokesman-Review,* 21 June 1998, reprinted 17 July 1998.

15. The Anti-Defamation League, Simon Wiesenthal Center, and Center for Democratic Renewal are other valuable resource organizations with national reach. Also see Carrier, *Ten Ways To Fight Hate.*

16. Paula T. Morelli and Michael Spencer, "Existing Anti-Bigotry Policies, Curriculum and Programs in Northwestern Schools," a Northwest Coalition Against Malicious Harassment Education Research Project.

17. The film and book, *Thousand Pieces of Gold,* told the life story of Polly Bemus, one of Idaho's most well-known Chinese residents, now buried in Grangeville just miles from where Wassmuth grew up.

18. Frank Pignatelli and Susanna Pflaum, ed., *Experiencing Diversity: Toward Educational Equity* (Corwin Press, Inc., 1994).

19. Thomas L. Friedman, *Understanding Globalization: The Lexus and the Olive Tree* (New York: Anchor Books, 2000).

5. Boise and Beyond

1. Leonard J. Arrington, *History of Idaho* (Moscow: University of Idaho Press, 1994), 284.

2. Jay P. Dolan, *In Search of an American Catholicism: A History of Religion and Culture in Tension* (New York: Oxford University Press, 2002), 201.

3. Martin Luther King Jr., Nobel Lecture, December 11, 1964, University of Oslo.

4. Dolan, *In Search of an American Catholicism,* 204.

5. Michael W. Cuneo, *The Smoke of Satan: Conservative and Traditionalist Dissent in Contemporary American Catholicism* (New York: Oxford University Press, 1997), 16.

6. The Role of Religion

1. James A. Aho, *This Thing of Darkness: A Sociology of the Enemy* (Seattle: University of Washington Press, 1994), chap. 10.

2. Susan DeCamp, "Locking the Doors to the Kingdom: An Examination of Religion in Extremist Organizing and Public Policy," *American Armageddon: Religion, Revolution and the Right,* ed. Eric Ward (Seattle: Northwest Coalition Against Malicious Harassment, 1998), 22.

3. Michael Barkun, *Religion and the Racist Right: The Origins of the Christian Identity Movement* (Chapel Hill: University of North Carolina Press, 1994).

4. James Coates, *Armed and Dangerous: The Rise of the Survivalist Right* (New York: Hill and Wang, 1987), 21.

5. Peter Y. Hong and Ken Ellingwood, "A Trip to the Birthplace of Racist Ideologies," *Los Angeles Times,* 13 August 1999.

6. Mike Barber, "Proud Architect of Hate at 81, Aryan Nations Founder Is Unrepentant," *Seattle Post-Intelligencer,* 27 August 1999.

7. Kim Murphy, "Last Stand of an Aging Aryan," *Los Angeles Times*, 10 January 1999.

8. James A. Aho, *The Politics of Righteousness: Idaho Christian Patriotism* (Seattle: University of Washington Press, 1990), 46.

9. For a more detailed description of the roots of Christian Identity religion, see the following works: James Coates, *Armed and Dangerous: The Rise of the Survivalist Right* (1987); Jerome Walters, *One Aryan Nations Under God* (2001); Michael Barkun, *Religion and the Racist Right* (1994); and Leonard Zeskind, *The Christian Identity Movement* (1986).

10. Timothy McVeigh claimed that his act of terror was inspired by William Pierce's *The Turner Diaries*, a fictional novel first published in 1978, that became the Christian Identity blueprint for violent overthrow of the government and inspired violence by The Order's Robert Mathews. Eric Rudolph, wanted in connection with the bombings at the Summer Olympic Games in 1996, attacks on several abortion clinics in the south, and the bombing of a gay bar in Atlanta, was raised with Christian Identity beliefs. Family members have attributed Rudolph's antigovernment views to a period in the mid-80s that he lived in the "Church of Israel" Christian Identity enclave in Missouri. Federal investigators say Rudolph maintained ties with Christian Identity leaders over the years, including the Aryan Nations. Buford Furrow, a Washington State man who opened fire on the North Valley Jewish Community Center in Granada Hills, Calif., then murdered a Filipino postman in Los Angeles in 1999, also had ties to the extremist movement. When Furrow turned himself in at the Las Vegas FBI office, police found Christian Identity literature in his van.

11. *The Northwest Imperative: Documenting A Decade Of Hate* (Portland, Oregon: Coalition For Human Dignity in association with The Northwest Coalition Against Malicious Harassment, 1994).

12. Ray C. Barker, "The Viper Connection," audio tape, Christian Covenant Church (circa 1990), as cited in *The Northwest Imperative, Documenting a Decade Of Hate*.

13. Raul Hilberg, *The Destruction of the European Jews* (New York: Holmes & Maier, 1985).

14. The National Council of Churches of Christ was one of the first groups to formally address the problem of religious-based hate when it published a pamphlet in 1986 called, "The Christian Identity Movement: Analyzing its Theological Rationalization for Racist and Anti-Semitic Violence."

15. David Ostendorf, "Christian Identity: An American Heresy," *Journal of Hate Studies* 1, no. 1 (2001-2002): 26.

16. Jerome Walters, *One Aryan Nations Under God* (Naperville, Illinois: Sourcebooks, 2001).

17. John Taylor, "Church Rebukes Militia: Members of Noxon Methodist Church Speak Up," *Billings Gazette,* 25 June 1995.

7. Coeur d'Alene

1. Mary Mitiguy Miller, "This Priest Is a Little Different," *Spokesman-Review* and *Spokane Chronicle,* 6 October 1985.

2. Michael W. Cuneo, *The Smoke of Satan: Conservative and Traditionalist Dissent in Contemporary American Catholicism* (New York: Oxford University Press, 1997), 109.

3. Bob Cubbage, fourth in a series of seven on the Tridentine Latin Rite Church, *Inland Register,* 1 May 1980.

4. The traditionalist group Schuckardt originally founded still exists today, and has, in fact, grown substantially under new leadership. The current Mt. St. Michaels community (now referred to as the Religious Congregation of Mary Immaculate Queen) still adheres to Latin Mass and believes Pope John Paul II is heretical, but vigorously distances itself from Schuckardt's beliefs and claims to have uprooted the cultlike practices he had introduced. A series of uncanonical bishops followed Schuckardt. Though its motherhouse remains in Spokane, Wash., today, the Religious Congregation of Mary Immaculate Queen serves nearly thirty churches and chapels throughout the United States and Canada.

5. Bob Cubbage, "Tridentine Political Beliefs Controversial," *Inland Register,* 24 April 1980, and editorial 10 April 1980.

6. According to Michael Cuneo, author of *The Smoke of Satan,* the Protocols, a fake document passed off at the turn of the century as proof of plans for a Jewish-Masonic world takeover conspiracy, is mentioned in one of the books most often cited by Catholic traditionalist conspiracists: *The Mystical Body of Christ in the Modern World,* written by Irish priest Dennis Fahey in 1935. Fahey essentially claims that modern history was a struggle between the forces of religious truth (a group consisting almost entirely of zealous Catholics) and materialism and subversion (a group consisting of "evil Jews"). Fahey argues that in "virtually every secular enterprise that has helped shape modern history, from Bolshevism to high capitalist finance, it is Jews who have been the principal power brokers; and in every case their ultimate objective has been the destruction of Catholicism and the creation of anti-Christian world order." These arguments echo those Schuckardt's ex-followers claim he taught.

7. In 1980, the *Inland Register,* official newspaper for the Spokane Roman Catholic diocese, published an in-depth investigative series about the Triden-

tine Latin Rite Church. Reporter Bob Cubbage spent two years developing and researching the series that quoted former members of the church. Cubbage's exposé of Schuckardt's anti-Semitic teachings prompted the mainstream media, including the *Spokane Chronicle,* to follow up on Cubbage's new allegations in April 1980.

8. "Tridentine 'Anti-Jew, Anti-U.S.'" *Spokane Chronicle,* 24 April 1980.

9. Cuneo, *The Smoke of Satan,* 109; author interview with Rathdrum resident Joseph Berchtold.

10. Judy Mills, "Idaho Cult Awareness Center Receives Praise and Criticism," *Spokesman-Review* and *Spokane Chronicle,* 7 March 1984.

11. Les Tidball, "Tridentine Case Hits Home for Post Falls Man," *Coeur d'Alene Press,* 10 April 1985, final edition.

12. O'Neil v. Schuckardt, No. 15580, Supreme Court of Idaho, 12 December 1986.

13. Tim Hanson, "A Bishop's Life on the Run," *Spokesman-Review,* 26 August 1984.

14. Jim Sparks, "Schuckardt Reportedly Running Scared," *Spokesman-Review,* 27 July 1986.

15. Jim Sparks, "Former Tridentine Bishop in Drug Bust," *Spokesman-Review,* 14 May 1987.

16. In Cuneo's *Smoke of Satan,* the author notes that Schuckardt later moved his ministry back to the Pacific Northwest where he and his followers lead a clandestine existence in Oregon and Washington as the Oblates of Mary Immaculate.

17. Joanne Davidson, "If You're Looking for a Great Place to Live—An Outdoor Paradise," *U.S. News and World Report,* 12 July 1982.

18. Ibid.

19. In 1986 alone, nearly 1,500 of Idaho's 23,000 farmers went bankrupt, giving the state the fifth highest percentage of failures in the nation.

20. Residents in Idaho's southern district elected one of the state's most embarrassing politicians in 1964: "Bircher" George Hansen, a right-wing Pocatello businessman who served nearly two decades in office before being convicted of tax evasion in 1983.

21. *The Northwest Imperative: Documenting a Decade of Hate* (Portland, Oregon: Coalition for Human Dignity in association with The Northwest Coalition Against Malicious Harassment, 1994), 1.17.

22. *Seattle Times,* 19 December 1984, from an interview with Gary Yarbrough in the Ada County Jail, Idaho.

23. As a result of the agent's find at Yarbrough's home, more than forty

people in seventeen states would be arrested and charged with crimes related to The Order's yearlong spree of bombings, robberies, and racist attacks.

24. A detailed review of Beam and Butler's early use of computer technology is covered in James Coates' *Armed and Dangerous: The Rise of the Survivalist Right* (New York: Hill and Wang, 1987), 206–212.

25. A human rights violation was filed over this incident with the Idaho Human Rights Commission in July of 1982.

26. James A. Aho, *The Politics of Righteousness: Idaho Christian Patriotism* (Seattle: University of Washington Press, 1990).

27. Ibid.

28. James A. Aho, *This Thing of Darkness: A Sociology of the Enemy* (Seattle: University of Washington Press, 1984).

29. Idaho was one of the first states to pass legislation that made malicious harassment of any person because of race, color, national origin, or creed punishable by up to five years in prison and a $5,000 fine. North Idaho lawmakers—particularly Sen. Mary Lou Reed, a Coeur d'Alene Democrat and Sen. Norma Dobler of Moscow—helped push through several crucial pieces of human rights legislation.

30. *United Press International*, "The Order Bought Idaho 'Training Camp,' FBI Says," published in the *Coeur d'Alene Press*, 9 April 1985.

31. Of the twenty-three members of The Order indicted on racketeering charges in 1984, ten were convicted in 1986 and sentenced from forty to one hundred years in prison.

32. Mark Shenefelt, "Idaho Image Needs Help," *United Press International*, 9 April 1985.

33. While appointed to the Prison Review Committee in 1979 and 1980, Wassmuth learned in committee meetings the media savvy he would later rely on during the news frenzy that surrounded the Aryan Nations. Wassmuth claimed he learned all he knew from a Lewiston businessman and legislator who was trained in media relations from working with tough editorial writers at the *Lewiston Morning Tribune*. The committee would work all day, then the Lewiston legislator would hold a press conference, later going to the bar to watch how the news was handled in the media.

> I remember one of the key things he told me was what we do in our meetings isn't nearly as important as what comes out in the media at the end of the day. You have to know what you want them to pick up and no matter what questions they ask, you have your point and then you get to that point and you say it in a small number of words so you can utilize it. When we watched the news media after our meetings, we could see

how it worked. He was very good at it, and it taught me how to work the media to an advantage.

34. Kootenai County Human Rights Task Force member Marshall Mend recalled the story at Wassmuth's Memorial Service, Thursday, 12 September 2002, Coeur d'Alene, Idaho.

35. David Lamb, "Spacious State is No Small Potatoes, Riddle of the Rockies: Just Where Is Idaho?" *Los Angeles Times,* 13 July 1988.

36. In 1988, Stone was awarded the U.S. Holocaust Memorial Council's Eisenhower Liberation Medal for his fight against Nazis in World War II, and neo-Nazis in Coeur d'Alene in the 1980s.

37. Several of the original members of the Kootenai County Human Rights Task Force continue to work for the advancement of human rights in Coeur d'Alene. Marshall Mend, Norm Gissel, and Tony Stewart, all longtime members of the task force, in 2002 traveled to meet with the Pennsylvania Human Relations Commission to share advice about their experience battling the Aryan Nations, which has since picked Pennsylvania as its new haven. These men are also at the forefront of the construction of a new human rights education center in the city and continue to speak nationally about the region's fight against hate groups.

38. Author interviews with Wassmuth's former parishioners, September 2002.

39. From news accounts as reported by D.F. Oliveria, "Racist Views Blasted at Rights Rally," *Spokesman-Review Spokane Chronicle,* 13 July 1986, and Nils Rosdahl for the *Idaho Register.*

40. Several churches also sent statements, including the Benedictine Sisters of the Priory of St. Gertrude in Cottonwood, who sent a handwritten parchment quoting passages from Genesis, Luke, and Galatians. The Priory of St. Gertrude is just a few miles from Wassmuth's hometown of Greencreek.

41. Bill Morlin, "Media Turns Spotlight on Aryan Meet," *Spokesman-Review Spokane Chronicle,* 12 July 1986.

42. Ibid.

43. Don Duncan, "Celebrating Unity and Hate-Gathering a Few Miles Apart Remain Poles Apart," *Seattle Times,* 13 July 1986.

44. Bill Wassmuth with M.J. Bryant, "Not in Our World," *Journal of Hate Studies* 1 (2001–2002).

45. Editorial, *Spokesman-Review,* 18 September 1986.

46. Bruder Schweigen is German for "Silent Brotherhood," which was one of the names used by The Order.

47. Tom Alibrandi with Bill Wassmuth, *Hate is My Neighbor* (Stand Together Publishers, 1999).

48. "2 Linked to Aryan Groups Plead Guilty in Plot," *New York Times,* 5 February 1987.

49. Alibrandi, *Hate is My Neighbor.*

50. This story has been retold and reprinted several times. I heard it firsthand from Wassmuth in interviews in 2001, but also as told by Mend at a memorial service for Wassmuth in Coeur d'Alene, 12 September 2002.

51. Associated Press, "Explosion Rips Priest's Home," 17 September 1986.

52. Susan Toft, "Wassmuth Uninjured in Explosion," *Coeur d'Alene Press,* 16 September 1986.

53. "Bomb Damages Rectory at St. Pius, Coeur d'Alene," *Idaho Register,* 19 September 1986.

54. Editorial, *Coeur d'Alene Press,* 17 September 1986.

55. Doug Clark, Editorial, *Spokesman-Review,* 18 September 1986.

56. Cynthia Taggart, "Blast Doesn't Weaken Belief in Strength of Non-Violence," *Spokesman-Review,* 21 September 1986.

57. Trudy Welsh, "Rev. Wassmuth Back at Pulpit Preaching Peace," *Coeur d'Alene Press,* 21 September 1986.

58. Trudy Welsh, "Hundreds Rally For Tolerance," *Coeur d'Alene Press,* 26 September 1986. Claims that Butler's pets had been mutilated surfaced again in 1998 when Butler's beloved German Shepherd, Hans, was found near the Aryan Nations compound fence, "shot twice, his heart pulled out of his rib cage and his body washed completely of blood," according to a 10 January 1999 *Los Angeles Times* story.

59. Russell Carollo, "Hundreds Gather To Answer Bomb With Friendship," *Spokesman-Review,* September 1986.

60. David Neuman, "Maryland Man Says He Helped With Bombings," *Spokesman-Review,* 7 October 1986.

61. Ric Clarke, *Coeur d'Alene Press,* 29 September 1986.

62. Associated Press, "Extremists Have Hit List, Judge Hears," *Chicago Tribune,* 10 October 1986, p. 4.

63. Neuman, "Maryland Man Says He Helped With Bombings."

64. *Spokesman-Review,* 18 May 1987.

65. Quoting testimony of FBI Special Agent David Jernigan, Associated Press, "Extremists Have Hit List, Judge Hears."

66. "2 Linked To Aryan Groups Plead Guilty in Plot."

67. Karen McGrath, Associated Press Writer, "Suspects Greeted By Jeers," as published in *Coeur d'Alene Press,* 4 October 1986.

68. "Extremists Have Hit List, Judge Hears."

69. The *Life Magazine* story drew ridicule from local residents, including Wassmuth, who were not happy with the author's portrayal of the region and its characters. The mayor fumed that author Pat Jordan needed a geography lesson because he referred to the city as in the Northern Rockies, and noted its "disorienting mountain air," though Coeur d'Alene is only at an altitude of about 2,200 feet. The article referred to the "big-bellied sheriff," in reference to one of the deputies, which perturbed the actual sheriff, a relatively fit man. Wassmuth, who was described as a priest in aviator sunglasses, told the Associated Press he was unhappy with the portrayal of the community and the task force's work.

70. *Seattle Times*, 20 October 1986.

71. Wassmuth would later appear on Geraldo Rivera's talk show about victims of hate crimes, while the Kootenai County Task Force on Human Relations was the center of a videotape produced by the Anti-Defamation League for distribution as an educational tool to other communities facing similar problems.

72. Wallenberg, a Swedish diplomat assigned to Budapest, Hungary, in 1944, is credited with saving more than 100,000 Jews during World War II before his arrest by advancing Russians in 1945.

73. D.F. Oliveria, "Coeur d'Alene Gathers Praise, Award in N.Y.," *Spokesman-Review*, 14 January 1987.

74. Law enforcement authorities later said Pires had been the getaway driver the day Kenneth Shray was killed in rural Bonner County, though Pires said he thought the Aryan Nations members only planned to beat the man, not kill him. In his plea agreement, Pires admitted to prosecutors that he was "present and an active participant" in the execution-style murder of Shray that August. Pires eventually was sentenced for life in prison for his role in Shray's murder, as well as state and federal charges up to twenty years for the Coeur d'Alene bombings, counterfeiting, and attempted bank robbery. The federal government agreed to cover Pires in its witness protection program.

75. After seven weeks of testimony and four days of deliberation, Butler and the others were acquitted of sedition charges in 1988. It was a major setback in the federal government's efforts to crack down on right-wing extremist groups, and a major letdown for Wassmuth and other human rights activists who thought Butler would be convicted.

76. According to NIC political science instructor Tony Stewart, as cited in a story by D.F. Oliveria, "5 States Form Board to Fight 'Hate Crimes,'" *Spokesman-Review*, 4 April 1987.

77. Hate crimes aimed at gays and lesbians have been on the rise in recent years, most notably, Matthew Shepard was beaten and murdered in Laramie,

Wyoming, and a lesbian couple's home was firebombed in Missoula, Montana, after the couple requested same-sex benefits at the local university. In both cases, law enforcement said the victims were targeted because of their sexual orientation.

78. Associated Press, "Idaho To Enact 'Toughest Anti-terrorism Bill' in Nation," 23 June 1987.

79. Idaho's malicious harassment law, and subsequent human rights legislation, did not extend any hate crimes protection to gays or lesbians. In most Western states, hate crimes laws do not cover violence directed at those because of their sexual orientation (except in Oregon and Washington).

80. Cuneo, *The Smoke of Satan*, 15.

81. Bill Morlin, "Aryan Rally Tame by Comparison," *Spokesman-Review*, 13 July 1987.

82. David Proctor, "1987 Citizen of the Year," *Idaho Statesman*, 1 January 1988.

83. Nils Rosdahl, "Father Bill to Leave CDA," *Coeur d'Alene Press*, 18 January 1988.

84. D.F. Oliveria, "Wassmuth Leaving Priesthood With Parish's Support," *Spokesman-Review*, 16 May 1988.

85. Ibid.

86. Rev. John Rizzo, priest at the traditionalist Catholic group SSPX, in a letter to the *Coeur d'Alene Press*, 26 May 1988.

8. The Role of Community

1. Tocqueville's classic two-volume work *Democracy in America*, written upon returning from a trip to the United States in 1831, is still used in classrooms today as an astute overview of American social and political institutions.

2. Jan Barry, *A Citizen's Guide to Grassroots Campaigns* (New Jersey: Rutgers University Press, 2000).

3. Robert Clifton and Alan Dahms, *Grassroots Organizations: A Resource Book for Directors, Staff, and Volunteers of Small, Community-Based, Nonprofit Agencies* (Illinois: Waveland Press, 1993), 9–11.

4. Barry, *A Citizen's Guide to Grassroots Campaigns*, 12.

5. K. Kingdon, *Agenda, Alternatives and Public Policies* (Boston: Little, Brown and Co., 1994).

6. Kootenai County Task Force on Human Relations, internal memos.

7. Ibid.

8. Ibid.

9. Ibid.

10. Ibid.

11. Barry, *A Citizen's Guide to Grassroots Campaigns*, 15.

12. Kootenai County Task Force on Human Relations, internal memo.

13. *Ten Ways to Fight Hate*, ed. Richard Cohen, a community response guide published by the Southern Poverty Law Center, 2001.

14. Ibid.

15. Clifton and Dahms, *Grassroots Organizations*, 9–11.

16. John Lunsford, "The Pink Swastika: The OCA's Defense Strategy," *The Dignity Report*, Spring 1999.

17. James A. Aho, *The Politics of Righteousness: Idaho Christian Patriotism* (Seattle: University of Washington Press, 1990).

18. Robert Crawford, "Who's Being Persecuted Here?" *The Dignity Report*, Spring 1999.

19. Jim Fisher, "Who But Bigots Carry Signs Saying, 'God Hates Fags'?" *Lewiston Morning Tribune*, 12 May 1999.

20. Bill Morlin, "Aryan Hopes To Seek Office in Panhandle," *Spokesman-Review*, 20 February 1992.

21. Jim Lynch and Bill Morlin, "Living on the Edge: Anti-Government Movement Struggles to Find Its Place in American Politics," *Spokesman-Review*, 11 December 1995.

22. Andrea Vogt, "WSU Shouts Down Holocaust Revisionists' Appearance by Hitler Apologist," *Spokesman-Review*, 14 April 1998.

23. David A. Neiwert, *In God's Country: The Patriot Movement and the Pacific Northwest* (Pullman: Washington State University Press, 1999), 56.

24. Jess Walter, *Every Knee Shall Bow: The Truth and Tragedy of Ruby Ridge and the Randy Weaver Family* (New York: HarperCollins, 1996).

25. Bill Morlin, *Spokesman-Review*, December 6, 1998.

26. Anti-Defamation League Law Enforcement Agency Resource Network.

27. Roundtable discussion with residents of North Idaho and Northeast Washington in: "A Lasting Legacy," Northwest Coalition for Human Dignity (2000), 17.

28. Gretchen Hellar, human rights supporter, as quoted in an *Associated Press* story, 14 November 1998.

29. David Sawyer, Sandpoint mayor, as quoted in an *Associated Press* story 22 November, 1998.

30. *Ten Ways To Fight Hate*, Southern Poverty Law Center.

31. Bill Morlin, *Spokesman-Review*, 9 December 2001.

32. Ibid.

33. Bill Morlin, "Racist Book Firm Moves to New Jersey," *Spokesman-Review*, 18 November 2001. The racist publishing organization 14 Word Press, now located in North Carolina, was started in 1995 by a woman named Katja Lane. She claimed to be the wife of David Lane, an imprisoned assassin and extremist who was one of the leaders of the racist group The Order. Her Internet operation and small press have been one of the primary supports behind Lane's attempts to propagandize and recruit new thugs for his racist aims while incarcerated for life at a federal penitentiary.

9. Seattle

1. In 1998, Wassmuth spoke at a rally in Lewiston against bigotry after three black men were beaten by an unruly crowd in downtown Lewiston. He called on law enforcement agencies to investigate and prosecute the assault as a hate crime because the men had been targeted because of their race.

2. Bill Morlin, "Ex-Aryan Discloses Death Plot," *Spokesman-Review*, 16 February 1992.

3. The FBI later suspended its investigation, saying its informant was no longer reliable.

4. Mike McLean, "Aryans Jailed in Killing," *Coeur d'Alene Press*, 19 December 1992.

5. In 1996, Kehoe set off a nail bomb at Spokane's City Hall, and three years later he was sentenced to life in prison for murdering an Arkansas family and plotting crimes to promote the white homeland that had been so often discussed at the Aryan compound.

6. Richard Butler had threatened to march down Coeur d'Alene's main drag in 1989 but called off his parade a month ahead of time, saying he did not want his conferees coming into contact with "AIDS-infected" counterdemonstrators from Seattle, San Francisco, and Portland. The more likely reason was the paltry showings for Butler's other most recent gatherings. Less than fifty attended the "Aryan Woodstock" near Napa, California, that March, and only about thirty attended a meeting on Whidbey Island, Washington, the previous December. Though the Aryans did not march, some residents tied orange ribbons on their cars, homes, trees, and bushes anyway to signify support for tolerance, while another group of Aryan Nations opponents—Citizens for Nonviolent Action Against Racism—sponsored their own march along U.S. Highway 95.

7. Bill Morlin, "Everybody Doesn't Love a Parade," *Spokesman-Review*, 11 February 1998.

8. Chris Peck, "In It Together: A Conversation about Race," *Spokesman-Review*, 17 July 1998.

9. Ken Olsen, "Man Wants To Squeeze Out Racists," *Spokesman-Review,* 1998.

10. Doug Cresswell, *Spokesman-Review,* 15 August 1999.

10. The Road Ahead

1. Kenneth S. Stern, *A Force upon the Plain: The American Militia Movement and the Politics of Hate* (New York: Simon & Schuster, 1996), 226.

2. *Neuer Zuercher Zeitung,* 3 March 2000.

3. Kenneth Stern, "Hate and the Internet," *Journal of Hate Studies* 1, no. 1 (2001).

4. Peter Ford, "Cybernazis Use Web to Reach into Europe," *Christian Science Monitor,* 26 March 1998.

5. Kenneth Stern, "Hate and the Internet," *Journal of Hate Studies* 1, no. 1 (2002), reprinted with permission of the American Jewish Committee.

6. Frederick M. Lawrence, *Punishing Hate: Bias Crimes under American Law* (Cambridge, Mass.: Harvard University Press, 1999), 6.

7. Center for New Community, *Soundtracks to the White Revolution: White Supremacist Assaults on Youth Music Subculture* (Chicago: Ill.: Center For New Community, 1999), 11.

8. Center for New Community, *Breaking New Ground, State of Hate: White Nationalism in the Midwest 2001-2002* (Chicago, Ill.). For more information on white power music, see *Soundtracks to the White Revolution* and the website http://www.turnitdown.com.

9. Center for New Community, *Soundtracks to the White Revolution.*

10. Center for New Community, *Breaking New Ground, State of Hate.*

11. *Atlas of the New West* (Center for the New West: University of Colorado at Boulder, 1997).

12. Robert E. Lang, Deborah Epstein Popper, and Frank J. Popper, "Is There Still a Frontier? The 1890 U.S. Census and the Modern American West," *Journal of Rural Studies* 13, no. 4 (October 1997): 377–386.

13. William Frey, "America's Bumper Crop," *Los Angeles Times,* 13 April 2001.

14. Kristopher Rengert and Robert Lang, "Cowboys and Cappuccino: The Emerging Diversity of the Rural West," *Fannie Mae Foundation Census Note 04,* May 2001.

15. Rengert, "Cowboys and Cappuccino."

16. Tom Kenworth, "Peaks, Valleys Define Today's West," *USA Today,* 18 May 2001.

17. Seymour Lipset, *The Politics of Unreason: Right Wing Extremism in America, 1790-1970* (New York: HarperCollins, 1970). In this seminal work on why

people hate, Lipset showed that racism often manifests itself in people afraid of losing their status of the honor accorded their lifestyle.

18. Carl Franklin, letter to the Editor, *Log Trucker Magazine,* December 1993.

19. Mark Warbis, Associated Press writer, "Officials Struggle With Sensitivity," *Idaho Statesman,* 2001.

INDEX

ANDREA VOGT, a North Idaho native, is a former
newspaper reporter and Fulbright Scholar whose
writing has appeared in *Review of Policy Research*,
National Geographic Traveler, the Associated Press,
and the German national news magazine *Der
Spiegel*.